THE
BIBLE FROM HEAVEN

A Summary of

PLAIN ARGUMENTS

FOR THE

BIBLE AND CHRISTIANITY

BY ELD. D. M. CANRIGHT.

"Forever, O Lord, thy word is settled in Heaven."—DAVID.
"For we can do nothing against the truth, but for the truth."—PAUL.

TEACH Services, Inc.
P U B L I S H I N G
www.TEACHServices.com • (800) 367-1844

World rights reserved. This book or any portion thereof may not be copied or reproduced in any form or manner whatever, except as provided by law, without the written permission of the publisher, except by a reviewer who may quote brief passages in a review.

The author assumes full responsibility for the accuracy of all facts and quotations as cited in this book. The opinions expressed in this book are the author's personal views and interpretations, and do not necessarily reflect those of the publisher.

This book is provided with the understanding that the publisher is not engaged in giving spiritual, legal, medical, or other professional advice. If authoritative advice is needed, the reader should seek the counsel of a competent professional.

Facsimile Reproduction

As this book played a formative role in the development of Christian thought and the publisher feels that this book, with its candor and depth, still holds significance for the church today. Therefore the publisher has chosen to reproduce this historical classic from an original copy. Frequent variations in the quality of the print are unavoidable due to the condition of the original. Thus the print may look darker or lighter or appear to be missing detail, more in some places than in others.

Copyright © 2023 TEACH Services, Inc.
ISBN-13: 978-1-4796-1672-5 (Paperback)

Published by

TEACH Services, Inc.
P U B L I S H I N G
www.TEACHServices.com • (800) 367-1844

To

THAT CLASS OF CITIZENS

WHO ARE KNOWN AS

CANDID SKEPTICS,

AND TO THE

Young Men and Women of our Time

BALEFUL INFLUENCE OF INFIDELITY,

—— IS ——

THIS LITTLE VOLUME

RESPECTFULLY

Dedicated

BY THE

AUTHOR.

PREFACE.

This work has been written after extensive reading and careful thought upon the subject of which it treats. The author has taken much pleasure in the preparation of these pages, as it has greatly strengthened his own faith in the Bible as an inspired revelation from Heaven, and as he hopes the work may inspire the same confidence in the hearts of many others. We appeal to parents and ministers in particular to place this work in the hands of the youth. It is written in an easy, simple style, with the design of creating an interest in the reader to peruse more extensive works, herein mentioned and quoted. May the blessing of Heaven attend it.

D. M. C.

Battle Creek, Mich., March 4, 1878.

CONTENTS.

CHAPTER I.

Are You Willing to Investigate? 9

CHAPTER II.

The Evidence of an Almighty Creator Revealed through the Telescope 17

CHAPTER III.

The Evidence of an Infinite God Revealed by the Microscope 30

CHAPTER IV.

The Exact Order in Nature Proves a Designer.... 34

CHAPTER V.

A Universal Cry for God 42

CHAPTER VI.

How to Find God 46

CHAPTER VII.

The Hope of the Infidel 51

CONTENTS.

CHAPTER VIII.
GOD CARES FOR US.................................... 53

CHAPTER IX.
WE NEED A REVELATION FROM GOD.................. 57

CHAPTER X
A UNIVERSAL THIRST FOR A REVELATION............. 64

CHAPTER XI.
THE CORRUPT NOTIONS AND PRACTICES OF THE HEATHEN. 68

CHAPTER XII.
MODERN HEATHEN NO BETTER THAN ANCIENT HEATHEN.

CHAPTER XIII.
THE WISEST HEATHEN PHILOSOPHERS IN THE DARK.....

CHAPTER XIV.
IMMORALITY AND CORRUPTION OF MODERN INFIDELS... 78

CHAPTER XV.
THE BIBLE COMPARED WITH OTHER SYSTEMS OF RELIGION. 82

CHAPTER XVI.
WHAT HAS INFIDELITY DONE?........................ 92

CHAPTER XVII.

When was the Bible Written?.................... 94

CHAPTER XVIII.

Testimony of Enemies to the Genuineness of the Bible..................................... 109

CHAPTER XIX.

Profane History Proves the Rise of Christianity in the First Century........................ 115

CHAPTER XX.

Who Wrote the New Testament?.................. 129

CHAPTER XXI.

Has the Language of the New Testament been Changed since it was First Written?......... 138

CHAPTER XXII.

The Apocryphal Books........................... 151

CHAPTER XXIII.

The Old Testament, when was it Written, and by Whom?.. 160

CHAPTER XXIV.

Has the Old Testament been Corrupted since it was Written?.................................. 176

CHAPTER XXV.
WHY WE REJECT THE APOCRYPHA.................... 183

CHAPTER XXVI.
CAN WE BELIEVE THE BIBLE?...................... 189

CHAPTER XXVII.
DID CHRIST DIE?................................ 208

CHAPTER XXVIII.
DID CHRIST RISE FROM THE DE.   215

CHAPTER XXIX.
INSPIRATION OF THE BIBLE PROVED BY PROPHECY..... 233

CHAPTER XXX.
OBJECTIONS CONSIDERED.......................... 277

THE BIBLE FROM HEAVEN.

CHAPTER I.

ARE YOU WILLING TO INVESTIGATE?

A SKEPTICAL friend, while in conversation with me not long since, said, "I do wish I could believe the Bible. I have tried hard to do so. I would give anything to have the strong faith in Christianity which some persons seem to have. Could I know it was the truth, I think it would be a glorious thing to believe it. But I cannot help my doubts; they will come up anyway. What shall I do? I cannot believe without evidence; and I cannot shut my eyes to objections and absurdities which are so plain to my mind."

And so infidels and skeptics generally talk. Very honest fellows they are, in their own opinion, and very anxious to know the truth. But, alas! they have so much good sense and thorough information that they cannot swallow the absurdities that simple-minded Christians do. So they say. Reader, is this your position? Are you really consoling yourself in this way? Let me tell you plainly that I have no faith whatever in such views. They are only self-deception. A little inquiry soon reveals the fact that those who cherish them have made no effort whatever to candidly and fairly investigate the evidences of Christianity. In ninety-nine cases out of a hundred they have never carefully and earnestly studied the Bible for themselves. Indeed, it will generally be found that they have never so much as read once through the Bible. They may have done so when they were small children, and incapable of judging of its merits; but since they came to manhood they have paid no attention to it, or at the most have only read a little here and there, hap-hazard, without giving it any fair investigation. They are therefore wholly unacquainted with the Bible.

These persons have gotten up a few objections here and there from some ranting infidel, and have never examined to see whether they were well founded or not. If they have read at all for information, it has been some infidel work against the Bible. This they call investigating; but it is all on one side. When I have met these doubters, I have taken pains to inquire of them what books they have read which have been written in defense of the Bible, and in answer to infidel objections; and though I have traveled extensively, and have met hundreds of these men, I have yet to find the first one who has ever, according to his own admission, given the subject a serious investigation. The great mass of skeptics have never so much as read one of the hundreds of books which prove the truthfulness of the Bible. A very few, perhaps, have carelessly read one or two small volumes of that nature. Upon such a flimsy foundation they are risking eternity.

"The millions of scoffers who have come, and who now live, are ignorant of Bible facts and Bible language. The profound and the unlettered, the wealthy and the indigent, the talented and the stupid, are ignorant of Bible facts and Bible language. To some, this may sound strange; but it is not hard to prove. The matter may be easily tested. These scoffers live now, and you may approach and converse with them. During a ten-years' search, you are not likely to find one exception to the general statement. There was one who tried this for eighteen years, to see if he could meet with any one who cast away the Bible, and who was at the same time acquainted with its contents, and with the ancient literature connected with the Bible. He found some who at first declared themselves acquainted with the subject, but who really were not. After asking them, in an affectionate manner, a few questions, they generally confessed that their knowledge did not extend far. But this fact can be seen more clearly while looking at examples of willful ignorance." [1]

Infidels make special pretensions to fair dealing and fair play. Now, would it be a fair way of investigating the character of any man, to go among his bitterest enemies, and hunt up every sneer, and scoff, and story, whether true or false, and then, without further ado, pronounce judgment upon him, and refuse to have any intercourse with him? Would it not be reasonable also to consult his friends, and see what they had to say, and especially to become personally acquainted with him, and also to investigate the character and accusations of his enemies, before giving credence to them, and see whether they were not prompted by envy, malice, or revenge, in the charges which they brought against him?

But how do skeptics investigate the Bible? Not one in a hundred of them has ever read it through

---

Nelson on Infidelity pp. 32, 33.

since he came to years of understanding. Not one in ten thousand of them could read it fluently and understandingly in the tongues in which it was written. They do not make it a study; they do not understand it; they cannot fairly represent it. It is a rare thing that an infidel quotes a passage of Scripture correctly. Even the passages they produce as objectionable are usually misunderstood, misquoted, or misrepresented. Probably not one infidel in five hundred could quote correctly from memory twenty passages of Scripture, giving chapter and verse where they occur. And the little they do know of the words of the Book is what was taught them in childhood, when their judgments were immature, instead of being learned by them when grown up, in the way of careful, diligent, painstaking investigation.

Now, we submit, that if men wish to investigate the Bible they should read it, study it, learn it, practice it, and inquire concerning it among its friends as well as its foes; and then let them investigate the condition and character of persons who live according to the Bible, and compare them with men who hate it, curse it, or are ignorant of it, and they will be better fitted to judge of its merits.

Reader, allow me to ask you personally, How is it with yourself? Are you a doubter? Are you skeptical? Do you sometimes question whether the Bible be true? Presuming your answer to be in the affirmative, let me ask, What pains have you taken to settle this question? Certainly you cannot fairly judge of the merits of the Bible unless you are thoroughly acquainted with it, have read it through, and carefully studied it. Have you done this? I fear you have not. Then when objections have arisen in your mind, have you referred to the proper authors to see how those objections could be answered? A few words of explanation in such a case will frequently remove what appeared to be a serious objection. My friend, are you honest and candid in saying that you would like to believe the Bible if you could? Are you really willing to make an effort to know the truth on this all-important question,—a question which affects the salvation of your soul hereafter, as well as your character in this life?

Do not say that you are not able to procure books by which you can make such an investigation. The cost would be but a trifle. Excellent books upon this subject can be obtained at any book-store, or from almost any library, at a cost of from fifty cents to a dollar and a half per book, any one of which, upon a careful perusal, would probably answer your objections satisfactorily, and two or three, studied with candor, would be likely to entirely settle your mind upon this subject. If you have not read the works of great writers and thinkers upon this important question, you are not aware of the strength of the evidence in favor of Christianity. You have never dreamed of the abundance of evidence which God has thrown around the truthfulness of his holy word. Do not say that you have not time to read; for almost any of the ordinary books in defense of the Bible can be read through in the odd hours or evenings of a single week. Are you not willing to give that amount of time to an investigation of the subject? If not, it shows that you care less about God and Heaven and your soul than you do about the most frivolous things of life,—an evening party, or a dime novel. If this is all the interest you have,

God will be just if he condemns you in the Judgment.

Do not refuse to read upon this question. You can better afford to read twenty volumes through carefully than to be in doubt upon so momentous a subject. Consider a moment its great importance. The Bible claims to be the infallible word of the great, the awful, and the eternal God, who reigns in Heaven. It plainly declares that all who do not love and serve that God shall be damned; that their souls shall be lost; and that they shall be cast into a lake of fire, and utterly burned up. It declares that this will be the doom of all skeptics and unbelievers.[2] Will you carelessly run the risk of such a terrible fate, taking no precaution to avoid it? The Bible declares, on the other hand, that he who, as a faithful Christian, believes and obeys God, shall have immortality and eternal life hereafter in a beautiful and glorious world; that there he shall never suffer pain, sickness, sorrow, nor death; but that he shall be eternally happy in God's kingdom. Who can estimate the value of such a prize? Is it not worth your while to examine into the matter, and see if these promises are true?

Again: If Jesus Christ has died for you, it is your duty to live for him, and to be a Christian every day of your life, and to strive to lead others to Christ; it is terribly wicked for you to go on talking doubts, sowing unbelief and skepticism among all your acquaintances, and leading others down to ruin with yourself. Friend, this is no light matter. As a Judgment-bound soul, you ought to stop and know what you are doing. If

---

[2] Rev. 21:8; Mark 16:16.

you will in the next six months but give a few shillings and odd hours that you may have to spare to the investigation of this matter, you may become thoroughly acquainted with the main arguments in favor of Christianity. Will you do it?

Parents, I appeal to you to do your duty to your children in this respect. This is the age of infidelity. Doubt and skepticism are increasing. Infidels walk on every side. Their papers and books are everywhere. Your children cannot walk the streets without hearing infidel views expressed, nor attend school without reading them. What effort are you making to fortify their minds against the determined foe, infidelity? Before you are aware of it, their minds have been poisoned by unbelief; they have read some caviling objection which will always be a stumbling-block in their way. Are you prepared to instruct them yourselves? Have you informed your minds so as to give an intelligent defense of your holy religion, or are you allowing your children to come up without any instruction upon the most vital question of their whole lives? By and by, when it is too late, you will wake up to find that your children are confirmed infidels. You alone will be to blame. You should take pains, while your children are young and under your own influence, to thoroughly establish them in a firm belief in the Bible. This you can easily do. There are many plain and interesting books upon this question, and you cannot afford to be without them. Every family should have at least half a dozen such volumes on their shelves. Then you should read them to your children, and have the older ones read them for themselves. Such a course would do much to save them from wickedness here and from hell hereafter.

Look to your sons and daughters, and see what they are reading.

Teachers and ministers, are you doing your duty in this matter? Are you yourselves informed upon the question? Are you able to answer the scoffs and cavils of ranting unbelievers? Have you warned your school and your flock as you should? Have you urged them to read and inform themselves concerning the evidences of the truth of the Christian religion? Call their attention to the proper books; set forth their advantages; interest all to read them; do your duty, and save souls from perdition.

List of books to be read. Do you inquire what books you should read upon the subject of infidelity? To aid you in the matter, I will here give a list from which you can readily make a selection. Any book-seller can obtain them for you. Most of them are small books, written in plain English, easily understood.

The Cause and Cure of Infidelity. By Nelson.

Fables of Infidelity; showing the absurdities of Atheism, Pantheism, and Rationalism. By R. Patterson.

The Evidences of Christianity. By Bishop M'Ilvaine.

•Ecce Cœlum. By E. F. Burr.

Pater Mundi. By E. F. Burr.

Horne's Introduction, Vol. I.

Evidences of Christianity (various authors). Am. Tract Society.

Paley's Evidences.

History of the Books of the Bible. By Prof. Stowe.

Alexander's Evidences.

Leland's Revelation.

Newton on the Prophecies.

Only a few are here named of those most easily obtained, and which will require the least hard study. The leisure hours of a few evenings will suffice to read any one of them. Then more extensive and critical works, such as Butler's Analogy, Lardner's Works, etc., can readily be obtained.

CHAPTER II.

THE EVIDENCE OF AN ALMIGHTY CREATOR REVEALED THROUGH THE TELESCOPE.

CHRISTIANS claim that there is a living God, and that he is in every attribute infinite, incomprehensible, eternally exalted far beyond the loftiest conception of the greatest minds, not only of men, but even of the angels. The most minute object does not escape his sight, while at the same time the eternal worlds on high are all under his care and control. The Holy Bible sets forth just such a being as the author of this world, and the one whom we should worship. Daniel prays to him as "the great and dreadful God,"[1] and Nehemiah as "the great, the mighty, and the terrible God."[2] And the Lord himself thus sets forth his own greatness. While we read this testimony, let us weigh it, not as hyperbolical language, but rather as coming far short of the real truth:—

---

[1] Dan. 9:4. [2] Neh. 9:32.

"Who hath measured the waters in the hollow of his hand, and meted out heaven with the span, and comprehended the dust of the earth in a measure, and weighed the mountains in scales, and the hills in a balance?" "Behold, the nations are as a drop of a bucket, and are counted as the small dust of the balance; behold, he taketh up the isles as a very little thing. And Lebanon is not sufficient to burn, nor the beasts thereof sufficient for a burnt-offering. All nations before him are as nothing; and they are counted to him less than nothing, and vanity. To whom then will ye liken God? or what likeness will ye compare unto him?" "Have ye not known? have ye not heard? hath it not been told you from the beginning? have ye not understood from the foundations of the earth? It is He that sitteth upon the circle of the earth, and the inhabitants thereof are as grasshoppers; that stretcheth out the heavens as a curtain, and spreadeth them out as a tent to dwell in." "To whom then will ye liken me, or shall I be equal? saith the Holy One. Lift up your eyes on high, and behold who hath created these things, that bringeth out their host by number; he calleth them all by names by the greatness of his might, for that he is strong in power; not one faileth." "Hast thou not known, hast thou not heard, that the everlasting God, the Lord, the Creator of the ends of the earth, fainteth not, neither is weary? there is no searching of his understanding."[3]

"Canst thou by searching find out God? canst thou find out the Almighty unto perfection? It is as high as heaven; what canst thou do? deeper than hell; what canst thou know? The measure

---

[3] Isa. 40: 12, 15-18, 21, 22, 25, 26, 28.

thereof is longer than the earth, and broader than the sea."⁴ "O the depth of the riches both of the wisdom and knowledge of God! how unsearchable are his judgments, and his ways past finding out! For who hath known the mind of the Lord? or who hath been his counselor?"⁵ In the supernal glory of his august presence, the highest seraphim stand in sacred awe with vailed faces, and cry, "Holy, holy, holy."⁶

This God is represented as working, creating worlds, beings, animals, plants, etc.⁷ Now if this be really so, then we shall expect to see everywhere wonderful works, worthy of such an almighty God. But if, upon carefully examining nature, we find those works to be small in extent, mean in execution, disorderly in arrangement, and easily searched out and comprehended, then we shall naturally conclude that the Bible has deceived us, and that there is no such God.

With these thoughts before us, let us now for a moment turn our eyes upon nature. We should especially do this as the Bible appeals to nature for proof that there is such a God as it sets forth.⁸ Yonder moon, to the naked eye, looks like a small affair; but turn one of our mighty modern telescopes upon it, and lo! it is a world, a planet, over 2,000 miles in diameter, and 6,000 miles in circumference! We find that it is, in round numbers, 240,000 miles distant from the earth. To form some idea of the actual distance indicated by these figures, a moment's calculation demonstrates that it would take a train of cars running constantly at the rate of twenty-five miles an hour, over a year

---

⁴ Job 11:7-9.   ⁵ Rom. 11:33, 34.   ⁶ Isa. 6:1-3.
⁷ Ex. 20:8-11; Ps. 19:1-3.   ⁸ Rom. 1:20.

to reach it! This moon, hung on nothing, is revolving around our earth at the rate of 54,000 miles per day.

Now look at our own planet, the Earth. See its far-stretching plains many hundreds of miles in extent; look upon its high-towering mountains, pushing their bald heads away above the clouds into the region of eternal snows; behold broad continents reaching thousands of miles in every direction, supporting to-day fourteen hundred million (1,400,000,000) souls. Sound the huge old foaming oceans, with their miles upon miles in depth of water. Who can comprehend the greatness of our earth? Eight thousand miles through the center! Twenty-five thousand miles around it! Who made it? Men? Angels? Nay, verily. Is it not worthy of an almighty God? Does it not loudly proclaim that there must be such a creator?

This great earth is hung upon nothing, is swinging in open space! What keeps it in position, and prevents it from falling? But more, it revolves upon its axis every day with the greatest exactness, never varying the hundredth part of a second in a thousand years. But more wonderful still, the earth is revolving around the sun once every year in an orbit, or circle, which is about one hundred and ninety million (190,000,000) miles in diameter! Were there a railroad from the earth to the sun, a train going night and day, thirty miles an hour, would require three hundred and thirty-eight years to reach the sun. To travel around this immense orbit, the earth moves about nineteen miles a second,—more than a thousand times faster than the fastest locomotive. It never fails to get around in exact time, even to a second.

EVIDENCE OF THE TELESCOPE.

Looking out through the telescope, we behold many other planets, similar to the earth, all revolving like ours around the sun. There is little Mercury, much smaller than the earth, thirty-seven million (37,000,000) miles from the sun, revolving around it every three months at the rate of 109,000 miles per hour. Next is Venus, sixty-eight million (68,000,000) miles from the sun, moving 80,000 miles per hour, and circling around the sun every seven months. Far out beyond our earth, one hundred and forty-five million (145,000,000) miles from the sun, hangs the large planet Mars. It goes whirling on its course around the sun, making its revolution every two years.

Leaving Mars, let us wing our way through space to the next planet, Jupiter, which is four hundred and ninety-five million (495,000,000) miles from the sun. On examination we find it 89,000 miles in diameter. What a monster! We thought our earth large, but it is a mere pigmy beside Jupiter. Then Jupiter has four moons, while we have only one; and it takes him twelve years, traveling eighty times as fast as a cannon-ball, to run his great circuit around the sun. And no wonder, for it is nine hundred and ninety million (990,000,000) miles straight across his orbit, and, of course, more than three times as far around.

Taking a long breath, let us plunge off through space till we halt at the next planet, Saturn, nine hundred million (900,000,000) miles in a straight line from the sun. We find it to be a huge body 79,000 miles in diameter, and having eight moons. It takes this planet twenty-nine years to make its circuit around the sun. Pushing on again in our aerial flight, we fetch up at Uranus, eighteen hundred million (1,800,000,000) miles from the sun.

It is no small affair, being 35,000 miles in diameter. Yet it is so far away that it is invisible to the naked eye. It has six moons. Uranus takes eighty-four years to run his race around the sun. Now we strike out for the last planet in our system, Neptune. We find that it is twenty-eight hundred million (2,800,000,000) miles distant from the sun. Its diameter is 31,000 miles, nearly four times that of the earth. It travels rather slowly, only about 11,000 miles per hour, and requires one hundred and sixty-four years to complete its circuit around the sun. Beyond the last planet of the solar system, however, we find an immense comet coursing its way forty-four billion (44,000,000,000) miles from the sun.

"You see that we have come to a new order of distances in our astronomy. The distances we have to deal with in our every-day life are such as we pass over in going to our fields, neighbors, schools, churches, markets, occasionally a neighboring city; and hours and miles answer very well to express such movements. Next, we learn that the earth we live on is nearly 8,000 miles through,—this lifts us to quite another plane of distances. Our common walks and rides are lost by the side of such mammoth lines. Then we learn that the moon is 240,000 miles away. See another plane and order of distances still! The word miles begins to empty itself of its meaning in such combinations.

"But we go on to learn that the moon is at our very door, as compared with other members of our planet system,—that the sun is four hundred times as remote; Neptune eleven thousand times; while the comet of 1680, that Minister of Foreign Affairs to his Solar Majesty, buries itself in that tremendous Ultima Thule, whose distance is one hundred and eighty thousand times that of the moon. Do you take the meaning of such enormous intervals? Have miles any meaning left to them? Does not the height of this last plane of our astronomical arithmetic seem almost too dizzy and cloud-mixed to stand upon? And when you are told that a car, running express from the sun to that frontier of this planetary system of ours, would not need to put on brakes for five hundred thousand years, do your conceptions seem any the less dizzy and astounded?"[9]

Besides the planets above named, there are a large number of smaller ones, about three hundred in all, belonging to the solar system, all revolving around our sun. Now what holds all these immense planets in their places, and keeps them revolving around the sun in such exact order and time? It is the great law of attraction by which larger bodies attract and hold to themselves smaller bodies, as the earth attracts an apple from the tree-top and pulls it to the ground. So the sun attracts all the planets of our system to itself, and keeps them from flying off at random into space. Is the sun, then, larger than all these immense planets which we have described? It must be, and so indeed it is.

Why, then, do not the planets all fall into the sun, as apples fall to the earth? Here comes into play another law. Tie a ball to the end of a string, and swing it around your head. The motion of the ball inclines it to pull away from you, but the string pulls the other way, and thus keeps it in position. So the swift motion of the planets

---

[9] Ecce Cœlum, pp. 108, 109.

inclines them to fly off from the sun, while the attraction of the sun pulls them in toward itself, and so they are kept in their orbits.

The telescope shows the sun to be a real body nearly 900,000 miles in diameter. Nine hundred thousand miles on a straight line through its center! Let us compare it with the size of our earth. "It would weigh down three hundred and fifty thousand earths! The philosopher sits with scales in his hands, as Homer says Jupiter did on Ida to weigh the contending fates of Greece and Troy. He puts the earth into one scale, and rolls the sun into the other. Instantly the earth flies aloft with tremendous precipitation. He throws in two worlds like ours—ten—one hundred—one thousand—with scarcely better success. In a fit of impatience, he trundles all the earths he has into the capacious scallop. At last an equipoise seems establishing: the scales hang see-sawing, and at last settle into motionlessness at the same level. With mingled curiosity and astonishment he counts up those terrestrial globes, and finds them three hundred and fifty-two thousand in number." [10]

A planet three hundred and fifty-two thousand times larger than our huge earth! Indeed, it is eight hundred times larger than all the planets taken together which revolve around it. This is the reason it is able to attract and hold them all in their orbits. None of the planets of which we have been speaking give light of themselves. All are dependent upon the sun for light. He is the prince over them all! They are but his attendants. Our sun itself is dashing on, and on, in its orbit, bearing all its planets with it at the rate of 3,000 miles

---

[10] Ecce Cœlum, p. 119.

per minute. "Could we plant ourselves immovably at a certain point in the celestial spaces, and see our sun go sailing by with all its glorious squadrons of planets and moons,—sailing down the abyss as if driven by ten thousand hurricanes,—would not the sight of such celerity almost irrecoverably daze both senses and spirit?" [11]

But, reader, now prepare for grander views than all this,—magnitudes, distances, and glories compared to which our sun with its three hundred rolling planets is a mere drop in the ocean, a candle beside the noon-day sun. It is now a demonstrated and unquestioned fact that our sun with its attendant planets is only one out of a vast number of suns with like planets revolving around each of them; and that many of these lesser suns, of which ours is one, are all revolving around another colossal central sun, who is king over them all. We find that the earth, in fact, is but a small planet, traveling around a small star, the sun; and that the whole solar system is but a mere speck in the universe, an atom of sand on the shore, a drop in the infinite ocean of space.

"From satellite neighborhoods we have risen to planet neighborhoods; and now, from these, we have evidently risen to grand solar neighborhoods, where orbed suns go grandly wheeling about suns; carrying with them in inseparable union their glittering retinues." [12] What a stupendous thought! Who can grasp it?

The nearest, after our own, of these suns, called fixed stars, is distant from our earth more "than one hundred thousand times one hundred and ninety millions of miles. A most bewildering dis-

---

[11] Ecce Cœlum, p. 190.   [12] *Id.* p. 129.

tance! It would take light itself, that fleetest of known travelers, that Mercury of science, whose pace is 192,000 miles a second, more than three years to sweep across it."[13] The more distant stars are so far away that their light, which travels as far as from California to England and back quicker than you can wink your eye, requires fifty thousand years to reach our eyes. Of all the stars which we can see with the naked eye, excepting a half-dozen which belong to our system, each one is a sun, with a huge system of planets revolving around it; and it in turn, with all its planets, revolves around another central sun. These are called Sun Systems.

There are known to be more than one thousand such systems. The Sirius system is equal in light to sixty-three of our suns; the Polar-star system to eighty-six. "Think of an eighty-fold sun! However, some stars are still more astonishing; Vega, for example, which blazes with the light of three hundred and forty-four suns; Capella, for example, which blazes with the light of four hundred and thirty; Arcturus, for example, which blazes with the light of five hundred and sixteen; Alcyone, for example, which blazes with the light of twelve thousand! As we have seen, our sun is no trifle. Its astonishing orb would nearly fill the whole lunar orbit; and would weigh down, eight hundred times over, its whole ponderous cortege of satellites, planets, and comets. And yet it is only one of the lesser lights of space. Not the smallest, indeed,—forbid it, little 61 Cygni,—but still a mere rush-light and glow-worm as compared with many of the huge luminaries which pour their glories

---

[13] Ecce Cœlum, p. 130.

adown the immensity of nature. It could not remain visible a moment in the presence of such golden-haired and majestic day-kings as even Sirius and Polaris, to say nothing of those huger monarchs whose effulgence floods the celestial spaces." [14] Reader, is not this a system worthy of such a God as the Bible reveals?

But do not think that we have arrived at the end of creation yet. Far from it. We have only looked at the A B C's, have only halted at the first station in a trip across a continent. Going still farther, we have the Group Systems. These are formed of many of the sun systems, all revolving around another great center, wheels within wheels, each ascending series growing grander and more vast than the one below it.

Cluster Systems, — we must go a step farther. Many of these great groups of central suns are revolving around another center, and of these great systems many must contain from ten to twenty thousand stars each. Think of a system made up of twenty thousand revolving suns!

"We advance another step, to systems of the Sixth Order,—Nebulæ Systems! Scattered, or rather arranged, over the sky by thousands, are those bright misty spots called nebulæ, which no power of the telescope has yet been able to resolve into stars." "In my view, they all consist of stars, so packed together by local neighborhood and unspeakable distance that all individuality of impressions on the eye is lost." [15]

"What is the Milky Way, so called, which we see belting our heavens? Nothing but the nebula to which we belong, expanded all round the sky

---

[14] Ecce Cœlum, pp. 132, 133.   [15] *Id.* pp. 140, 141.

and easily resolved into stars by the fact that we are in the midst of it." [16]

"According to the best estimates of our own nebula, it contains some eighteen million suns; and the thickness of its golden wheel is about eight million diameters of the earth's orbit, while its diameter is one hundred and seventy million such diameters. One of its Border States would require not far from one hundred millions of years to put orbit about metropolis Alcyone." [17]

Ulterior Systems. "We have found all the suns, and groups of suns, and clusters of groups of suns in each nebula engaged in revolution about its center of gravity. Is this center itself in motion on another orbit still larger? Is each nebular fleet, instead of riding at anchor in the sky, sailing away on a circumnavigation more stupendous than we have yet noticed? It is even so." [18]

"Eighteen million suns belong to our firmament. More than four thousand such firmaments are visible; and every increase of telescopic power adds to the number. Where are the frontiers—the last astronomical system—that remote spot beyond which no nebula, no world, glitters on the black bosom of eternal nothingness?" [19]

"What right have we to stop just where the power of our instrument happens for the moment to have stopped, and say, 'This is the end—these are the Pillars of Hercules! Turn back, O adventurous explorer—nothing but night and void in this direction—thou hast reached the last outpost of the kingdom of the Eternal! *Ne plus ultra!*' No; thrice no. On still through peopled infini-

---

[16] Ecce Cœlum, p 142.
[17] *Id.* p 145.
[18] *Id.* p. 146.
[19] *Id.* p. 148.

tude, through raining galaxies and tornado nebulæ; and while thou goest outward still through the charging, storming hosts of suns as long as thought can fly, or angels live, say ever to thyself, 'Lo, these are parts of His ways; but how little a portion is heard of him!'" [20]

"But is there not something at the bottom of our hearts better than science, which invites us to believe that what would be so fitting and beautiful is also triumphantly actual; namely, that at the center of this august totality of revolving orbs and firmaments—at once the center of gravity, the center of motion, and the center of government to all —is that better country, even the heavenly, where reigns in glory everlasting the supreme Father and Emperor of Nature; the capital of creation; the one spot that has no motion, but basks in majestic and perfect repose while beholding the ponderous materialism which it ballasts in course of circulation about it? All hail, central Heaven! All hail, innermost Sun Palace and celestial Alhambra! All hail, believer's Last Home!" [21]

Just such a universe as this is what we would naturally expect an infinite being to make. "Certainly such a universe as this does not cry out against the existence of a God whose essential attribute is immensity; on the contrary, it is just such a universe as one would have expected to come from such a being. Nay, given a deity who is practically at home in every point of space, whose attributes are laid out on a scale of unbounded vastness, to whom it is just as easy to make and govern a trillion of worlds as it is a grain of sand; and the imperial fitness of things

---

[20] Ecce Cœlum, pp. 149, 150.   [21] Id., pp. 150, 151.

would demand that he people vacancy with very much that profusion and breadth of being we actually see. The work ought to express and honor the workman." [22]

Who made all these blazing suns and rolling worlds on high? Who set them in such perfect order? Who keeps them there? What can the atheist say to this? Nothing, only that it happened so! Who ever saw a watch happen to make itself? Who ever saw a machine happen to come together and go to running in perfect order? No one. Did, then, this wonderful machinery of the heavens make itself? Did it all happen so? The man who can believe thus has more credulity than ten robust Christians. How much easier and more rational to believe that there is an almighty God who made all these!

CHAPTER III.

THE EVIDENCE OF AN INFINITE GOD REVEALED BY THE MICROSCOPE.

But Unbelief asks, "How can the God of such a universe as this condescend to notice the small things of this earth, such as men, men's thoughts, words and actions, beasts, birds, and insects? Is it not preposterous to suppose that he will hear our prayers if we do pray to him?" O Unbelief, how blind thou art, and how ready to stumble! Know thou that an infinite God is infinite not simply in

---

[22] Ecce Cœlum, pp. 161, 162.

one direction, but in every direction, in small things as well as in large ones.

Dr. Burr well says: "Another characteristic of nature, deserving of notice, is the perfection of its details. The exquisite finish of nature in its minutest parts is about as wonderful as its vastness and variety. Scan that leaf. Examine the wing of that butterfly. Let the tinted and polished antennæ of that moth glitter in the focus of your instrument. Subject to the skillfulest notice of science and art the smallest veins of any animal or vegetable. Push the analysis just as far as possible, and submit that last visible minimum of organization in the crystalline lens of the cod, with its five millions of muscles and sixty thousand millions of teeth, to the most searching criticism of the superbest microscope. What exquisite details! What elaborate refinement of workmanship!

"In masterpieces of human painting, the main points only are cared for, while all the subordinate are too rude to bear close inspection. Not so with the works of nature. A real landscape you may analyze to your heart's content, and inspect its details as critically as eye, armored with lens, can do, without finding workmanship growing less exquisite the further you push inquiry. A real man —you may descend to the minutest particulars of his organization, and get as near its primary elements as an Ehrenberg with his superb instruments and practiced vision can carry you, without finding the least falling off from that delicacy of execution which appears on the larger masses and outlines of the body.

"So everywhere among natural objects — the great and the small, the outlines and the minute filling up, as far as utmost optical resources can carry our observation, are wrought with apparently the same overflowing outlay of attention and skill. It is not so in a few instances merely, nor in a thousand,—it is so universally. That there are any so preposterous as to think that this feature of nature makes positively against the idea of a sparrow-watching, hair-numbering, and thought-weighing God, is, of course, not to be imagined. Of course, it is a feature that fully harmonizes with such an idea.

"A nature finished exquisitely, down to the most infinitesimal of its details, is just what one would have predicted from a God of this description. Announced the fact that he was about to create, and expectation would have stood on tiptoe to look for just such a nature as we see. A God for whose vision nothing is too small, who necessarily gives as complete attention to the affairs of an atom as to those of an empire, who can concentrate his almightiness with as much freedom and accuracy on a mathematical point as on a world, who is embarrassed no more by unlimited multiplicity than by unlimited minuteness of details, who can with equal ease paint a landscape on the point of a needle,—say, if you please, forty thousand of such landscapes at once, with all their innumerable and minima particulars, back of the reticulated eyes of a single butterfly,—can with equal ease do this, and roll a solar system on its triumphant path about the Pleiades; do I not know that a being with such a striking attribute as this, would surely give it expression in his works?"[1]

Ah! little man, do not fear that God is so great that he will overlook you,—that Being whose

---

[1] Ecce Cœlum, pp. 168–170.

almighty power and infinite wisdom are not only manifest in the great things of creation, but are just as marvelously manifest in the construction of a flea or an animalcule. Lay that speck of a flea under a microscope. He has a perfect body, head, eyes, mouth, stomach, legs, etc. Yet he is so small that you can scarcely feel him with your finger. What skill in workmanship! Is not the hand of God seen here?

Take a drop of water from that stagnant pool, and look at it under a powerful microscope. Who would have believed it? There are thousands of living, moving animals in that drop of water, each animal just as perfect in its way, just as full of life and motion, as yourself, yet so small that were they to move in close single file, twenty thousand of them would not reach more than half an inch. Several hundred millions of these tiny creatures might be packed into a space the size of the head of a pin. In a single drop of water four thousand millions would have room to exercise at will; while more than eight trillions might occupy a cubic inch without uncomfortable crowding. I do not know which is the more astonishing, the infinite power of God as manifested in the rolling, blazing suns on high, or as seen in the perfection of the infinitesimal animals invisible to the naked eye. Instinctively I bow my head, and worship this infinite God.

But you say you cannot comprehend such infinitudes, either of vastness or of exiguity. Exactly, yet you know that they exist; and that is the very reason we must believe without understanding everything. If God should undertake to explain all his wonders to us, it would only the more bewilder us, as we could not comprehend them.

Every one must believe in one thing that is infinite; viz., space. Reader, think a moment; where is the end of space? Go in a straight line on, and on, and on, far beyond all suns, all worlds, all matter, out far into the open void. Then what? Have you reached the end? There is no end. Space is infinite. So may there also be an infinite God, though we cannot fully comprehend the one more than the other. Everywhere, then,—above, below, on every side, in the immense worlds as seen through the telescope, or in a drop of water as viewed through the microscope,—we see the proof of an intelligent, infinite Creator. Shall we not adore and serve him?

CHAPTER IV.

THE EXACT ORDER IN ALL NATURE PROVES A DESIGNER.

We behold, upon a little closer observation, a wonderful wisdom in the works of nature around us. A perfect harmony prevails in all things; each particular object is specially adapted to the place it fills; and everything around it exactly fits it. Take the birds of the air. How admirably are they adapted to flying, in shape, feathers, bones, wings, and in every other way. How admirably adapted to swimming are the fishes in the water, with their thin, paddle-like shape, hard, smooth sides, and slippery scales and fins. How well prepared for walking and running upon the earth are the land animals. Their lungs are exactly fitted to breathe its air, their stomachs to digest its food.

Look at man himself. How wonderfully is he adapted to his position! What could he do were his hands like horses' feet, or had he any other than just the sort of limbs and shape he has? Of all forms, his is just the one that can be adapted to almost everything. He can swim in the water, walk and run upon the land, climb trees, endure the cold and the heat, travel over the world, and use everything for his advantage.

Who can fail to admire the wonderful mechanism of the eye? Notice where it is placed in the body. Had it been on the top of the head, on our backs, on our feet, or in almost any other place except just where it is, how terrible a calamity it would have been! Then see how it is protected by bones protruding beyond it; how it is arranged so that it can be turned in a twinkling in any direction. You can readily adjust it to perceive objects near by, or miles away. It is furnished with just that particular shape, out of ten thousand possible shapes, which science has demonstrated to be the only one which can refract all the rays to a single surface, and thus afford distinct vision. Were everything in the world just as it is to-day, with the exception of eyesight, were all living creatures wanting in this, the world would go to ruin in a week. What wisdom, then, what goodness, is shown in this simple arrangement! But this is only one instance out of ten thousand where we see the same wisdom displayed.

And then notice how everything is governed by exact law. Nothing is left to go at random. "On the earth's surface, in its dark interior, in the air and vault above, in the instant present and the ancient past,—everywhere, law waves its mighty scepter. Atoms and masses, the ponderables and imponderables, the organic and inorganic, the living and dead,—all are evidently subjected, in their modes of being and action, to certain fixed rules." "All known changes in the planetary orbits have been found to be bound in a law of periodicity which is apparently invariable. So beyond the solar system. Law still; nothing but law; law everywhere on ten thousand blazing thrones; largely the same laws that prevail in our system! As far as we can observe,—and it is no little that has been observed,—those distant orbs reverence the various principles of gravitation and mechanics, and keep as rigidly to their behests as when the earliest astronomy gazed at them from its rude Uraniberg of a hill-top. And every man of science is well persuaded that, could his observation alight on particular orbs of those remote and twinkling hosts, he would find their minutest details bound up in the chains of the same adamantine regularity that rules our own globe."[1]

Does not this fact of a universal rule, or fixed and settled law, show that everything has been planned and arranged by a great Intelligence? Throughout the universe, from the mightiest blazing suns in celestial glory down to the minutest object in a drop of water, we behold perfect order and exact regulation. The sun courses in its regular orbit, never varying a minute in its vast course of untold millions of miles. Think of our huge earth hissing and bounding on its way at the rate of 68,000 miles an hour, in an orbit that embraces nearly four hundred million (400,000,000)

---

[1] Ecce Cœlum, pp. 182-184.

ORDER IN NATURE. 37

miles in circumference every year; and yet in making that enormous round it has never varied the hundredth part of a second. Each year it finishes its round in exactly the same time. Wonderful! The superscription of an infinite God is here!

The same order and wisdom are observed everywhere. A volume might be written upon the wonderful mechanism of the human body, or even the hand, and then not exhaust its wonders. The most consummate wisdom is shown in the construction of every muscle, of every joint, and every capillary of the body. Now, how did all these things come? Were they so from eternity? How did they get a start? Did they happen so? Did they come by chance? Let us illustrate the folly of such a supposition.

Suppose a man had never seen, nor heard of, a watch. He is walking through a field, and finds a beautiful silver watch which is running. He picks it up and examines it. He observes the second-hand moving rapidly; observing more closely, he finds that the minute-hand is moving regularly, though not so fast. Further observation shows that the hour-hand also is moving. Studying it for some time, he learns that the second-hand goes clear round while the minute-hand goes from one minute mark to another. He sees that it never varies from this; it is always exactly the same. Further, he soon learns that the minute-hand makes just one entire revolution while the hour-hand is going from one hour mark to another. There is no variation in that. He opens the watch, and, lo! here are a large number of wheels with cogs; all of them are in motion; each one exactly fits the other. With his penknife he stops one of the wheels, and the whole machine stops. He finds that each one of the hands is a separate piece by itself, that each wheel is a separate part. The hands are steel, the wheels are of brass, the body of the watch is of silver; the face, of glass. In short, he soon perceives that it is a very delicate piece of machinery, adapted to keeping time, marking off the seconds, minutes, and hours of each day.

Now what would be his natural conclusion about this matter? If he should conclude that this watch came together thus by chance, without any living designer, without any maker; that by the mere force of certain laws among the different parts they arranged themselves in this perfect order, and set themselves thus to work,—if he should draw this conclusion, would not every one pronounce him a fool? Would not any sensible man, upon discovering such an instrument, in perfect running order, immediately conclude that some intelligent person, with great ingenuity and careful labor, had planned and constructed this machine, and that too, for a definite purpose?

Certainly, we could not find one intelligent man in the whole world who would draw any other conclusion. This would be the only legitimate conclusion he could draw; for look at the facts: He has seen a great many machines and engines,—sewing-machines, threshing-machines, etc., and yet he never saw one grow of itself. He knows that every such machine which he ever saw was planned and built by an intelligent being, and for a specific object. Accordingly, if it was suggested to him that this machine was the work of chance, he would reason: "How is it possible that these delicate parts of the watch should all happen to come together so orderly, the delicate little brass wheels, with their still more delicate little cogs, and each one in just the shape, and in just the place, to fulfill its particular function? How could it be possible that those three steel hands should have happened to come together and arrange themselves in just that manner? How does it happen that the glass crystal placed itself over those hands just where it was needed?" And thus he might go on reasoning, showing conclusively that there was not one chance in a hundred million that the watch made itself, or was made by chance.

But, reader, what is the mechanism of that little watch, compared to the wonderful machinery of the universe which we have examined, commencing with the eternal worlds on high and ending with the ten hundred thousand animals in a drop of water, everything made after the most consummate wisdom, showing the most perfect adaptation in all its parts, and kept moving according to the strictest law? Shall we pronounce it preposterous that the little watch made itself, and then contradict ourselves by affirming that a mechanism infinitely higher and more wonderful came together by chance, or made itself? Men have been able to make watches, sewing-machines, steam engines; but all the wisdom of the world has never been able to create one living thing. Among all the millions of objects around us, we never saw one thing that was self-created. Shall we pronounce it impossible that a watch should be the work of chance, and that its component parts should be drawn together by laws of so-called natural selection, and then turn our eyes upon nature and swear there is no God,—that nature made itself? How desperately the human heart must have hated a holy God, before it dared to breathe to itself such a preposterous supposition.

How readily the atheist may be confounded by a few simple questions. For instance: Where did the first hen come from? Does he say she was hatched from an egg? Then we ask, Where did the egg come from? What will he say now? He cannot say that a hen laid it, for then we ask, Where did the hen come from? Men have lived thousands of years upon the earth, and they have seen millions of eggs and hens; but they never saw a hen that was not hatched from some egg; nor did they ever see an egg, that would produce a chicken, that was not laid by a hen. So we repeat the question, Where did the first hen come from? So of any other species of animals. We do not see men or beasts growing on trees, or sprouting out of the ground. All animals have some living father and mother. Where did the first dog come from, the first horse, the first man? The atheist cannot tell; but God's book tells, and it is a sensible story. God made the first hen, the first horse, the first man.

> "Deny God—all is mystery beside;
> Millions of mysteries! each darker far
> Than that thy wisdom would unwisely shun.
> If weak thy faith, why choose the harder side?
> We nothing know but what is marvelous;
> Yet what is marvelous we can't believe." [2]

Why, how natural, how fitting it is that there should be a living creator who has designed and executed all this wonderful machinery of the universe for a definite object! The idea of an almighty God meets every emergency of the case,

---

Campbell's Debate with Owen, p. 119.

and immediately answers all its wants. It explains everything. Granting that there is such an infinite and almighty creator, how readily it solves the whole problem. It ends the chapter immediately, and winds up all our doubts and speculations. Why not accept such a logical solution? But another conclusion follows:—

If there is an almighty, holy God, as the Bible sets forth, then there is a day of Judgment; then sin must be accounted for; then wicked men will be punished. Here is the rub, and that is the sum of the difficulty. It is to evade this dreaded conclusion that men resort to all these miserable shifts, dodges, and preposterous suppositions.

At one time these haters of God boldly asserted the eternity of all things. But that opinion was exploded long ago. Few hold it now. Next, it was confidently affirmed that everything came by chance. Here, again, the enemies of God had a jubilee. There was no God, no Judgment, no one to be called to account for crimes. Chance created all things, and ordered all things. But that child of perdition was dead and buried long ago. No one knows of its now having even a distant relative alive. People wonder that anybody was so foolish as to give it birth, or attempt to keep it alive. But now, all hail, ye last-born of hell! God is dead, after all. "Law, law, almighty law!" This is now the grand battle-cry of atheists. No living, intelligent God to fear! Nothing but law and fate! This is the golden calf around which unbelievers and atheists are now dancing and feasting. But their rejoicing will be short. This rival to the blessed God will soon go the way of all its predecessors.

CHAPTER V.

A UNIVERSAL CRY FOR GOD.

The universal belief of all nations in all ages, that there exists a supreme, intelligent ruler of the universe, has a strong bearing upon this question. It certainly is not proof positive that there is such a being, but it affords strong presumptive proof to that effect. Search the records of the most hoary antiquity, go backward in the fabulous ages, beyond all history, and you can find no fragmentary record of a nation, or an age, where there was not generally held a belief in some kind of a supreme being. Doubters could be found the same as now, but only a few, here and there. The great mass of the people, and the teachers, the philosophers, and kings upon their thrones, have all held a general belief in a deity.

"And the Jews, the Christians, the Mohammedans, the Hindoos with their affiliated races—to say nothing of smaller peoples—the believing nations covered by these names include in their mighty circumference nearly all the science, and civilization, and semi-civilization, and respectable morals the world can boast. Further, the whole body of mankind, past and present, with a few trifling exceptions, firmly believe in at least one great Intelligence of a grade indefinitely superior to the human, and worthy of worship. Every nation has some divinity. There is no country without temples, altars, priests. In all climates, under all governments, through all stages of society, from the most barbaric to the most cultivated, man humbles himself before great invisible personal powers.

The traveler into unexplored countries about as much expects to find them supplied with deities as he expects to find them supplied with men. The traveler into distant ages, whatever direction he takes, about as much expects to find men worshiping as he does to find them eating and drinking. Whether Livingstone or Humboldt—he encounters the supernatural at every step. Whether Niebuhr or Muratori—at every step he meets the immemorial traditions of the supernatural descending upon him like Amazons from every point of the compass. The *cultus* is everywhere. And whether it points at the fetich, or the idol, or the star, or the Grand Lama, or Brahma, or Boodh, or Odin, or Osiris, or Jupiter, or Allah, or Jehovah—it expresses the faith of all nations and ages in at least one great superhuman Intelligence, who holds sanctuary within such holy names, before whose power and wisdom the greatest of men should uncover, and from whose undefined and dreamy greatness one should not be surprised to see issuing any conceivable wonders. I use universal language. It is because the dissenters from this generic Theism are so few as to be absolutely inappreciable in the presence of the empires and continents and generations who hold it with a profound and ineradicable faith.

"What means this great Plebiscitum? What means this universal faith in at least one worshipful superhuman Intelligence,—this chain of such faiths stretching away back into the mists of history, and even the *adyta* of primeval tradition,—this chain ever expanding toward Christian Theism as it passes through the more enlightened times and lands? If any man says that it means nothing, or that it does not flex itself significantly in the direction of God, my eyes dilate upon him with astonishment. Is he serious? Does he mean what he says?"[1]

How came this universal belief? If it is all a lie, and without any foundation in nature, why so universal? If a few philosophers or priests started the notion, how did it become so wide-spread from the very beginning? How is it that in the densest forest of America the least of the savage Indians believe in the Great Spirit? The cannibals in the Pacific islands reverently believe in the same Being. The blackest negro in the heart of Africa has faith in a deity. Not a tribe has ever been found upon the face of the earth that has not faith in some kind of a deity. My infidel friend, you should make some reasonable disposal of this mighty and indisputable fact. It means something; it proves something; viz., that the power which made man, impressed deep in his nature the fact that there is a being high above himself.

In perfect harmony with this fact, the science of phrenology shows that man was created to worship a supreme being. Any examination of the organs of the mind as they are manifest in the development of the brain, shows that a well-balanced mind is just as naturally inclined to revere and worship, as it is to reason and to love. Look upon any phrenological chart or bust, and there you will see marked the organ of veneration. It is a healthful development of this organ which inclines us to worship. All human beings, of every race, have this organ in a greater or less degree of development, which indicates a desire to worship some God. They could no more refuse to worship than they could refuse to

---

[1] Pater Mundi, pp. 277-279.

love their offspring. Some men there are, indeed, who have so perverted and warped their nature that they scarcely feel one sentiment of love for anything; but these are rare exceptions.

There is, then, naturally in the constitution of man in his normal condition, a desire for a God to worship; a reaching out toward a being higher than himself, a heavenly creator. Is there then no God in the universe to meet this universal want in our nature? Such a conclusion is absurd, unscientific, and contrary to nature. Says a devout scholar: "On observation, we find that there are, outside of this case and two or three other mooted cases,—such as that of the desire for immortality,—no desires natural to a sound human constitution for objects which do not exist. Thus a desire for food, for friendship, for knowledge, for reputation, for society, for liberty, for freedom from pain, is natural to every sound human constitution; and the object of each of these desires actually exists. The food exists to meet the hunger; the beauty exists to meet the taste for beauty; there is knowledge, society, health, to meet the natural relish for each of these things. Indeed, you cannot point out a single desire natural to a sound human nature to which there is not an answering object somewhere; but, on the contrary, such answering object is certainly known to exist, outside of the two or three disputed cases, like that under consideration. Hence we must conclude that the desire for God, which is natural to virtuous or normal minds, has over against it in the outward universe such a God to fulfill it."[2]

---

[2] Id. pp. 206, 207.

CHAPTER VI.

HOW TO FIND GOD.

"THE fool hath said in his heart, There is no God."[1] The Holy Bible, in which Christians believe, teaches that there is one living God, who is almighty, infinite in every perfection, eternal in his nature, the Creator of everything which exists, and the Father of all. This Bible claims to be a revelation of his will to man. It teaches that those who do his will shall be rewarded for it, both in this life and also eternally in the life to come; and that those who disobey him shall be punished, both here and hereafter.

But what evidence have we that the Bible is what it claims to be,—the word of God, a revelation from our Creator? Infidels pretend that there is not sufficient evidence to justify this claim. We affirm, and shall show, that there is an abundance of evidence that the Bible is the word of God. Indeed, there is so much evidence in proof of this, that many volumes would not suffice to contain it all. However, we shall state only a few of the plainest evidences for Christianity. Our acquaintance with infidels has thoroughly convinced us that it is not merely evidence which is needed to convince them, but that the difficulty lies far back of that. If an overwhelming amount of evidence could cure infidelity, the disease would long since have ceased to exist.

"Well," says the skeptic, "if there is a God, why do n't he show himself? If he will appear in

---

[1] Ps. 14:1.

mid-heaven, if he will come personally and talk with me, then I will believe him. I will stand in the door and call upon him to cause it to thunder out of a clear sky, to flash his lightnings where there are no clouds, to make the earth shake in answer to my questions,—let him do this, and then I will believe."

"Suppose God should take as much of his nature as we can understand, and bring it to us in the way of adequate personal manifestation to the senses. Could we endure the exhibition? Why, we can hardly bear such sights and sounds as we ourselves can produce. We can kindle such glory of conflagration, can detonate such might and majesty of sound, as will destroy sight and hearing, and even shock the weakly out of life. And surely if God should come upon our senses with such imperialism of sights and sounds as would appropriately represent the utmost power and knowledge we can conceive,—as would worthily express our ideas of Eternity and Almightiness and Omniscience,—that moment would be our last.

"Even now, when the common lightning shoots before our eyes, how they quiver back from the blinding flame; and when the common thunder comes upon us in some great crash, how our ears and hearts quail under the terrible bass! And were God himself to come flashing and pealing on the world in all that outward majesty that rightfully belongs to him, and fitly signifies to sense the presence of a virtually infinite being, who of us would see another moment in the body? We should straightway be dazzled out of life. Our frighted senses and hearts would give one leap, and then become motionless forever—and this though they were a thousand-fold stronger than they are.

". . . . The men who ask that God should personally manifest himself to their senses as God, know not what they ask. . . . Should a being of virtually infinite glory and majesty come on our senses, or our thoughts, with any but the most inconsiderable fraction of his greatness, our feeble souls would infallibly go into unhingement."[2]

Foolish man, you have no right to thus put tests to your God, to say just how he must prove himself to you. Do you know that God himself has given many tests by which he offers to prove to any man that he does exist; and that he will manifest himself to all who will put him to the proof? Now if you despise the way that God has chosen, and demand some other test, of your own invention, do not expect God to come to your terms and change from what he has declared he will do. You would better first try the tests which God submits. If you will do this thoroughly, we are willing to warrant that the results will be perfectly satisfactory. They have never failed and they never will fail in the case of any individual who will put them to thorough trial.

Try the following test: The Lord says, "If any man will do his will, he shall know of the doctrine, whether it be of God, or whether I speak of myself."[3] Now, skeptic, here is a chance for you to try an experiment. Commence to walk carefully according to the light you already have on matters of duty, and see whether faith in the Bible, and the God of the Bible, does not spring up in your heart. Begin to act upon the Bible as a rule of life, and see if it does not harmonize with your better nature. Promise this hour, that for the next six

---

[2] Pater Mundi, pp. 122-124.   [3] John 7: 17.

months you will go once a day, and, upon your knees, alone, humbly ask that if there is a God he will help you to the light, will help you to find him, will help you to know the truth; if the Bible is his word that he will help you to believe it, and open it to your understanding so that you may see it is the truth. My skeptical friend, do this and your infidelity is gone.

"Who cannot put God and the Scriptures on the test of this actual experiment? Who so poor, so weak, so ill-informed, so uncultured, so busy, that he cannot try these things by his liberality, by his prayer, by his conscientious living? Such a variety of easy practical methods enables all the world to become critics in religion."[4] But I have little hope that any skeptic will try this test. And why? Because he is not so willing or anxious to believe as he pretends. God must come to his terms or he will have nothing to do with him. The trouble, my friend, is not in the head; it is deeper than that, in the secret springs of your heart. Yours is a corrupt, sin-loving heart, which does not desire communion with a holy, sin-hating God. However loudly you may talk and prate, the Judgment will show that this was the trouble.

Who is it that wants to get rid of God? "There are persons who would as soon be without God as not; nay, there are those who could hardly hear pleasanter news than that the whole Theistic argument has been fairly overturned from the foundation, and the impossibility of a God proved beyond all possibility of denial. Oh, how scoffing Voltaire, and licentious Rousseau, and bloated Paine would

---

[4] Pater Mundi, pp. 20, 21.

have clapped their hands and shouted, could they have fallen on some wonderful geometry which by its rigid demonstrations could compel even the most unwilling to give up their last plea for Deity! Oh, how the high-handed evil-doers of every name, sinning and impetuously bent on sinning, would congratulate themselves, could it be made as plain as day that such a machine as a thinking, embodied man was created by chance; that chance fitted up the earth as his convenient home, and hung out the heavens above him with the blazon of stars and suns!

"But as soon as a sinner has made up his mind conclusively against sin, and has fully committed himself for endless war upon it in all its forms, then he ceases to be averse or indifferent to the divine existence; then he begins to positively like the idea, as including that of a righteous, divine government; then he begins to cling to it, to bless it, to feel that he cannot do without it; and as he goes on to higher and higher grades of virtue, the feeling in behalf of God gradually deepens into a profound hunger and thirst. He says, 'My soul thirsts for God, for the living God.' To him an offer to disprove God would be an offer to make the universe an awful solitude and desert." [5]

It is neither impossible nor difficult to find God to the entire satisfaction of your mind, if you are really in earnest about it. If you will humbly study the word which God has given, and try the many tests there proposed by God himself, you will soon lose all your doubts, and receive in exchange firm faith in God.

---

[5] Pater Mundi, pp. 203, 204.

CHAPTER VII.

THE HOPE OF THE INFIDEL.

The hope of the infidel,—what is it that he should love it, and cling to it so pertinaciously? Let us unmask it, and view its bald and hideous features, its grim skeleton. It is a hope that the universe is fatherless, without a ruler, without a guiding hand; the hope that creation has come by chance, and is governed by chance, that there is none higher than man himself to call the sinner to account; the hope that there is no judgment for the ungodly, no reward for the pious, that there is no hereafter for any one; the hope that our darling children whom we have laid in the grave have died like beasts, that we shall never see them more; the hope that in the hour of distress there is no rock higher than ourselves to which we can anchor for safety, that there is no loving heart in Heaven to respond to our cries in trouble; the hope that there is no hereafter, no future life, no blessed immortality, no Heaven, no angels, no Saviour, nothing but blank, cold, dark nothingness.

This is the prospect which the infidel offers us in exchange for the Christian's hope. What a bargain! For this shall I give up the faith which sustains me through trials and sorrows, which lightens up the valley of the shadow of death, which gives me a loving, sympathizing, almighty, heavenly Father, which puts into my hands an infallible guide for my feet, which gives me a Saviour to heal the wounds of sin, and to cleanse my guilty heart; a hope which holds out to me an immortal life hereafter, a glorious Heaven of light and beauty, and inexpressible joy, a reunion with my lost, cherished friends, redemption from the power of death; a faith which places an infinite, holy, and benevolent God at the helm of the universe?

The least observation will show that atheism and infidelity are simply systems of doubt, opposition, and fault-finding. Infidels take no positive positions themselves; they affirm nothing; they simply doubt everything, and object to everything. They do not offer us any system of faith, any code of morals, any hope of a hereafter, any book of instruction, any remedy for sin, any redemption from death. No; they do not profess to have these to offer. They simply find fault with our house, and propose to demolish it without providing us any substitute for it, even so much as a scanty shelter to cover our heads from the scorching sun, or the pelting rain. No; they only give us doubt for faith, uncertainty for certainty, despair for hope, chance for the living God, and death for life.

Read their books; hear their lectures; talk with a thousand of them; and you will find that this is always the truth. Infidelity never satisfies the longings of a sin-burdened heart. With all their endeavors, infidels never feel at ease; they are dissatisfied, restless, and fearful; they are not certain of anything, but afraid of everything. "It has been usual for leading unbelievers to confess the excellent moral tendency of the doctrine of a righteous divine ruler. And ask any man of ordinary sense and observation, putting him on his honor and conscience to speak frankly,—ask him whether he does not really think that a solid faith in such a being would, on the whole, be a greatly better thing for his son and all connected with him than disbelief or unbelief would be,—what would be the answer? He might not speak it, but ere a moment could elapse he would think it. 'Practically,' would he say to himself, 'it is better that my child should believe. Whatever may be the abstract truth in the case, I cannot deny that such a belief is likely to be followed by better results to himself and to all within his sphere of influence than the absence of that belief.'"[1]

I have myself frequently heard infidels say that although they did not believe in Christianity themselves, they wanted their children brought up under religious influences; for it would have a tendency to make them more refined and elevated, and to teach them good principles. Intelligent infidels the world over feel thus. Why is this so if there is no God, if the Bible is false, and if religion is a fable? Why do they prefer the influence of Christianity for their children? Why do they prefer a lie to the truth, if it be a lie, as they claim? It is because they see that religion is good for man even in this life.

CHAPTER VIII.

GOD CARES FOR US.

We have abundantly shown in the previous chapters that there is an intelligent creator who has made our world and all things in it,—the living God, who made man in his own image. The greatest wisdom and the most careful design are manifest in everything we behold; but the greatest and

---

[1] Pater Mundi, pp. 208, 209.

most wonderful of all the works of God upon this earth, is man. He stands high above all other creatures in his physical organization, and in his mental powers. God's choicest work was evidently bestowed upon him. This is in harmony with the Bible record of creation.[1] Here only the simple fact is mentioned that God created the other animals; but when it comes to man we have a minute description of how God made him, and for what; and it is further stated that he was made in the image of God himself.

These simple facts afford strong presumptive proof that this God must be interested in us, must have a fatherly care for us. Consider this point carefully: He stands in the double relation to us of creator and father. He is our Father in a much higher sense than is our earthly father, because he is absolutely the source, not only of our existence, but of everything around us upon which the continuance of our life depends. And all those things which sustain life, and make it desirable, he has made for us. Having thus made us so wisely, and placed us in this beautiful world, surrounded by everything for our comfort, does he then abandon us, and take no further thought or care concerning our welfare? A human parent who would do that would be called a brute or a monster. We should say that he was a hardened wretch. Shall we accuse our God and heavenly Father of this?

"Look about you among human parents. Do they not, almost without exception, tenderly love their little, dependent, helpless children? Is not that person considered almost a monster who approaches a state of heartlessness toward those who

---

[1] Gen. 1, 2.

lisp toward him the name father? Is not parental love an instinct through all the graded parentage of the brute kingdoms? The birds, the quadrupeds, the fishes,—animals, domestic or wild, how the feeblest and most timid of them will flame forth in reckless self-exposure to defend their young!

"Even the philosopher who is parent of an ingenious theory, the author who is parent of a creditable book, the inventor who is parent of a useful machine, the discoverer who is parent of an important science or fraction of a science, the artist who is parent of an excellent statue or painting, the statesman who is parent of a wise measure of national policy, the mechanic who is parent of a beautiful ship or house or watch,—all such persons find themselves having an affection for the things toward which they sustain this relation of paternity. They are the root from which that beautiful greenness has come; their image is on it; their life is in it; their body, their soul, their genius, their patience, their knowledge, their character, is diffused through it; in short, they have in all those green leaves and yellow fruits so many promising little children of their own. And they almost invariably conceive an affection for them as such. The abuse of them is the abuse of themselves; the praise and beauty of them are the praise and beauty of themselves.

"Such is the law of paternity everywhere within the range of our observation,—the parent loving its offspring. Among all the animal tribes, in earth and air and sea—whether the child be flesh and blood, or only the cell of the bee, the nest of the bird, the dam of the beaver, or the hand-work, mind-work of the ingenious man, it is loved by its author. And now we have to ask, Is God the sole exception to this sweeping law of paternity? Is the Being who established this law, and armed it with flails of remorse—is he himself out of harmony with it? Does he, too, not love his children, whether their name be men, or oxen, or birds, or flowers, or oceans, or stars? The induction, the science, is overwhelmingly against it."[2]

Yes, blessed be God! we are not orphans, we are not fatherless; we have an almighty and affectionate Parent who loves us; and of this he has given thousands of proofs. All nature cries out that he loves us, and the Bible confirms the testimony of nature.

"First, the great Father professes to love us. To lay no stress on hundreds of written declararations, 'I love you, I love you,' professing to come from him, the flowers, the songs, the golden light, the precious perfumes, the delicious tastes, all grace and beauty of form and feature and motion abroad in nature,—these are so many loving words, smiles, caresses of the All-Maker and All-Father toward the intelligent creatures who are aware of them. Who does not know it,—vocal speech is not the only language; the lighting up and wreathing of a face is not the only smile; the pressure of an arm of flesh is not the only embracing! O bright-faced sky, O smiling earth, O scented and singing and festival springs and summers, O innumerable anthems and poetries of delightful Nature,—ye also are God's tender looks and words and sacred kisses to us!

"Next, see what a beautiful home he has fitted up; ceiled with sapphire, floored with emerald, walled and curtained with sunsets and sunrises,

---

[2] Pater Mundi, pp. 103–105.

upholstered and garnished superbly and almost unboundedly for our shelter, our convenience, our dignity, and our delight. Then see what stores of healthful and pleasant food he provides for us in the manifold grains and fruits; of suitable and comely clothing in the bolls of cotton, the fleeces of flocks, the moils and spoils of the silk-worm; of useful and exalting knowledge in the eyes and ears and other organs by which he puts us in communication with the wonders of this wonderful universe." [3]

Yes, nature and the Bible are in perfect agreement. They not only declare that there is a God, but that he loves us with the love of a father. The conclusion therefore is inevitable, that he must be interested in our welfare, must care for what we do, must think of us, and be solicitous with regard to our conduct; and it cannot be that he has created us only to forsake us.

CHAPTER IX.

WE NEED A REVELATION FROM GOD.

What is God's will, then, concerning us? What will please him? What will displease him? How shall we gain his favor? How shall we appease his wrath? If we have sinned against him, how shall we atone for our sin? What is to become of us hereafter? Oh that we might know about these things! But for some reason, because of sin, we

---

[3] Id. pp. 111, 112.

cannot come into his presence; we cannot see him, nor speak with him. How, then, shall we learn about these important matters? We must have a direct revelation from God, that will answer all these inquiries. In this way he can plainly tell us what is his will, and declare to us our duty and destiny. Without this we are absolutely in the dark. We may conjecture that there will be a hereafter for us, but we cannot know it. We may fancy what would please God, and what would displease him, but there would be no certainty in our surmises. A few words directly from Heaven would alone set our minds at rest upon these things.

Having made us, and caring for us and loving us as he does, how reasonable it is that God should make such a revelation to man. The Bible declares that all men are sinners against God and his holy law; and our consciences rise up and declare that this is the truth. I have an audience of a thousand,—where is there a person among them all who does not know that he has done wrong, that he has sinned? Is there such a man in the audience? Let him rise up. Not a man will rise; and why not? Because the consciences of all condemn them; yea, their bosom friends and their neighbors know them to be sinners. Not one of them dare deny it. Here our Bibles and our consciences agree. But if we have sinned against our Creator, how shall we obtain pardon? Can we buy it with silver? Can we purchase it with gold? We are in the dark. Like one of old we cry out, "Wherewith shall I come before the Lord, and bow myself before the high God? shall I come before him with burnt-offerings, with calves of a year old? Will the Lord be pleased with thousands of rams, or with ten thousands of rivers of oil? shall

I give my first-born for my transgression, the fruit of my body for the sin of my soul?"[1] Who can answer? God alone must speak.

But to the shame of humanity we must confess that some infidels deny that we need a revelation from God, and claim that nature, reason, our own consciences, or our "inner light," as they are pleased to term it, are sufficient to guide us in all the matters of life. Furthermore, they assert that it is impossible for the Almighty to make a satisfactory external revelation to man. They declare that they cannot and will not receive such a revelation upon the word of another; that it is constitutionally impossible for them to trust any one to this extent, be he prophet, apostle, or anybody else.

"Now, we are tempted to ask, who are these wonderful prodigies, so incapable of receiving instruction from anybody? And to our amazement we learn that some forty odd years ago they made their appearance among mankind as little squalling babies, without insight enough to know their own names, or where they came from, and were actually dependent on an external revelation from their nurses for sense enough to find their mothers' breasts. And as they grew a little larger they obtained the power of speaking articulate sounds by external revelation, hearing and imitating the sounds made by others.

"Further, upon a memorable day they had a 'book revelation' made to them, in the shape of a penny primer, and were initiated into the mysteries of A B C by 'the instructions of another, be he who he may.' There was absolutely not the least 'insight,' or 'spiritual faculty,' or 'self-conscious-

---

[1] Micah 6: 6, 7.

ness,' in one of them by which they then could, or even to this hour did, 'find true within them' any sort of necessary connection between the signs, c, a, t,—d, o, g, and the sounds *cat*, *dog*, or any other sounds represented by any other letters of the alphabet. Faith in the word of their teachers is absolutely the sole foundation and only source of their ability to read and write. On 'the word of another, and as his second, be he who he may,' every one of them has accepted every intelligible word he speaks or writes." [2]

This reasoning is just, and the facts undeniable. Not a man of all these boasted reasoners but that has received instruction from others for nearly everything he knows. How did he learn to write? By the instruction of another. How did he learn that arsenic is poison? By taking it himself? If he had done so he never would have lived to receive any benefit from his knowledge. How did he learn that the earth is round? Has he been around it himself? How did he learn that there ever was such a man as Washington? Did he ever see him? How did he obtain the knowledge that there is such a place as London? Was he ever there? How does he know that seals are caught in the northern seas? Did he ever catch one? The fact is, not one thing in a thousand which we virtually know to be true, has been proven so by our own individual senses. We have been obliged to take the evidence of others on the subject; or, in other words, it has been revealed to us. If we had not received our knowledge in this way, we could not have received it at all. It is therefore inconsistent to refuse instruction from God, through his chosen me-

---

[2] Fables of Infidelity, pp. 64, 65.

diums, when we have to practice a similar faith continually toward our fellow-creatures.

Another important fact is worthy of particular note: Modern infidels, living in these Christian lands, where the light of the Bible is shining brightly everywhere,—a light which they have enjoyed ever since they came into the world,—boast of their great wisdom, and of what reason has done for them. They talk very knowingly about our duties to God and to one another; about virtue, right, and law. They claim that they need no revelation from God to teach them what is right; that they know right from wrong as well as Christians do with the Bible before them. This may be true; but let us not be deceived upon this point. Where did they obtain this knowledge, this light? We assert that they obtained it from the Bible, and we can readily prove it.

Look at the facts in the case: If nature, and reason, and conscience can sufficiently teach men what is right and wrong, then those who have never had the benefit of the Bible should be as wise and virtuous as those who have had it. This is a fair test of the matter. Go, then, to heathen lands, and see what you will find. Nature is as widely open to them as to the infidel in our land; they have the same natural reason and conscience of which these skeptics boast so loudly. Now what have nature, reason, and conscience, or the "inner light," done for those men who have had nothing but these to instruct them? We find those heathen everywhere making gods to themselves with their own hands out of wood and stone, and then falling down to them in worship. Our infidels know better than to do that, but where did they learn better? If reason taught them, why does it not also teach the heathen?

Again: Heathen represent their gods as cruel monsters, committing adultery, stealing, lying. Our infidels are horrified at such ideas of God. How does it happen that they have so much higher notions of God than their heathen brethren? Again: Some heathen offer their children in sacrifice to their gods. Our infidels shudder at such cruelty. Many heathen go stark naked without shame. Our infidels would blush at the thought. Some live in mud shanties in a state of squalor, ignorance, and degradation. Why do not nature, and reason, and the "inner light," do for them what the infidel, living in Christian lands, claims they have done for him?

Reader, the difference is, that infidels in Christian lands have stolen from the Bible all they know about morals and religion, and then deny the source of their knowledge. The glorious light of the word of God has shone all around them for generations. By this light they see. This is why they are so much wiser and more virtuous than those who have not had the benefit of that book. They are like the man who turns his back upon the sun and declares he has no need of it. He can see with his own eyes without the sun. Poor simpleton! How much good would his eyes do him if there were no sun? Just so these infidels turn their backs upon the Bible and declare they do not need its instruction, while they are indebted to it for every ray of light they have.

That great Christian philosopher, Mr. Locke, truly observed that "a great many things which we have been bred up in the belief of from our cradles (and are notions grown familiar, and, as it were, natural to us under the gospel) we take for unquestionable truths, and easily demonstrable, without considering how long we might have been in doubt or ignorance of them, had revelation been silent."[3]

"It is one thing to see that these rules of life, which are beforehand plainly and particularly laid before us, are perfectly agreeable to reason, and another thing to find out these rules merely by the light of reason, without their having been first any otherwise made known."[4] After the truth is once known, it is easy to talk very wisely about it, and wonder that anybody should not know it; but it is not so easy to find it out. So in this case. After the word of God has revealed to us the great truths of Christianity, and infidels have learned them from this source, then it is easy for them to talk learnedly about them.

Could we have a revelation directly from God, all must admit that it would be of the greatest conceivable value. There would be no guess-work about such a revelation. It would express the mind of God himself. We should then know just what was right, and what was wrong. God could tell us plainly what would please him, and what would displease him. He could tell us how, when we had sinned against him, to become reconciled to him. He could tell us concerning our future, what would be the consequences of sin, and what the reward of obedience. If God himself should speak and tell us that he loved us, and pitied us, and would pardon and save us on certain reasona-

---

[3] Locke's Reasonableness of Christianity, in his works, vol. ii. p. 535, 3d ed.
[4] Dr. Clarke's Discourse on Natural and Revealed Religion, prop. vii. p. 818, 7th ed.

ble conditions, we could rest upon such a revelation. All must admit that such a revelation is exceedingly desirable, and that it would be prized above all earthly blessings by every honest, candid soul who really desires to know what is right.

That God can make such a revelation to man if he chooses, must readily be admitted by every candid person. "No one who believes that there is a God, and that he is a being of infinite power, wisdom, and knowledge, can reasonably deny that he can, if he thinks fit, make a revelation of himself and of his will to men, in an extraordinary way, different from the discoveries made by men themselves, in the mere natural and ordinary use of their own rational faculties and powers. For if the power of God be almighty, it must extend to whatever does not imply a contradiction, which cannot be pretended in this case."[5] This point is so plain that we do not deem it necessary to further discuss it.

CHAPTER X.

A UNIVERSAL THIRST FOR A REVELATION.

An unanswerable argument, proving that men do need a revelation from the Creator, is found in the fact that all people and nations in every age of the world, both barbarous and civilized, have constantly been seeking after such a revelation. It has not been a few isolated individuals here and there who have manifested a desire for such a reve-

---

[5] Horne's Introduction, vol. i. p. 2.

lation, and have sought earnestly to obtain one; but it has been the universal sentiment of the race. Go back to the remotest antiquity, and you cannot find a nation that had not its gods, its temples, its priests, its prophets, and pretended revelations from God. All men were running after them and consulting them, from the king on his throne to the beggar in his hovel. Search through the nations of the earth, and not one can be found that has not been constantly seeking to obtain revelations from God in some manner. Even the wild Indian prays to the Great Spirit; the degraded negroes of Central Africa have their priests and pretended revelations; the Greeks and the Romans, the most enlightened of all heathen nations, were noted for their temples, their priests, their pretended communications from God, etc. The learned Dr. Horne, who has so thoroughly studied this question, thus remarks:—

"Now, if any credit be due to the general sense of mankind in every age, we shall scarcely find one that believed the existence of a God, who did not likewise believe that some kind of commerce and communication subsisted between God and man. This was the foundation of all the religious rites and ceremonies, which every nation pretended to receive from their deities. Hence, also, the most celebrated legislators of antiquity,— Zoroaster, Minos, Pythagoras, Solon, Lycurgus, Numa, etc., etc., all thought it necessary to profess some intercourse with Heaven, in order to give the greater sanction to their laws and institutions, notwithstanding many of them were armed with secular power. And what gave birth and so much importance to the oracles, divinations, and auguries, in ancient times, was the conscious sense entertained by mankind of their own *ignorance*, and of their *need* of a supernatural illumination; as well as the persuasion that their gods held a perpetual intercourse with men, and by various means gave them intelligence of future things.

"The probability of a divine revelation further appears from this circumstance, that some of the wisest philosophers, particularly Socrates and Plato, confessed that they stood in need of such a revelation to instruct them in matters which were of the utmost consequence. With regard to the state of morals, they acknowledged that, as the state of the world then was, there were no human means of reforming it. But they not only saw and acknowledged their great want of a divine revelation, to instruct them in their conduct toward God and toward man; they likewise expressed a strong hope or expectation that God would, at some future time, make such a discovery as should dispel the cloud of darkness in which they were involved."[1]

"In so doing they have undoubtedly attempted to meet the wishes of the greater part of mankind, who have in all lands and in all ages longed for some outward revelation from God, and testified their desire by running after all sorts of omens, auguries, and oracles, consulting witches, and treasuring sibylline leaves, employing writing mediums, and listening to spirit rappers. . Surely, such a universal craving after an external revelation testifies to a felt necessity for it, and renders it probable, or at least desirable, that God would supply the deficiency. Is the religious appetite the only one for which God has provided no supply?"[2]

---

[1] Horne's Introduction, vol. i. pp. 3, 4.
[2] Fables of Infidelity, pp. 65, 66.

And think you that everybody would be running for a physician if there was no such thing as disease? As the abundance of patent medicines is proof of disease and the need of a remedy, so the abundance of things that come pretending to be a revelation from God, shows how deeply mankind feel the necessity of such a revelation. Why this universal craving for a revelation from God?

Socrates acknowledged the insufficiency of human reason in the following language: "We must of necessity wait till some one from Him who careth for us shall come and instruct us how we ought to behave ourselves toward God, and toward men." Plato said, "We cannot know of ourselves what petition will be pleasing to God, or what worship we should pay to him; but it is necessary that a law-giver should be sent from Heaven to instruct us. . . Oh, how greatly do I long to see that man." Again: "This law-giver must be more than man, that he may teach us the things that man cannot know by his own nature."[3]

There exists some object by which every natural desire may be gratified. We desire to breathe; the air is all around us. We desire to hear; sounds are produced. We desire food; it is provided for us in abundance. We desire clothing; it is easily procured. We desire friends; and we find them. And so the desire for reputation, for society, for liberty, for beauty, for health, etc., is natural to all men; and the object of each of these desires actually exists. Indeed, you cannot point out a single desire natural to a sound man, to which there is not an answering object somewhere; such objects are certainly known to exist. Hence we

---

*Id. p. 68.

must conclude that the desire for a revelation from God, which has been so universally felt among all classes and nations of our race, is not a sole exception to this rule. There must be some way to gratify this natural desire, or it never would have been so deeply planted in our natures.

CHAPTER XI.

THE CORRUPT NOTIONS AND PRACTICES OF THE HEATHEN WHO ARE WITHOUT THIS REVELATION.

Another convincing proof that we need a revelation from God is found in the fact that those who have no such revelation have always been lamentably ignorant concerning the nature of God and how to properly worship him. They have not been able to discover the plainest principles of morality. They have shown a surprising ignorance of the simplest truths. They have blundered, and stumbled, and fallen where a child with the Bible in its hand would have walked safely; and the morals and conduct, even of the best of them, have been fearfully corrupt. Notice how foolish and ignorant are their views with regard to God, as seen in the objects and manner of their worship.

The Chaldeans "gave up the worship of God, adored the sun, and moon, and stars of heaven; and in process of time degenerated still further, and worshiped dumb idols. From this rock we were hewn; the common names of the days of the week, and especially of the first day of the week, will forever keep up a testimony to the necessity of that revelation which delivered our forefathers and us from burning our children upon the devil's altars on Sundays."[1]

Our modern enlightened infidels know better than to worship the objects of heathen idolatry; but where did they get this knowledge? None of them could possibly be induced to fall down and worship the sun, moon, or stars. Yet this is what the wisest of the heathen did.

"The monuments confirm the satirical sketch of the poet, as to the 'monsters mad Egypt worshiped; here a sea-fish, there a river fish; whole towns adore a dog. This place fears an ibis saturated with serpents; that adores a crocodile. It is a sin to violate a leek or onion, or break them with a bite.' Cruel wars were waged between different towns, as Plutarch tells us, because the people of Cynopolis would eat a fish held sacred by the citizens of Latopolis. Bulls, and dogs, and cats, and rats, and reptiles, and dung beetles, were devoutly adored by the learned Egyptians. A Roman soldier, who had accidentally killed one of their gods, a cat, was put to death for sacrilege. Whenever a dog died, every person in the house went into mourning, and fasted till night. So low had the 'great, the mighty, and transcendent soul' been degraded that there is a picture extant of one of the kings of Egypt worshiping his own coffin! Such is man's knowledge of God without a revelation from him.

"And the same remarks will apply to the Romans. Their gods were as detestable as they were numerous. Hesiod tells us they had thirty thousand. Temples were erected to all the passions,

---

[1] Fables of Infidelity, pp. 68, 69.

fears, diseases, to which humanity is subject. Their supreme god, Jupiter, was an adulterer, Mars a murderer, Mercury a thief, Bacchus a drunkard, Venus a harlot; and they attributed other crimes to their gods too horrible to be mentioned. Such gods were worshiped with appropriate ceremonies, of lust, drunkenness, and bloodshed. Their most sacred mysteries, carried on under the patronage of these licentious deities, were so abominable and infamous that it was found necessary, for the preservation of any remnant of good order, to prohibit them."[2]

"Besides the numbers of men who were killed in the bloody sports and spectacles instituted in honor of their deities, human sacrifices were offered to propitiate them. Boys were whipped on the altar of Diana, sometimes till they died. How many lovely infants did the Carthaginians sacrifice to their implacable god, Moloch! What numbers of human victims, in times of public danger, did they immolate, to appease the resentment of the offended deities!"[3]

"Further: The Egyptians, the Athenians, the Lacedemonians, and, generally speaking, all the Greeks, the Romans, Carthaginians, Germans, Gauls, and Britons,—in short, all the heathen nations throughout the world, offered human sacrifices upon their altars; and this, not on certain emergencies and imminent dangers only, but constantly, and in some places every day. Upon extraordinary accidents, *multitudes* were sacrificed at once to their sanguinary deities. Thus, during the

---

[2] Fables of Infidelity, pp. 69, 70.
[3] Horne's Introduction, vol. i. p. 6.

battle between the Sicilian army under Gelon and the Carthaginians under Amilcar, in Sicily, the latter remained in his camp, offering sacrifices to the deities of his country, and consuming upon one large pile the bodies of numerous victims (Herod. lib. vii. c. 167).

"When Agathocles was about to besiege Carthage, its inhabitants, seeing the extremity to which they were reduced, imputed all their misfortunes to the anger of Saturn; because, instead of offering up children of noble descent (who were usually sacrificed), there had been fraudulently substituted for them the children of slaves and foreigners. Two hundred children of the best families in Carthage were therefore immolated, to propitiate the offended divinity."[4]

Our sense of piety and virtue is outraged by the recital of such vile abominations; yet this is just what has been done by the wisest of nations that have not had the light of the Bible. Just such scenes as have been described would be enacted this day in New York and St. Louis, had we never been taught better by the Holy Scriptures. Infidels have reason to thank God for the very revelation which they despise and reject. If we turn our eyes to the modern heathen world, we find them no higher in intelligence, no more improved in morals, than those before them.

---

[4] Id. vol. i p. 6, note.

CHAPTER XII.

MODERN HEATHEN NO BETTER THAN ANCIENT HEATHEN.

"It may be supposed that the human race is wiser now than in the days of Socrates and Cicero, and that such abominations are no longer possible. Turn your eyes, then, to India, and behold one hundred and fifty millions of rational beings, possessed of 'spiritual faculties,' 'insight,' and 'the religious sentiment,' worshiping three hundred and thirty millions of gods, in the forms of hills, and trees, and rivers, and rocks, elephants, tigers, monkeys and rats, crocodiles, serpents, beetles and ants, and monsters like to nothing in heaven or earth, or under the earth.

"Take one specimen of all. There is 'the lord of the world,' Juggernaut. 'When you think of the monster block of the idol, with its frightfully grim and distorted visage, so justly styled the Moloch of the East, sitting enthroned amid thousands of massive sculptures, the representative emblems of that cruelty and vice which constitute the very essence of his worship;—when you think of the countless multitudes that annually congregate there, from all parts of India, many of them measuring the whole distance of their weary pilgrimage with their own bodies;—when you think of the merit-earning assiduities constantly practiced by crowds of devotees and religious mendicants, around the holy city; some remaining all day with their heads on the ground, and their feet in the air; others with their bodies entirely covered with earth; some cramming their eyes with mud and their mouths with straw, while others lie extended in a puddle of water; here one man lying with his foot tied to his neck, another with a pot of fire on his breast, a third enveloped in a network of ropes;—when, besides these self-inflicted torments, you think of the frightful amount of involuntary suffering and wretchedness arising from the exhaustion of toilsome pilgrimages, the cravings of famine, and the scourgings of pestilence;—when you think of the day of the high festival—how the horrid king is dragged forth from his temple, and mounted on his lofty car, in the presence of hundreds of thousands that cause the very earth to shake with shouts of 'Victory to Juggernaut, our lord!'—how the officiating high priest, stationed in front of the elevated idol, commences the public service by a loathsome pantomimic exhibition, accompanied with the utterance of filthy, blasphemous songs, to which the vast multitude at intervals respond, not in the strains of tuneful melody, but in loud yells of approbation, united with a kind of hissing applause; —when you think of the carnage that ensues, in the name of sacred offering,—how, as the ponderous machine rolls on, grating harsh thunder, one and another of the more enthusiastic devotees throw themselves beneath the wheels, and are instantly crushed to pieces, the infatuated victims of hellish superstition;— when you think of the numerous Golgothas that bestud the neighboring plain, where the dogs, jackals, and vultures seem to live on human prey; and of those bleak and barren sands that are forever whitened with the skulls and bones of deluded pilgrims that lie bleaching in the sun,'— you will be able to see an awful force of meaning in the words of our text, and to realize more fully the necessity of a revelation from God, for the very preservation of animal life to man. Literally, where there is no vision, the people *perish*. Man doth not live by bread only, but by every word that proceedeth from the mouth of God." [1]

How we hold up our hands in horror at such terrible scenes of superstition, folly, and idolatry! But what has saved us from the perpetration of like acts? Nothing but the teachings of that Bible which skeptics despise and hate. One can hardly believe how fearfully corrupt such idolatrous worship has always been. The blackest crimes, the most fearful pollution, has always been connected with idolatrous worship.

Prof. Julius H. Seelye, of Amherst College, in a recent lecture before the Yale Divinity School, on the subject of Missions, spoke particularly of the condition and needs of the unchristian world. "He presented a vivid picture of the degradation of these nations, based not merely on his own observation, which has been extensive, but supporting his statements by reference to authorities accessible. China, as one of the most promising of pagan nations, and whose civilization has been so widely lauded, was shown to be shockingly corrupt in its social and private life. Lying, insincerity, licentiousness, and almost every other vice mentioned in Scripture, is practiced without restraint. Their virtue is entirely external. India is in a similar condition. Before the establishment of the English in that country, not less than ten thousand infants were put to death by their parents per month in the single province of Bengal. This condition is true not only of modern half-civilized pagans, but it is

---

[1] Fables of Infidelity, pp. 70-72.

found where civilization has shown some of its most renowned trophies. In Greece and Rome, society was all pollution. The most classic writings reveal it. Even their philosophers taught the most unmentionable vices. The first chapter of Romans is not an untrue portraiture of pagan corruption."[2]

All who have read the history of ancient heathendom, or have traveled among modern heathen, agree in saying that the awful description of heathen in general, as penned by inspiration eighteen centuries ago, was literally true then as to-day. What a fearful picture it presents! Read it carefully. Rom. 1: 21–32. This is the condition of men and nations who know not our God, and who have not had the benefit of our Bible. Reader, is this not overwhelming evidence that we need a revelation from the Creator?

At this very day, the people in heathen lands worship the sun, moon, and stars, young birds, fishes, and even serpents. Many of them pray and offer sacrifices to evil spirits and to the devil. Sorcery, divination, and magic are almost universal. Polygamy, divorce, and infanticide are everywhere prevalent. Human life is held of little account, and is sacrificed on the slightest occasion. This has always been the condition of every nation which has not had the Bible; and this would be our condition to-day were it not for the light of that blessed book. Let infidels mark this, and lay it to heart.

---

[2] *Christian Union*, Dec. 16, 1874.

CHAPTER XIII.

THE WISEST HEATHEN PHILOSOPHERS IN THE DARK.

The wisest and most enlightened of the heathen philosophers and teachers were not able to discern the simplest truths of morality. In confirmation of this fact, read the following: "From the ignorance and uncertainty which, we have seen, prevailed among some of the greatest teachers of antiquity, concerning those fundamental truths which are the great barriers of virtue and religion, it is evident that the heathen had no perfect scheme of moral rules for piety and good manners. Thus, with the exception of two or three philosophers, they never inculcated the duty of loving our enemies and of forgiving injuries; but, on the contrary, they accounted revenge to be not only lawful, but commendable.

"Pride and the love of popular applause, the subduing of which is the first principle of true virtue, were esteemed the best and most noble incentives to virtue and noble actions; suicide was regarded as the strongest mark of heroism; and the perpetrators of it, instead of being branded with infamy, were commended and celebrated as men of noble minds. But the interior acts of the soul, the adultery of the eye and the murder of the heart, were little regarded. On the contrary, the philosophers countenanced, both by arguments and example, the most flagitious practices. Thus theft, as is well known, was permitted in Egypt and in Sparta. Plato taught the expedience and lawfulness of exposing children in particular cases, and

Aristotle, also, of abortion. The exposure of infants, and the putting to death of children who were weak or imperfect in form, was allowed at Sparta by Lycurgus; and at Athens, the great seat and nursery of philosophers, it was enacted that 'infants which appeared to be maimed should either be killed or exposed;' and that 'the Athenians might lawfully invade and enslave any people, who, in their opinion, were fit to be made slaves.' "[1]

The gratification of the sensual appetites, and of the most unnatural lusts, was openly taught and allowed. Aristippus maintained that it was lawful for a wise man to steal, commit adultery and sacrilege, when opportunity offered; for that none of these actions were naturally evil, setting aside the vulgar opinion, which was introduced by silly and illiterate people; and that a wise man might publicly gratify his libidinous propensities.

" Truth was but of small account among many, even of the best heathen; for they taught that, on many occasions, a *lie* was to be *preferred to the truth itself!* To which we may add that the unlimited gratification of their sensual appetites, and the commission of unnatural crimes, was common, even among the most distinguished teachers of philosophy, and was practiced even by Socrates himself, 'whose morals' (a living opposer of revelation has the effrontery to assert) 'exceed anything in the Bible; for they were free from vice'!"[2]

Dr. Whitby has collected many maxims of the most eminent heathen sages, in corroboration of the fact above stated. The following examples are taken from his note on Eph. 4 : 25 :—

---

[1] Horne's Introduction, vol. i. pp. 13, 14.   [2] Id. pp. 15, 16.

"A lie is better than a hurtful truth."—*Meander.*
"Good is better than truth."—*Proclus.*
"When telling a lie will be profitable, let it be told."—*Darius,* in Herodotus, lib. iii. c. 62.
"He may lie, who knows how to do it in a suitable time."—*Plato apud Stobæum,* serm. 12.
"There is nothing decorous in truth but when it is profitable. Yea, sometimes, truth is hurtful, and lying is profitable to men."—*Maximus Tyrius,* diss. iii. p. 29.[3]

With this picture before us, how forcible are the words of the Bible: "The world by wisdom knew not God." 1 Cor. 1:21. Never was a declaration more true.

CHAPTER XIV.

IMMORALITY AND CORRUPTION OF MODERN INFIDELS.

THE most educated and talented of modern infidels, right in the midst of Christianity, have indirectly proved its truthfulness by their dissolute lives, and have added another evidence of man's need of a revelation from God. These men have been fearfully corrupt. We will briefly notice some of the most noted of modern infidels.

Lord Herbert taught that the indulgence of lust and anger is not to be blamed. Mr. Hobbes asserted that the civil law is the only rule of right and wrong, and that every man has a right to all things, and may lawfully get them if he can. Lord Bolingbroke taught that ambition, lust of power,

---
[3] Horne's Introduction, vol. i. p. 16, note 1.

sensuality, and avarice, may be lawfully gratified if they can be safely gratified; that modesty is only feigned; that polygamy is not wrong. He intimates that adultery is no violation of the law of nature.

Hume taught that price is not wrong; that adultery must be practiced if men would obtain all the advantages of life; that if practiced secretly and frequently it would cease to be thought a crime. Voltaire advocated the unlimited gratification of the sensual passions. Rousseau made feelings the only standard of right. Said he, "I have only to consult myself concerning myself what I do. All I feel to be right is right."

Let not the reader think that the picture is overdrawn, for, alas! we have men among us to-day in America of the same stamp, teaching these damnable doctrines. I refer to modern Spiritualists. They have cast away the Bible, and now boast of the sufficiency of reason to guide men in all matters of morality. One of the leading lights of this school, Dr. Child, in a work entitled "Christ and the People," puts forth the following blasphemous doctrine. It is thus indorsed by the *Banner of Light*, the highest authority among these infidels: " This book should find its way to every family. . . Its liberality reaches the very shores of infinity. It is born of Spiritualism, and reaches for the manhood of Christ."

Dr. Child says: "Ere long, man will come to see that all sin is for his spiritual good. . . To see that holiness lays up treasures on earth. . . . Sin destroys earthly treasures, and causes them to be laid up in Heaven."[1] "There is no criminal act

---

[1] Christ and the People, pp. 32, 33.

that is not an experience of usefulness. The tracks of vice and crime are only the tracks of human progress. . . There has been no deed in the catalogue of crime that has not been a valuable experience to the inner being of the man who committed it."[2] "Man has yet to learn and yet to admit that *all* sins which are committed are innocent; for all are in the inevitable rulings of God."[3] "He who wars with sin leaves nothing lovely in his tracks."[4]

Hell itself must blush at such depths of infamy. Of a great national convention of these atheists I thus read: "At the National Spiritual Convention, at Chicago, called to consider the question of a national organization, the only plan approved by the committee especially provided that no charge should ever be entertained against any member, and that any person, without any regard to his or her moral character, might become a member."[5] This is the standard which modern infidels are trying to erect in our country. Reader, if you wish to see what the result will be, turn your eyes to a nation which once claimed and supported these very principles.

In the entire history of the world there is but one case where a whole nation has turned atheist and has installed infidelity as the religion of the land. This was infidel France. Let us see what was the result. This afforded a fair test of the question whether a nation can prosper best with or without the Bible. Solomon says, "Where there is no vision, the people perish; but he that keepeth the law, happy is he."[6] We shall now have a

---

[2] Christ and the People, p. 137. [3] Id. p. 175.
[4] Id. p. 191.   [5] W. B. Potter, in "Astounding Facts."
[6] Prov. 29 : 18.

forcible illustration of this Scripture truth. The scenes of horror that filled France during the reign of terror far exceeded anything of the kind in the annals of history.

"While infidelity was enthroned in power, it wielded the sword of vengeance with infernal ferocity against the priests of the Romish Church, who were butchered wherever found, hunted as wild beasts, frequently roasted alive or drowned in hundreds together, without either accusation or trial. At Nantes, no less than three hundred and sixty priests were shot, and four hundred and sixty drowned. In one night forty-eight were shut up in a barge and drowned in the Loire; two hundred and ninety-two priests were massacred during the bloody scenes of the 10th of August and the 22d of September, 1792; and eleven hundred and thirty-five were guillotined under the government of the National Convention, from the month of September, 1792, till the end of 1795, besides vast numbers, hunted by the infidel republicans like owls and partridges, who perished in different ways throughout the provinces of France."[7]

"The number of persons guillotined during the reign of terror in France was 1,022,351. This does not include the massacre at Versailles, at the Abbaye, the Carinelite, or other prisons, on September 2, the victims Glaciere of Avignon, those shot at Toulon and Marseilles, or the persons slain in the little town of Bedoin, the whole population of which perished."[8]

Dr. Dick, in speaking of the results of this Rev-

---

[7] Dick on Diffusion of Knowledge, p. 155.
[8] Thiers' French Revolution, vol. iii. p. 106.

olution, says: " Such was the rapidity with which the work of destruction was carried on, that within the short space of ten years not less than *three millions* of human beings (one-half more than the whole population of Scotland) are supposed to have perished in that country alone, chiefly through the influence of immoral principles, and the seductions of a false philosophy."[9]

But this state of things could not long continue; the world would soon have been emptied of its inhabitants. "Callot-d' Herbois died calling on that very God whom he had impiously blasphemed."

Now let the scenes of France be acted in America. Let the Bible be burned and the goddess of reason adored, and the scenes of Paris and Lyons will soon transpire in New York and Philadelphia. Then we apprehend that even infidels will " wander from sea to sea, and from the north even to the east, for the word of the Lord."[10] And we are certain that no minister will be needed to expound the text, " Where there is no vision, the people perish."

CHAPTER XV.

THE BIBLE COMPARED WITH OTHER SYSTEMS OF RELIGION.

HAVING abundantly shown in the previous chapters the imperative necessity for a divine revelation from our Creator, one that is clear and unequivocal, we now inquire if such a revelation has

---

[9] Improvement of Society, p. 154.   [10] Amos 8: 11, 12.

ever been given. All intelligent persons know that numerous books and systems have claimed to give such revelation, and among them all, the Holy Bible stands prominent. But infidels argue that the fact of there having been so many confessedly false revelations, and false systems of religion, and false gods, proves that all are deceptions; that there are no genuine ones. How foolish the conclusion! Shall we conclude there is no genuine coin because there is so much spurious? Shall we deny that there are any genuine bank-bills because the land is flooded with counterfeit bills? We would pronounce a man insane who would reason thus. The very existence of a counterfeit proves the existence of the genuine. Men never counterfeit that which does not exist. And so the existence, in all ages of the world, of so many counterfeit revelations, and systems of false religion, is in itself proof that the genuine exists somewhere. But how shall we determine which is the true, and which is the false? The Lord says, "Prove all things." And Jesus gives a good rule, "By their fruits ye shall know them."

All infidels admit that the Bible is much the best of all books claiming to be sacred. They admit that much of its teaching is pure and sublime, far better than can be found anywhere else. Take all the atheists, deists, infidels, and skeptics of Christendom, and not one of them has a particle of faith in any other sacred book than the Bible. So, they themselves being judges, if God has ever spoken to man this must be his word. If not, then we are without a revelation from Heaven. This latter conclusion, however, is here inadmissible, since it contradicts the abundant proof we have already given on the other hand.

Since men forsook the worship of the true God,

immediately after the flood, many false gods have come up, and many systems of worship have flourished in the earth at different times. Let us briefly notice them, and inquire what has become of them.

If we go back to the remotest antiquity, so far as the records reach, we find that Egypt stood far above all other nations in reputed learning, wisdom, and human science.[1] The Egyptians had their gods, their temples, and their priests.[2] The Jews fell into the worship of the Egyptian gods. They made the golden calf in imitation of one of the gods of Egypt.[3] For hundreds of years the worship of these Egyptian gods was professed by millions, and was maintained with the greatest pomp, while the God of Israel, his worship and his people, were held in contempt. But where are the gods of Egypt now? Where are their worshipers? Where are their temples? Gone; all gone; not a vestige of them left upon the face of the earth; not a temple, not a priest, not a book, not a worshiper,—blotted out of existence. But the God of Israel and his holy Book still live.

Coming a little farther down, we are all familiar with the god of the Philistines, viz., Dagon. For several hundred years there was a sharp contest between the worship of this famous god and the worship of Jehovah. Many times it looked as though Dagon and his followers would triumph. On one occasion a grand feast was made to this god in honor of the glorious victory over Israel. "Then the lords of the Philistines gathered them together for to offer a great sacrifice unto Dagon their god, and to rejoice; for they said, Our god hath delivered Samson our enemy into our hand."[4] But

---

[1] Acts 7:22. [2] Gen. 41:45. [3] Ex. 32:4. [4] Judges 16:23.

his triumph was short. Where now is Dagon? Where are his temples? What has become of his worshipers? Not a vestige of any of them left beneath the sun. The deep waves of oblivion have rolled over their silent graves for three thousand years; but Jehovah and his holy Book still live and reign in the hearts of as many millions now as of hundreds then.

Baal was another famous god at one time. The king and queen were on his side, and the power of the law supported him. The great mass went after him, while the Lord's prophets were slain, his altars thrown down, and his worshipers driven into caves. Elijah makes this mournful appeal to the people: "How long halt ye between two opinions? if the Lord be God, follow him; but if Baal, then follow him. And the people answered him not a word. Then said Elijah unto the people, I, even I only, remain a prophet of the Lord; but Baal's prophets are four hundred and fifty men."[5]

What a mighty difference! Apparently what an unequal contest! But God alone is a majority against the world with all its false gods, and hell with all its demons. Twenty-eight centuries have rolled by since then, and where is Baal? What has become of his worship? It, too, has gone down, and the dust of more than twenty-five centuries lies piled upon its forgotten grave. But the Lord lives, and his worship has spread from pole to pole.

Moloch was another renowned god, who came up, and flourished for a season. Many of Israel ran bowing to him, and courted his protection. The Phœnicians and Carthaginians also worshiped

---

[5] 1 Kings 18: 21, 22.

him. But who can find Moloch now? Where is there a nation, a city, a town, or a solitary individual among all the nations of the earth, who believes in Moloch? Nowhere. He, too, with his worshipers, is buried beneath the dust of ages; while the Lord Jehovah is exalted on high.

How lordly and magnificent the gods of Assyria! What treasures of gold were poured out upon their shrines! What millions did them reverence! How they lorded it over the Hebrews, and despised the God of Israel! But where are they now? Echo answers, WHERE? They are dead, and forgotten, and their worshipers are scattered. But our God still sits upon his throne, and all over the earth millions daily bow to him.

Great Diana at Ephesus was one of the most renowned goddesses of the world. All Asia bowed at her shrine. Kings paid her homage, princes brought her offerings, and the fame of her magnificence was world-wide. Her temple is said to have been the richest that the sun ever shone upon. A learned author thus describes it: "It was reckoned one of the wonders of the world. It was built of pure white marble, about five hundred and fifty years before Christ; and though burned by a fanatic on the night of the birth of Alexander the Great, B. C. 356, it was rebuilt with more splendor than before. It was four hundred and twenty-five feet long, by two hundred and twenty broad; and the columns, one hundred and twenty in number, were sixty feet in height, each of them the gift of a king, and thirty-six of them enriched with ornament and color. It was what the bank of England is in the modern world; the larger portion of the wealth of Western Asia being stored up in it. It was constantly receiving new decorations.

and additional buildings, statues, and pictures by the most celebrated artists. It created unparalleled admiration, enthusiasm, and superstition. Its very site is now a matter of uncertainty."[6] A mighty commotion was raised by the worshipers of Diana when the religion of the humble Man of Nazareth was introduced at Ephesus by the apostle Paul. Hear what those worshipers said:—

"So that not only this our craft is in danger to be set at naught, but also that the temple of the great goddess Diana should be despised, and her magnificence should be destroyed, whom all Asia and the world worshipeth."[7] What a mighty goddess was this! The zeal of her worshipers was so great that for the space of two hours they cried out, "Great is Diana of the Ephesians!" The town clerk said that these things must not be spoken against. The plain worship of the humble Christians seemed contemptible in comparison with that of this goddess. How could a few fishermen make headway against such a mighty system as this? But eighteen centuries have rolled by since that period, during which time the religion of Jesus has spread all over the face of the earth. And what has become of Diana? Where now is her temple? Where her followers? They are among the antiquities of the past. They are known only in history. Not a vestige of this worship is left upon the face of the earth to-day. And this fact is another monument to the power of our God, and to the eternal stability of his religion.

Let us go with the apostle to Athens, at that time the most polished and educated city upon the

---

[6] Com. on the Old and New Testaments, by Jamieson, Fausset, and Brown, on Acts 19:27. [7] Acts 19:27.

earth. Very devout indeed were these Athenians. One historian declares that they had thirty thousand gods. So jealous were they of the honor of these gods that they put to death one of their most renowned men, Socrates, for supposed contempt of them. The whole power of the government was enlisted to support them. The greatest philosophers, the wisest statesmen, the most eloquent orators, with the treasures of Greece, were on their side. But where are they now? Like all the others named, a few centuries ended their glory, exposed their corruption, scattered their worshipers, and leveled their temples with the ground. Who now believes in any of the numerous gods of ancient Greece? They live only in history. We now read of them, and wonder that any people were so foolish as to believe in them. Why does not the religion of the Bible go down as have all these systems of worship? Is it not remarkable that, on the other hand, it has grown stronger with each succeeding generation?

What shall we say of the gods of Rome? This was the grand metropolis of all the gods. Here each god was protected by law, and had an honorable place assigned to it. Faithful devotees worshiped at each shrine, and were zealous in their service. But who can now find a heathen god in Rome? The glory of these gods is gone; their altars are thrown down; their worshipers are dead. They are known only from history. "False religion" has been written on all their tombs. Time would fail us to mention the scores and hundreds of like cases which are familiar to all the world.

Now, reader, on the other hand, look a moment at the wonderful history of our Bible, and of the worship of God which it promulgates. Beginning in

Eden, there has been an unbroken succession of faithful worshipers through all the generations of men. After the flood, Abraham stands forth as a prominent pillar of the faith. The knowledge and worship of the Lord was preserved in Egypt through four hundred years of the hardest bondage. Next, Moses appears, and commences to write the very record we have in the Bible to-day, by hundreds of years the oldest writing in the world. Herodotus and Homer are thought to be very ancient writers, but Moses was about a thousand years earlier than they. The world was then in its infancy; all nations were then barbarians, unlettered and uncivilized. Rome was a howling wilderness. Greece had not learned the first letter of the alphabet. Is it not wonderful that so far back in hoary antiquity, and in the deep darkness of barbarism, any man could have studied out such sublime precepts of morality and religion as Moses gave his people? Look at the ten commandments, for instance. They have been the admiration of the world ever since their promulgation. Their equal has never been found, nor ever will be found. What other religion ever had such precepts as these?

Follow that chosen people through fifteen hundred years of their history, to the birth of Jesus. They were in bondage under the Philistines many times, carried into Babylon for seventy years, hunted, persecuted, and slain by their enemies on every side. The Holy Scriptures were proscribed and burned. It was death for any man to be found in possession of a copy of them; but still they survived. At the coming of Christ, they burst all national bonds; they put on new glory, and went forth conquering and to conquer.

The people rose to oppose them; priests cursed

them by their gods; armies marched against them; kings from their thrones condemned their followers to death. But nothing hindered their progress. The Scriptures of the Old and New Testaments were rapidly translated into the languages of the different nations where their ministers went. If one missionary is murdered, a hundred spring up from his ashes, catch the falling banner, and carry it forward with renewed zeal. Nation after nation yield to their mighty power, lay down their defense, and take the gospel into their hearts. Paganism vanishes before it like dew before the rising sun. On it rolls, gathering impetus and volume with each succeeding generation. Opposition only gives it strength. While other systems decay, it strengthens; while others lie down in the dust, it rises higher; while others are circumscribed to one nation, the religion of the Bible spreads among all people.

The Bible, the Book of God, the Book for all nations, where can it not be found within the circle of this mighty earth? It is enthroned in millions of hearts of every nation, kindred, tongue, and people. The sun never sets where it is not. How different from all other religions is the Bible religion! How different from all other professedly sacred books is the Bible! Ah, dear reader, this vitality is of Heaven,—it is the power of God. Let us bow our heads in solemn awe.

Let us notice one more point: How are you to account for the fact that civilization, refinement, education, the sciences, everything that is good and great, has gone where the Bible has gone, and stopped where it has stopped? Who is it that have schoolhouses, colleges, and hospitals? It is those who live where the Bible holds sway. Who is it that ride in the chariots that go like the lightnings? What nations have the benefit of steamboats, of printing-presses, of telegraphs, of sewing-machines, of astronomical instruments? Who have good houses and carpeted floors, easy carriages, fine clothes, and good food? They are the nations who have the Bible.

"If you will take the map of the world and a pencil, then sit down and draw a black line around that portion of the earth where the Bible has been in the longest and most plentiful circulation, where every class, high and low, are able to read, and do read the volume most commonly, and with most ease, such as England, Scotland, and the United States of America, *there* you will find men most enlightened and most amiable in demeanor. There, wherever are most Bibles, men are less cruel, less polluted, and less unprincipled. There they are less inclined to kneel before images of wood and stone, and more ready to understand and to practice the law of forgiveness and of love. Then sit down and draw a line around those countries where there are no Bibles, where none have been for generations, and there you will find most cruelty, most pollution, most absurd notions of Deity, and most darkness. Finally, mark off those sections of earth where that book has a partial circulation, as in Catholic countries, where it is read by a portion of the people, and with a medium frequency only, and there you will find a twilight in everything. The moralist is either afraid to look long at or to follow out such facts, or he says, 'It happened so.'"[8]

---

[8] Nelson on Infidelity, p. 116.

CHAPTER XVI.

WHAT HAS INFIDELITY DONE?

Infidelity comes to us, not only with the profession of a friend, but also as a great benefactor. When any system claims our patronage and discipleship, we naturally inquire, What is its object? what does it propose to do for us? what has it already done for others? If it cannot bring good credentials in this respect, we do well to give it a wide berth. We inquire, therefore, What has infidelity done for those who have embraced it in the past? what does it propose to do in the future?

The least investigation shows, that, so far as infidelity is a system at all, it is merely a system of doubt, of fault-finding, and of opposition to Christianity. Evidently it exists only for this purpose. It has no missionaries of its own, no code of morals, no rites of worship, no God, no hope, no hereafter. It has no scruples as to what means it employs, or whether it employs any, provided it accomplishes its object. Who ever heard of infidels sending out missionaries to enlighten the dark corners of the earth? What foreign missions have they established? What heathen nation have they ever been the means of civilizing? What apostles of infidelity have ever toiled and sacrificed in heathen lands for the enlightenment of its people, or spent their lives to elevate the barbarous nations of the earth?

The very question provokes a smile. They never dreamed of such a thing. For all their efforts to the contrary, cannibals might continue to eat their fellow-men; idolatry might continue to rule over millions of their fellow-mortals; and mothers might continue to sacrifice their children to bloody idols to the end of time. What churches or schools have they ever established in which to give moral and religious instruction and to reform the wicked? Not any. They have no burden in that line; they care for none of these things. Their only burden is to oppose the Bible and the work of Christians.

What does their system do for man? Does it teach him that he is in the image of his Creator, that there is a happy future before him, and a glorious hope of immortality in store for him? Oh, no; it teaches him that he is only one among the beasts that perish; and that at death he will utterly cease to exist, and lie down in the dust. It teaches him that all the enjoyment he ever has is in this life; that if he can here escape the penalty of the law which he has broken, he will never suffer it hereafter. It quenches the highest aspirations of the human soul; it dethrones God, blots out Heaven, and blasts the most cherished hopes of the race. It mocks at our fear of the Judgment, and sneers at our hope of eternal life. And after destroying our dearest aspirations and hopes, the apostles of infidelity offer us nothing to atone for this destruction.

"They promise to him who disbelieves the Founder of the Christian religion; to him who neglects and disdains the salvation of the gospel; to him who tramples under foot the blood of the new institution, and insults the Spirit of favor; to him who traduces Moses, Daniel, and Job; to him who vilifies Jesus, Paul, Peter, James, and John; to him who devotes his soul to the lusts of the flesh; who disdains Heaven; who deifies his appetites; who degrades himself to a mere animal, and eulogizes philosophy,—to this man they promise eternal sleep,—an everlasting death. This is the faith, the hope, the joy for which they labor with so much zeal and care and pain."[1]

This is all that infidelity offers us. But there is no agreement among its advocates. How shall we know which one to believe? One promulgates one theory, another something essentially different. "There is no agreement among deists as to what their natural religion consists in, or as to the truth of what some of them consider its most fundamental doctrines. Their chief writers are altogether at variance as to whether there is any distinction between right and wrong, other than in the law of the land or the customs of society; whether there is a providence; whether God is to be worshiped in prayer and praise, or the practice of virtue is not the only worship required; whether the practice of virtue forbids or encourages deceit, suicide, revenge, adultery, and all uncleanness; . . . . whether God has any concern with human conduct."[2] What, then, are the inducements to embrace infidelity? If it be true, it will do no good. If it be false, it will lead us to hell.

CHAPTER XVII.

WHEN WAS THE BIBLE WRITTEN?

CHRISTIANS claim that the New Testament was written about eighteen hundred years ago by the disciples of Jesus Christ, who were personally ac-

---

[1] Campbell's Debate with Owen, p. 17.
[2] M'Ilvaine's Evidences, p. 26.

quainted with him; and that the Old Testament was written in Hebrew by the Jews several hundred years before that time. While infidels do not pretend seriously to dispute this, they often put on a look of great wisdom, and raise many doubts concerning it. They say, "Who knows that this is so? Where is the proof of it?" Some suggest that King James was the one who first collected the books of the Bible; others say that Constantine did it, while others say that there is nothing certain about it anyway. But it will be noticed that the wisest of them never dare argue the question with another; they never pretend to show who did write these books, nor just when they were written. We might leave the question right here, and demand of them to prove that these books were not written at the time and by the persons claimed by Christians. But we should have to wait forever. They will never attempt it.

We shall now show the reader that there is most overwhelming testimony conclusively proving that the Bible was written at the time claimed by Christians, and by the very men claimed by them to have written it. Our motto is, One thing at a time, and the nearest one first. We will begin, then, with an undeniable fact :—

The Bible exists to-day. It lies upon our tables; it is read in our Sabbath-schools, and is preached from every Sunday in thousands of pulpits. You can buy it in any book-store throughout the world. Who will deny these facts? No one. But further, the Bible not only exists to-day in the English language, but it is translated into over two hundred and fifty different languages, including all the great languages of the world. But more than that, all the great, leading, civilized nations of this age not only receive it as the word of God, but have largely founded their laws upon its teachings. This is true of the United States, of England, of Germany, of France, of Russia, etc. There are about four hundred million people to-day who receive and believe this book. "Is there any other book so generally read, so greatly loved, so zealously propagated, so widely diffused, so uniform in its results, and so powerful and blessed in its influences? Do you know any? If you cannot name any book which in these respects equals the Bible, then it stands out clear and distinct, and separate from all other authorship; and with an increased emphasis comes our question: *Who wrote it ?*"[1]

Reader, is it not worth our while to carefully inquire where such a wonderful book as this came from? Let us go back a little farther in the history of the world. John Wesley, of whom everybody has heard as being a strong believer in this book, and a great Christian preacher, lived about one hundred years ago. Did he not make the Bible? No; because his father had it when he was a child, and out of it his mother taught him when he sat upon her knee. Wesley was the father of the Methodist Church, but the Episcopal Church existed two hundred years before John Wesley's time, and it had the very Bible which Wesley used. So we must go still farther back to find its origin.

Going back, then, about three hundred years, to the time of King James, of England, we find that by his authority some forty-seven learned men were selected to translate the Bible into English. This reminds me that I have heard infidels state that

---

[1] Fables of Infidelity, p. 82.

King James was the man who first had the books of the Bible collected into one book and translated into English. Any intelligent reader would laugh at such a foolish claim. See how easily its absurdity can be shown. This same Bible was translated into the English language back, far back, of that, by Wycliffe, more than three hundred years before King James's time. So King James was not the author of the Bible, nor the one who first collected its books or translated it into English.

Some three hundred and fifty years ago, Martin Luther translated that same Bible into the German language. Luther found it printed in the Latin language, and it was by the reading of this book that he was converted to God. Nor was it a rare or new volume in Luther's day. Far from it. At that period it was scattered nearly all over the known world, and was implicitly believed by the leading civilized nations of the earth, as it is to-day. There were many millions of Catholics, and they all received it; and so there were millions of Greeks, who also received it. Besides this, it was translated into scores of different languages, and circulated in many lands.

Ancient Manuscripts of the Bible. Another proof that the Bible was written many hundred years ago is found in the fact that we now "have nine hundred and seventy-two entire manuscripts of the different volumes of the Greek Testament, of which forty-seven are more than one thousand years old."[2] Among these is the Alexandrian manuscript, written about A. D. 325; the Vatican manuscript, written about A. D. 300; the Sinaitic

---

[2] Hist. of the Books of the Bible, by Prof. Stowe, p. 63.

manuscript, written at least as early as either of the other two; the Ephraim manuscript, about A. D. 350; and the Beza manuscript, written about A. D 490.

"Here, then, we have accessible to us five manuscript copies of the Greek Testament, the most recent more than twelve hundred years old, and the most ancient reaching to an age of fifteen centuries. The proudest and most costly architectural structures of men have within that period either crumbled and moldered away, or become obsolete and unfit for their original use, though built of the most solid materials and put together with the utmost care; while we of this age can read the same fragile page of books which were in the hands of men forty-five and fifty generations before us."[3]

"It is about two hundred years from the death of the apostle John to the first full manuscript we have of the whole New Testament, though we have fragments and quotations from the very earliest periods, from the time of the apostle John himself."[4] It is absolutely certain, then, that the very last of the books of the Bible were written, and in general circulation, and were read throughout all the churches, as early as fifteen hundred years ago.

This takes us back to the middle of the fourth century, or to A. D. 350. Here we might quote numerous celebrated authors of that very period, who not only mentioned the Bible, and quoted copiously from it, but wrote commentaries upon it. Thus did the celebrated scholar Jerome, who was born A. D. 330 and died A. D. 420, one of the most learned of all the church fathers, particularly in

---

[3] Hist. of the Books of the Bible, by Prof. Stowe, p. 78.
[4] Id. p. 61.

everything pertaining to the Bible. His greatest work was the revision of the common Latin translation of the Bible, called the Vulgate. Besides this he wrote prefaces for the several books of Scripture, containing all that could be ascertained concerning the authors, times of writing, etc. He dwelt a long time in Palestine, the very place where Jesus and the apostles lived and taught. He gives a catalogue of the books of the New Testament in which he mentions the same books which we now have. The old Bible, then, was not new at that date.

Passing over many witnesses which we might introduce, let us go back a little farther, to another important era, to the Council of Nice, A. D. 325. This is one of the most noted eras in the history of the church or of the world. It was just the time when the paganism of the Roman Empire gave way before the triumphant progress of Christianity, after a struggle of three hundred years. Constantine, the Roman emperor, had publicly indorsed Christianity just previous to this epoch. A great council of bishops, priests, and leading ministers of the world, was convened at Nice. Three hundred and eighteen bishops of all nations, from Spain to Persia, were gathered here. The Emperor Constantine presided in person. Many days were spent in earnestly discussing the doctrine of the trinity, and other matters pertaining to Christianity. The list of the books of the Bible was carefully re-examined by this council, and again published to the world. "Ah," says the infidel, "that is probably the time the Bible was made. Here is the origin of Christianity, or at least this is the council which decided what books should be received as Scripture, and what should not." But there is not a word of truth in either of these assertions. Let us look at the facts:—

"There did exist then, undeniably, in the year 325, large numbers of Christian churches in the Roman Empire, sufficiently numerous to make it politic, in the opinion of infidels, for a candidate for the empire to profess Christianity; sufficiently powerful to secure his success, notwithstanding the desperate struggles of the heathen party; and sufficiently religious, or, if you like, superstitious, to make it politic for an emperor and his politicians to give up the senate, the court, the camp, the chase, and the theater, and weary themselves with long prayers and longer speeches of preachers about Bible religion. Now that is certainly a remarkable fact, and all the more remarkable if we now inquire, How came it so? for these men, preachers, prince, and people, were brought up to worship Jupiter and the thirty thousand gods of Olympus, after the heathen fashion, and leave the care of religion to heathen priests, who never troubled their heads about books or doctrines after they had offered their sacrifices. In all the records of the world, there is no instance of a general council of heathen priests to settle the religion of their people. How happens it, then, that the human race has of a sudden waked up to such a strange sense of the folly of idolatry and the value of religion? The Council of Nice and the Emperor Constantine and his counselors making a Bible, is a proof of a wonderful revolution in the world's religion,—a phenomenon far more surprising than if the Secretaries of State, and the Senate, and the President should leave the Capitol and post off to Boston, to attend the meetings of a Methodist Conference assembled to make a hymn-book. Now, what is the cause of this remarkable conversion of prince, priests, and people? How did they all get religion? How did they get it so suddenly? How did they get so much of it?

"The infidel gives no answer, except to tell us that the austerity, purity, and zeal of the first Christians, their good discipline, their belief in the resurrection of the body, and the general Judgment, and their persuasion that Christ and his apostles wrought miracles, had made a great many converts. [Gibbon.] This is just as if I inquired how a great fire originated, and you should tell me that it burned fast because it was very hot. What I want to know is, how it happened that these licentious Greeks, and Romans, and Asiatics became austere and pure,—how these frivolous philosophers suddenly became so zealous about religion,—what implanted the belief of the resurrection of the body, and of the Judgment to come, in the skeptical minds of these heathen scoffers,—and how did the pagans of Italy, Egypt, Spain, Germany, Britain, come to believe in the miracles of one who lived hundreds of years before, and thousands of miles away, or to care a straw whether the written accounts of them were true or false? According to the infidel account, the Council of Nice and the Emperor Constantine's Bible-making is a most extraordinary business,—a phenomenon without any natural cause, and they will allow no supernatural,—a greater miracle than any recorded in the Bible.

"If we inquire, however, of the parties attending that council, what the state of the case is, we shall learn that they believed—whether truly or erroneously we are not now inquiring, but they believed —that a teacher sent from God had appeared in

Palestine two hundred and ninety years before, and had taught this religion which they had embraced."⁵

But a difference of opinion had grown up as to the exact nature of this teacher in whom they believed; whether he were an angel from Heaven, or God himself. They assembled to discuss this solemn question, and "through the whole of the discussions, both sides appealed to the writings of the apostles, as being then well known, and of unquestioned authority with every one who held the Christian name. These facts, being utterly indisputable, are acknowledged by all persons, infidel or Christian, at all acquainted with history.

"Here, then, we have the books of the New Testament at the Council of Nice well known to the whole world; and the council, so far from *giving* any authority to them, *bowing to theirs*,—both Arian and Orthodox with one consent acknowledging that the whole Christian world received them as the writings of the apostles of Christ. There were venerable men of fourscore and ten at that council; if these books had been first introduced in their lifetime, they must have known it. There were men there whose parents had heard the Scriptures read in church from their childhood, and so could not be imposed upon with a new Bible. The New Testament could not be less than three generations old, else one or other of the disputants would have exposed the novelty of its introduction, from his own information. The Council of Nice, then, did not make the New Testament. It was a book well known, ancient, and of undoubted authority among all Christians, ages before that coun-

---

⁵ Fables of Infidelity, pp 87, 88.

cil. *The existence of New-Testament Scriptures, then, ages before the Council of Nice, is a great fact.*" [6]

From the Council of Nice we go back ten years, to A. D. 315, which brings us to the world-renowned Eusebius, bishop of Cæsarea, an intimate friend of the Emperor Constantine. Eusebius was a man of extraordinary learning, diligence, and judgment, and singularly studious in the Scriptures. His invaluable Ecclesiastical History, written at that date, is a volume of over four hunded pages, containing a particular account of Jesus Christ, his twelve apostles, the early rise and wonderful progress of Christianity in the world. He gives a minute account of each book of the New Testament, calling each by its name, telling who wrote it, how sacred it was held by the whole church, etc. Chapter twenty-five of Book III. he devotes particularly to a catalogue of these books. His list is exactly the same as that which we now have. Here, then, is another nail in a sure place.

We will now push our inquiry about fifty years farther back, bringing us to A. D. 260, or to the middle of the third century, to the testimony of Victorinus, bishop of Pettau in Germany. "Victorinus wrote commentaries on different books of the Old Testament, an exposition of some passages of St. Matthew's gospel, a commentary on the Apocalypse, and various controversial treatises against the heretics of the day; in which we have valuable and most explicit testimonies to almost every book of the New Testament."[7] No doubt, then, about the old Bible thus far.

Going back to a still more remote period, we

---

[6] Id. pp. 89, 90 [7] Horne's Introduction, vol. i. p. 80.

come to the great and learned Origen. Of all the fathers who flourished in the third century, he is unquestionably the most learned and renowned. He was born A. D. 184, and died about A. D. 253. Thus it will be seen that he lived within a hundred years of the death of St. John, and was therefore so near the time of the publication of the books of the New Testament that he could hardly avoid obtaining the most accurate knowledge of their origin and authors. So great was the esteem in which this man was held, even by the heathen, that their philosophers dedicated their writings to him. He traveled all over the Eastern world, collecting different manuscripts and versions of the Bible. He compiled a Bible called the Hexapla. It contained six columns to a page, one in Hebrew, one in Hebrew with Greek characters, and the other four the versions of the Bible by Aquila, Symmachus, the Septuagint, and Theodotion.

"Besides these, which in themselves form a decisive testimony to the authenticity of the Scriptures, he wrote a threefold exposition of all the books of the Scripture; viz., scholia, or short notes; tomes, or extensive commentaries, in which he employed all his learning, critical, sacred, and profane; and a variety of homilies and tracts for the people. Although a small portion only of his works has come down to us, yet in them he uniformly bears testimony to the authenticity of the New Testament, as we now have it; and he is the first writer who has given us a perfect catalogue of those books which Christians unanimously, or at least the greater part of them, have considered as the genuine and divinely inspired writings of the apostles."[8] What more abundant testimony to the ex-

---

[8] Horne's Introduction, p. 81.

istence of the Scriptures at that time could any Christian ask?

From this we proceed to the second century. Here we find Tertullian, of the city of Carthage. He lived within fifty years of the last of the apostles, and was a vigorous writer in defense of Christianity. His work abounds in quotations and long extracts from the books of the New Testament. It is said that "his quotations occupy nearly thirty folio pages." Lardner says, "There are more and larger quotations of the small volume of the New Testament in this one Christian author, than of all the works of Cicero in the writers of all characters for several ages."[9] Irenæus and Clement both lived in this century. They often quote from the apostolic writings; but our limits forbid giving quotations from these and others of this century.

Tertullian says, in his Apology to the Roman Presidents, "Look into the words of God, our Scriptures, which we ourselves do not conceal, and many accidents bring into the way of those who are not of our religion." Does not this appeal to the heathen rulers to read "the words of God," show that these writings were then in circulation? In the time of Tertullian it is believed that the original manuscripts were still in existence. He says: "Well, if you be willing to exercise your curiosity profitably in the business of your salvation, visit the apostolic churches, in which the very chairs of the apostles still preside, in which their truly authentic letters are recited, sounding forth the voice and representing the countenance of each one of them. Is Achaia near you? you have Corinth. If you are not far from Macedonia, you have Philippi, you have Thessalonica. If you can visit Asia, you

---

* Vol. i. p. 435.

have Ephesus; and if you are near Italy you have Rome, from whence also you may be easily satisfied."[10]

"If Tertullian did not mean that the original manuscript, but only *authentic copies* of the epistles to the Corinthians, Philippians, etc., were to be seen by application, why send inquirers thither? Could an *authentic copy* of the epistle to the Philippians be seen nowhere but at Philippi? or of that to the Corinthians nowhere but at Corinth?"[11]

One step farther back and we are in the generation immediately succeeding the apostles. Here we find Justin Martyr, born ten years before John was banished. "After becoming a Christian, he occupied a high stand in learned writing and holy living. His remaining works contain numerous quotations from, as well as allusions to, the four gospels, which he uniformly represents as containing 'the genuine and authentic accounts of Jesus Christ and of his doctrine.' The same is true in relation to the Acts of the Apostles, and the greater part of the epistles. The book of Revelation is expressly said by Justin to have been written by 'John, one of the apostles of Christ.' Having lived before the death of that apostle, he had the best opportunity of knowing.'"[12]

"Further, in his [Justin Martyr's] first apology he tells us that the memoirs of the apostles and the writings of the prophets were read and expounded in the Christian assemblies for public worship; whence it is evident that the gospels were at that time well known in the world, and not designedly concealed from any one."[13]

---

[10] De Præscriptione, cxxxvi, p. 245.
[11] Alexander on the Canon, p. 143.
[12] M'Ilvaine's Evidences, p. 72.
[13] Horne's Introduction, p. 85.

"We finish the second century with Papias, bishop of Hierapolis in Asia, whom Irenæus speaks of as a hearer of John, and a disciple of Polycarp, a pupil of John the apostle. How he obtained his information will appear from the only fragment of his writings remaining. It is found in Eusebius. 'If at any time I met with one who had conversed with the elders, I inquired after the sayings of the elders; what Andrew or what Peter said; or what Philip, Thomas, or James had said; what John or Matthew, or what any other of the disciples of the Lord were wont to say.' Thus we have a witness who lived near enough to the beginning to inquire of those who had conversed with the apostles, if not to listen to St. John himself. Too little remains of his writings to furnish many testimonies, especially as he had it not in view to confirm the authenticity of any part of the Scripture; but still he gives a very valuable testimony to the gospels of Matthew and Mark, and the first epistles of Peter and John. He alludes to the Acts and the book of Revelation.

"Thus we have ascended to the *apostolic age*. But we may reach still higher. We have in our possession the well-authenticated writings of four individuals and fathers in the primitive church, who, because they were contemporary with the apostles, are called *apostolical fathers*. Two of them, Clement and Hermas, are mentioned by name in the New Testament; the third, Polycarp, was an immediate disciple of St. John; the fourth, Ignatius, enjoyed the privilege of frequent intercourse with the apostles. There is scarcely a book of the New Testament, which one or another of these writers has not either quoted or alluded to. Though what is extant of their works is very little, it contains more than two hundred and twenty quotations, or allusions to the writings of our sacred volume, in which they are uniformly treated with the reverence belonging to inspired books, and entitled, 'The Sacred Scriptures;' 'The Oracles of the Lord.'

"Their testimony, having been given incidentally, without any view to its being testimony, does not apply to all the books. They had no design of enumerating for posterity, or for their contemporaries, the books of Scripture. There was no controversy on that subject in their age. It would have seemed a needless waste of words, had they attempted to decide a question which no one asked. It is very natural therefore, considering the brevity of their remaining works and the incidental character of their quotations, that some of the shorter writings of the New Testament should not be alluded to; while the fact that by one or another almost every book is quoted or alluded to, and that the whole number of quotations or allusions is upwards of two hundred and twenty, accompanied with every mark of reverence and submission, is a most impressive proof that the authenticity and inspired authority of the New-Testament books were then notorious and unquestioned among Christians.

"Thus we have ascended the line of testimony, into the presence of the apostles. Our evidence has been collected from only a few out of the many witnesses that might have been cited. It has been derived from writers of different times, and of countries widely separated,—from philosophers, rhetoricians, and divines, all men of acuteness and learning in their days, all concurring in their testimony that the books of the New Testament were equally known in distant regions, and received as authentic by men and churches that had no intercourse with one another. The argument is now, therefore, reduced to this: The apostles and disciples of Christ are known to have left some writings. That those writings have been lost, none can give a reason for believing. It is not pretended that any other volume than that of the New Testament contains them. The books contained in this volume were considered to be the writings of the apostles, by the whole Christian church, as far back as those who were their contemporaries and companions, being continually quoted and alluded to as such. It was impossible that such witnesses should be deceived. Contemporaries and companions must have known whether they quoted the genuine works of the apostles, or only forgeries pretending to their names. Our evidence, therefore, is complete. What I have presented exceeds, above measure, the evidence for the authenticity of any other ancient book. Should the fiftieth part of it be required for the proof of the authenticity of any book of ancient Grecian or Roman origin, it could not abide the trial."[14]

CHAPTER XVIII.

TESTIMONY OF ENEMIES TO THE GENUINENESS OF THE BIBLE.

THE testimonies in the previous chapter, showing that the New Testament was written in the days of the apostles, some eighteen centuries since, were from Christian writers. In this chapter we propose

---

[14] M'Ilvaine's Evidences of Christianity, pp. 72-75.

to bring testimony from infidels themselves, from the bitterest enemies of Christ, confirming the genuineness of the New Testament; that is, showing that it was written by Christians in the first century.

Everybody is aware of the fact that within the last century two noted infidels, Thomas Paine and Voltaire, have written books, not only against Christianity, but against the Bible itself. They have referred to the Bible and taken quotations from nearly every book in it. This very fact proves beyond dispute that Christianity and the Bible did exist in their time; for they would not have written against that which had no existence. Just so in different ages we find infidels and opposers writing against Christianity and against the Bible, by which we may know certainly that both of these had an existence at that time. We might stop and find such writings as these in every century from our day back to that of the apostles. But as no one disputes that the Bible existed with a wide-spread influence over millions of believers and whole nations of Christians as early as the fourth century, we will first stop there.

In the year 361 the Emperor Julian wrote a very bitter book against the Bible. Julian was brought up a Christian; but he afterward apostatized and became a zealous pagan, an earnest supporter of the heathen religion. He became emperor of Rome, the mightiest empire of the world. The previous emperor had been a Christian; but when Julian came to the empire he was so bitter against Christianity that he resolved to use his power and that of the empire to destroy it. But his effort was a failure. Julian united intelligence, learning, and power, with persecuting zeal, in his resolute effort against Christianity. In the year 361 he wrote his book against Christianity. We may be very certain that he would say everything possible against it. Though his work is not extant, yet we have lengthy quotations from it in both Jerome and Cyril, from which it is evident that he bore witness to the genuineness of the New Testament.

He quotes from the four gospels and from the Acts, and also refers to the epistles to the Romans, Corinthians, and Galatians. "He concedes, and argues from, their early date; quotes them by name as the genuine works of their reputed authors; proceeds upon the supposition as a thing undeniable, that they were the only historical books which Christians received as canonical; the only authentic narratives of Christ and his apostles, and of the doctrine they delivered. . . He nowhere insinuates that the authenticity of any portion of the New Testament could reasonably be questioned."[1] "He himself expressly states the early date of these records. He calls them by the very names which they now bear. He does not give the slightest intimation that he suspected the whole or any of them to be forgeries."[2] No doubt, then, about the existence of the Bible at that date. Let us go back a little farther.

"Hierocles, president of Bithynia, and a learned man of about the year 303, united with a cruel persecution of Christians the publication of a book against Christianity, in which, instead of issuing even the least suspicion that the New Testament was not written by those to whom its several parts were ascribed, he confines his effort to the hunt of internal flaws and contradictions. Besides this

---

[1] M'Ilvaine's Evidences, p. 107.
[2] Horne's Introduction, vol. i. p. 94.

tacit acknowledgment, his work, or the extracts of it that remain, refer to at least six out of the eight writers of the books of the New Testament." [3]

Thus, in the providence of God, this opposer has left his testimony to the existence of the Bible in that day. But we have not yet reached the fountain-head. If we go back to A. D. 270, to within two centuries of the apostles, we find another noted infidel, Porphyry, universally admitted to be the ablest and most formidable opponent of Christianity in ancient times. In that year he wrote a book against Christianity, from which it appears that he was very familiar with the books of the Bible. He was well versed in profane history, and had conversed with the Christians in all parts of the world.

"Is it credible, then, that so sagacious an inquirer could have failed to have discovered a forgery with respect to the New Testament, had a forgery existed,—a discovery which would have given him the completest triumph, by striking at once a mortal blow at the religion which he attempted to destroy? So far, however, is this from being the case, that Porphyry not only did not deny the truth of the gospel history, but actually considered the miracles of Jesus Christ as real facts. The writings of the ancient Christians, who answered his objections, likewise afford general evidence that Porphyry made numerous observations on the Scriptures." [4]

We will now go back about a century earlier, to the year 176 A. D., where we find Celsus, a philosopher of great learning and notoriety,

---

[3] M'Ilvaine's Evidences, pp. 107, 108.
[4] Horne's Introduction, vol. i. pp 93, 94.

who wrote a lengthy work against the Christians. He flourished about seventy-five years after the death of the last apostle. His zeal against Christianity was unbounded. "None can complain against his testimony as deficient in antiquity. An industrious, ingenious, learned adversary of that age must have known whatever was suspicious in the authorship of the New-Testament writings. His book, entitled 'The True Word,' is unhappily lost; but in the answer composed by Origen the extracts from it are so large that it is difficult to find of any ancient book, not extant, more extensive remains. The author quotes from the gospels such a variety of particulars, even in these fragments, that the enumeration would prove almost an abridgment of the gospel narrative."[5]

He proceeds in all his argument upon the supposition that the New Testament was written by the apostles, and at the very time it claims to have been written. He never advances a supposition to the contrary, though he was one of the bitterest enemies who ever wrote against the Bible. Living at that early day, he certainly had the best opportunity to know whether those books were genuine or not. Think of it: His book was written within about seventy-five years of the death of St. John. He speaks of Christ as having lived but a few years before his time, and mentions all the principal facts of the gospel history, relative to Christ. He admits that Christ was considered a divine person by his apostles. "He acknowledges the miracles wrought by Jesus Christ, by which he engaged great multitudes to adhere to him as the

---

[5] M'Ilvaine's Evidences, p. 109.

Messiah. That these miracles were really performed, he never disputes or denies, but ascribes them to the magic art which, he says, Christ learned in Egypt."[6]

Hence it appears, "by the testimony of one of the most malicious adversaries the Christian religion ever had, and who was also a man of considerable parts and learning, that the writings of the evangelists were extant in his time, which was the next century to that in which the apostles lived; and those accounts were written by Christ's own disciples, and consequently in the very age in which the facts there related were done, and when, therefore, it would have been the easiest thing in the world to have convicted them of falsehood, if they had not been true."[7]

Here, then, we have the testimony of the most learned infidels of the world, commencing with Paine in our own age, and running back through the ages, embracing Julian in the fourth century, Porphyry in the third century, Celsus in the second century, and the last reaching to within one generation of the apostles themselves—all testifying to the existence of Christianity and of the Bible, away back to the apostles in the first century. It seems that the testimony presented is absolutely conclusive, and should remove from the most skeptical mind the least doubt as to the early origin of Christianity and the New Testament.

---

[6] Horne's Introduction, vol. i. p. 201.
[7] Answer to "Christianity as Old as the Creation," by Leland, vol. ii. chap. v. pp. 150-154.

CHAPTER XIX.

PROFANE HISTORY PROVES THE RISE OF CHRISTIANITY IN THE FIRST CENTURY.

The New Testament professes to contain the history of the remarkable person, Jesus Christ of Nazareth. It gives a narration of his wonderful life and of the origin of the Christian religion. It tells how rapidly that religion spread, not only over Palestine, but into Africa, Asia, and Europe, among both Jews and Gentiles.

"Now," says the infidel, "if this is so, why do not profane historians speak of it, historians who are not Christians or friendly to the cause?" Assuming that there is no such mention in history, they boldly pronounce the whole thing a forgery, gotten up by Catholic monks in the Dark Ages. But any one at all acquainted with the facts in the case can but pity the ignorance that dares to make such an assertion.

"That an extraordinary person, called Jesus Christ, flourished in Judea in the Augustan age, is a fact better supported and authenticated than that there lived such men as Cyrus, Alexander, and Julius Cæsar; for although their histories are recorded by various ancient writers, yet the memorials of their conquests and empires have, for the most part, perished. Babylon, Persepolis, and Ecbatana are no more; and travelers have long disputed, but have not been able to ascertain, the precise site of ancient Nineveh, that exceeding great city of three days' journey. Jonah 3:3. How few vestiges of Alexander's victorious arms are at present to be seen in Asia Minor and

India! And equally few are the standing memorials in France and Britain, to evince that there was such a person as Julius Cæsar, who subdued the one and invaded the other. Not so defective are the evidences concerning the existence of Jesus Christ. That he lived in the reign of Tiberius, emperor of Rome, and that he suffered death under Pontius Pilate, the Roman procurator of Judea, are facts that are not only acknowledged by the Jews of every subsequent age, and by the testimonies of several heathen writers, but also by Christians of every age and country, who have commemorated, and still commemorate, the birth, death, resurrection, and ascension of Jesus Christ!"[1]

Beginning with our own times, let us now consider the facts in the case. Christianity is to-day the greatest power of earth. It is believed in by the mightiest nations of the earth, by four hundred millions of the most learned, intelligent people of the world. Surely, it started somewhere and by some cause. Where and what were they? Well, we have Protestant Christians; they began with Luther, three hundred years ago. So Christianity is certainly as old as that. Then we have Roman Catholic Christians. How old are they? Everybody knows that in the ninth century there was a division between the Eastern, or Greek, Church, and the Western, or Roman, Church. Each of them, at that time, numbered millions of believers. Hence Christianity existed as early as that day.

We will make no account of the fact that in the fourth century Christianity had become so powerful and wide-spread that it took possession of the Ro-

---

[1] Horne's Introduction, vol. i. p. 68.

man Empire, the mightiest power of the world; that it had already sent its missionaries into all the known world; that about this time Sozomen and Socrates wrote extensive histories of Christianity; nor of the fact that in A. D. 315 Eusebius wrote a large volume, giving a history of Christ and his church; nor of the testimony of one hundred Christian authors during the first three centuries of the Christian era. We will set these all aside, and prove the origin of Christianity in the first century by profane authors alone. We will give the testimony of eleven of the most noted authors and historians of antiquity, reaching from the middle of the fourth century back to the very days of Christ himself.

JULIAN, A. D. 361. We have already stated that Julian was emperor of the Roman world at this period; that the great effort of his life was to put down Christianity. For this purpose he employed the greatest talents, and the most mighty scepter ever wielded. He wrote a book against Christianity, in which he acknowledged that there were multitudes of Christians in Greece and Italy in the days of the apostles, and that many of them were men of high character, such as Cornelius, a Roman centurion, and Sergius Paulus, proconsul of Cyprus.[2]

PORPHYRY, A. D. 270. This learned writer acknowledges that Christians were very numerous in the Roman Empire; admits the miracles wrought by the apostles, which he ascribes to the magic art; and endeavors to expose them to reproach as the cause of the calamities that befell the Roman Empire.[3]

---

[2] Lardner's Works, vol. viii. pp. 394-411.
[3] Horne's Introduction, vol. i. p. 209.

GALEN, A. D. 220, acknowledged the virtuous principles of the Christians.[4]

MARCUS ANTONINUS, A. D. 161, mentions the Christians as furnishing examples of an obstinate contempt of death.[5]

EPICTETUS, A. D. 109, mentions the fortitude and constancy of the Christians under persecution. He calls them Galileans.[6]

LUCIAN, A. D. 176, in his numerous writings bears testimony to the leading facts and principles of Christianity. He says that Christ was crucified in Palestine, and is worshiped by the Christians. He mentions their contempt for this world, and how they courageously suffered for their religion; and affirms that they were noted for honesty and probity; that their Master had taught them mutual love, which they universally practiced. He says that they were well known in the world by the name of Christians; that they were then numerous in Pontus and Paphlagonia, and the adjoining countries. He ridicules many of their practices and doctrines.[7]

PLINY, A. D. 107. The celebrated Pliny the Younger was born A. D. 62, and was very distinguished in many ways. Trajan the emperor made him governor of Bithynia A. D. 106–108. Trajan cruelly persecuted the Christians, and Pliny had to carry out his edict against them. He found vast numbers of them in his province. He wrote the following letter concerning them to the emperor, A. D. 107 :—

---

[4] Lardner's Works, vol. viii pp. 90, 91.
[5] Id. vol. vii. p. 398.
[6] Horne's Introduction, vol. i. p. 209.
[7] Id. vol. i. p. 208.

"*Pliny, to the Emperor Trajan, wisheth* **health and happiness:**

"It is my constant custom, Sire, to refer myself to you in all matters concerning which I have any doubt. For who can better direct me when I hesitate, or instruct me when I am ignorant?

"I have never been present at any trials of Christians, so that I know not well what is the subject-matter of punishment, or of inquiry, or what strictures ought to be used in either. Nor have I been a little perplexed to determine whether any difference ought to be made upon account of age, or whether the young and tender, and the full-grown and robust, ought to be treated all alike; whether repentance should entitle to pardon, or whether all who have once been Christians ought to be punished, though they are now no longer so; whether the name itself, although no crimes be detected, or crimes only belonging to the name, ought to be punished.

"In the meantime, I have taken this course with all who have been brought before me, and have been accused as Christians: I have put the question to them whether they were Christians. Upon their confessing to me that they were, I repeated the question a second and a third time, threatening also to punish them with death. Such as still persisted, I ordered away to be punished; for it was no doubt with me, whatever might be the nature of their opinion, that contumacy and inflexible obstinacy ought to be punished. There are others of the same infatuation, whom, because they are Roman citizens, I have noted down to be sent to the city.

"In a short time, the crime spreading itself, even while under persecution, as is usual in such cases, divers sorts of people came in my way. An information was presented to me, without mentioning the author, containing the names of many persons who, upon examination, denied that they were Christians, or ever had been so; who repeated after me an invocation of the gods, and with wine and frankincense made supplication to your image, which, for that purpose, I have caused to be brought and set before them together with the statues of the deities. Moreover, they reviled the name of Christ. None of which things, as is said, they who are really Christians can by any means be compelled to do. These, therefore, I thought proper to discharge.

"Others were named by an informer who at first confessed themselves Christians, and afterward denied it. The rest said they had been Christians, but had left them, some three years ago, some longer, and one or more above twenty years. They all worshiped your image and the statues of the gods; these also reviled Christ. They affirmed that the whole of their fault or error lay in this: that they were wont to meet together on a stated day, before it was light, and sing among themselves alternately, a hymn to Christ as God, and bind themselves by a sacrament, not to the commission of any wickedness, but not to be guilty of theft, or robbery, or adultery, never to falsify their word, nor to deny a pledge committed to them, when called upon to return it. When these things were performed, it was their custom to separate and then to come together again to a meal, which they ate in common, without any disorder; but this they had forborne since the publication of my edict, by which, according to your command, I prohibited assemblies. After receiving this account I judged it more necessary to examine two maid-servants, which were called ministers, by torture, but I have discovered nothing besides a bad and excessive superstition.

"Suspending, therefore, all judicial proceedings, I have recourse to you for advice; for it has appeared to me a matter highly deserving consideration, especially upon account of the great number of persons who are in danger of suffering. For many of all ages and every rank, of both sexes likewise, are accused, and will be accused. Nor has the contagion of this superstition seized cities only, but the lesser towns also, and the open country. Nevertheless, it seems to me that it may be restrained and arrested. It is certain that the temples, which were almost forsaken, begin to be frequented. And the sacred solemnities, after a long intermission, are revived. Victims, likewise, are everywhere bought up, whereas for some time there were but few purchasers. Whence it is easy to imagine what numbers of men might be reclaimed, if pardon were granted to those who shall repent."[8]

Here follows Trajan's answer:—

"*Trajan, to Pliny, wisheth health and happiness:*

"You have taken the right course, my Pliny, in your proceedings with those who have been brought before you as Christians; for it is impossible to establish any one rule that shall hold universally. They are not to be sought after. If any are brought before you, and are convicted, they ought to be punished. However, he that denies his being a Christian, and makes it evident in fact, that is, by supplicating to our gods, though he be suspected

---

[8] Lardner's Works, vol. vii. p. 18.

to have been so formerly, let him be pardoned upon repentance. But in no case of any crime whatever, may a bill of information be received without being signed by him who presents it, for that would be a dangerous precedent, and unworthy of my government." [9]

The importance of this testimony should be well weighed. This letter and the reply were public documents, open to all. Notice the following points: 1. These letters were written within eighty years of the death of Christ, and within ten years of the death of the last apostle, John. 2. Christianity had already spread a great distance from Judea, as this was far off in Asia Minor. 3. Immense numbers of persons of all classes had embraced Christianity prior to this event. 4. So extensive had its influence already become that the heathen temples were nearly forsaken, and animals were no longer bought for sacrifices. 5. This sect had not lately come up; some of those examined had been Christians twenty years before. This takes us back into the very days of the apostles. 6. What a noble testimony is here borne to the honesty, the purity and innocence of these devoted Christians! This testimony alone is sufficient to prove the existence of the Christian religion as far back as the first century, in the days of the apostles.

SUETONIUS, A. D. 65. The first general persecution of Christians was in A. D. 65, under Nero, the tyrant under whom Paul was martyred. Concerning this persecution, we have the testimony of two Roman historians, Suetonius and Tacitus. Of this the former says, "The Christians likewise were se-

---

[9] Lardner's Works, vol. vii. p. 24.

verely punished,— a sort of people addicted to a new and mischievous superstition." [10]

TACITUS, A. D. 65, was contemporary with the apostles, and one of the most noted profane historians of the Roman world. His history can be bought at any book-store. I quote only a part of what he says upon the point. Of the single extract which we take from Tacitus, Gibbon says: "The most skeptical criticism is obliged to respect the truth of this important fact, and the integrity of this important passage of Tacitus. The former is confirmed by the diligent and accurate Suetonius, who mentions the punishment which Nero inflicted upon Christians. The latter may be proved by the consent of the most ancient manuscripts; by the inimitable character of the style of Tacitus; by his reputation, which guarded his text from interpolations of pious fraud; and by the purport of his narration." [11]

Tacitus, after relating the burning of the city of Rome, and the attempt to convict the sect "commonly known by the name of Christians," of the crime, says:—

"The author of that name was Christ, who, in the reign of Tiberius, was put to death as a criminal, under the procurator, Pontius Pilate. But this pestilent superstition, checked for a while, broke out afresh, and spread not only over Judea, where the evil originated, but also in Rome, where all that is evil on the earth finds its way and is practiced. At first, those only were apprehended who confessed themselves of that sect; afterward,

---

[10] Suetonius, in Nerone, chap. xvi.; Lardner's Works, vol. vii. chap. viii. p. 265.
[11] Decline and Fall, vol. ii. p. 19.

a vast multitude, discovered by them; all of whom were condemned, not so much for the crime of burning the city as for their enmity to mankind. Their executions were so contrived as to expose them to derision and contempt. Some were covered over with skins of wild beasts, that they might be torn to pieces by dogs; some were crucified; while others, having been daubed over with combustible materials, were set up for lights in the night time, and thus burned to death. For these spectacles, Nero gave his own gardens, and at the same time exhibited there the diversions of the circus, sometimes standing in the crowd as a spectator, in the habit of a charioteer; and, at other times, driving a chariot himself, until at length these men, though really criminal and deserving of exemplary punishment, began to be commiserated, as a people who were destroyed, not out of regard to the public welfare, but only to gratify the cruelty of one man." [12]

The above testimony of Tacitus, covered as it is by contemporary authors, is an important confirmation of the evangelical record. This historian says, 1. That Jesus Christ was put to death as a malefactor, by Pontius Pilate, under Tiberius; 2. That the people called Christians took their name from Christ, and also derived their principles from the same source; 3. That this religion first had its rise in Judea, where it spread extensively, notwithstanding severe opposition; 4. That from Judea it spread to Rome, where, in the days of Nero, the Christians were very numerous; that there were indeed vast multitudes of them as early as that period; and, 5. That these Christians were re-

---

[12] Lardner's Works, vol. iii. p. 611.

proached and hated and terribly persecuted. How could profane historians say more! What additional evidence could we ask to prove the truthfulness of the New Testament? What do infidels do with these unanswerable facts? Nothing.

JOSEPHUS, the Jewish priest who lived in the very days of the apostles, and in the land of Judea, in his History of the Jews, after referring to their sedition against Pontius Pilate, bears testimony to Jesus Christ thus:—

"Now there was about this time Jesus, a wise man, if it be lawful to call him a man; for he performed many wonderful works. He was a teacher of such men as received the truth with pleasure. He drew over to him many of the Jews, and also many of the Gentiles. *This was the Christ.*

"And when Pilate, at the instigation of the principal men among us, had condemned him to the cross, those who had loved him from the first did not cease to adhere to him. For he appeared to them alive again, on the third day; the divine prophets having foretold these and ten thousand other wonderful things concerning him. And the tribe, or sect, of Christians, so named from him, subsists to this time." [13]

The learned Dr. Horne has shown that this testimony is genuine. [14]

PONTIUS PILATE, the very man by whose authority Christ was crucified, has left on record a careful account of that event. The Romans were very careful to make a record of all important events occurring within the empire. This record was preserved in their "Acts of the Senate," or in the

---

[13] Josephus' Antiq., lib. xviii. chap. iii. sect. 3.
[14] Horne's Introduction, vol. ii. part i. chap. vii.

"Daily Acts of the People," which are carefully kept at Rome. It was customary for the governors to send to the emperor an account of any remarkable occurrence within their jurisdiction. Pilate sent to Rome an account of affairs in Judea, among the rest that concerning Jesus Christ and his death. That this is unquestionably true is proven by the many ancient witnesses. Eusebius quotes it in his Ecclesiastical History, Book II., chap. 2.

The primitive Christians, in their disputes with the Gentiles, frequently appealed to this statement of Pilate as undoubted testimony. Thus Justin Martyr wrote an Apology for the Christians, A. D. 140, and sent it directly to the emperor at Rome. In speaking of the death of Christ, he says, "And that these things were so done, you may know from the Acts made in the time of Pontius Pilate."[15] In the year 200, the learned Tertullian, in his Apology for Christians, says, "Of all these things relating to Christ, Pilate himself, in his conscience already a Christian, sent an account to Tiberius, then emperor."[16]

These testimonies of Justin and Tertullian, in their public apologies for the Christians, were presented either to the emperor and senate of Rome, or to the magistrates of public authority in the Roman Empire. Now it is not reasonable that they would have made such an appeal as this to the very men in whose hands this record must have been, unless there was such a record in existence. How quick those heathen would have exposed such a falsehood; but, on the contrary, no one ever denied the statements of these writers upon the point.

---

[15] Justin Martyr, Apol. Prima, pp. 65–72.
[16] Tertullian's Apol. chap. xxi.

The testimony of the Jews. Of all classes and nations, the Jews are the very ones who ought to know best whether there ever was such a man as Jesus Christ, and whether he was put to death in Judea as the New Testament affirms. Jesus was a Jew. He lived among the Jews. It was the Jewish religion which he undertook to reform. It was the Jews who instigated his death. All his apostles were Jews; and it was among the Jews entirely that Christianity was first founded. Now suppose all this to be false,—that Christ never lived; but that Christianity was gotten up somewhere else many years afterward;—what would be the testimony of the Jews on the subject of Christ's life and ministry? Could they be persuaded that all these things had occurred right among their people, yet without their knowledge? No; the whole nation would rise up and declare that no such person as Jesus Christ ever lived or died among them. This would settle the point. But now go into that clothing store, enter that synagogue, and ask every Jew you meet if he believes that such a man as Jesus of Nazareth, a Jew, lived in Judea eighteen hundred years ago, and that he was put to death on the cross. Every Jew in the world will say, "Yes, we have no doubt of that, though we do not believe he was the true Messiah." In proof of this, read the following from a learned Jew, addressed to myself upon this point:—

"Battle Creek, Mich., Feb. 1, 1877.

"Eld. D. M. Canright:

"*Dear Sir,*—In answer to your inquiry I would state that our Jewish people all admit and believe that there was such a man as Jesus, who lived in Judea, that he had great influence over the people, and that he was finally put to death under Pontius Pilate.

"The Talmud, which is our stronghold, mentions his name very frequently. In some places he is called יֵשׁוּעַ הַנָּצְרִי, *Jesus the Nazarene;* in other places by the name תָּלוּי, *he was hung*, the *passive* participle of the verb תָּלָה, to *hang*, to *suspend*. The last name is more commonly used.

"Now, considering that the chief writers of the Talmud were Rabbi Gamaliel, and many others like him, who lived at the same time that Jesus did, we, therefore, as a people, although denying his divinity,—his being the Son of God, and his resurrection from the dead,—cannot and do not deny his existence.

"M. B. LICHTENSTEIN."

Thus even among the profane authors and historians do we find the most undoubted testimony to the truthfulness of the New-Testament record. They all agree in saying that there was such a man as Jesus Christ; that he lived in Judea; that he was crucified; that from him started the sect of Christians; and that these things occurred in the reign of Tiberius, just where the New-Testament record places them.

What can infidels do with this overwhelming testimony? Just nothing at all. A great majority of them have never troubled themselves to inquire as to whether there is any such testimony; and when their attention is called to it, they pass it with a sneer, and some trivial objection. We repeat, that no event in the history of the world, or even of a nation, is so well authenticated as that of the life and death of Christ, and the rise of the Christian religion in the land of Judea, in the first century.

CHAPTER XX.

WHO WROTE THE NEW TESTAMENT?

Skeptics would have us believe that it is an utter impossibility to know anything about who wrote the New Testament; that we cannot positively prove that the apostles wrote it; and hence that the authorship of these books is altogether uncertain. But, like all the rest of their assertions, this is mere fog and vapor, which the clear rays of truth immediately dispel. Nothing can be shown more conclusively than that the New Testament was written by the apostles in Judea, in the early part of the first century. We have not half as much proof that Milton wrote "Paradise Lost," Cicero the orations ascribed to him, or Tacitus his "Annals of History," as we have that the different books of the New Testament were written by the apostles of our Lord.

The following reasons compel us to believe that John Milton wrote the poem bearing the title, "Paradise Lost": 1. The title-page ascribes it to him. This, in the absence of counter testimony, is proof enough. 2. It has been received by our fathers of their fathers as his production. 3. Contemporary writers ascribe it to him. 4. Writers of every succeeding age quote it, and refer to it as his work, and, 5. Its spirit and style display the distinctive features of Milton's mind and character. All of these evidences can be brought in favor of the apostolic origin of the New Testament.

1. We have received the New Testament from our forefathers, with their unanimous consent, as

being the writings of the apostles. How did they all, without a single dissenting voice, come to receive them as such, if it were not so?

2. As we have shown in a previous chapter, an unbroken line of authors, from our time back to the times of the apostles themselves, quote these books as the writings of those apostles. All who have quoted them, and they are not few, have quoted them as productions of the apostles. Not only Christian authors have so regarded them, but the bitterest enemies of Christianity, as we have shown, such as Porphyry, Celsus, etc., acknowledge them to be their writings. This alone is sufficient to prove that they were such.

3. All the authors contemporary with the apostles, or immediately succeeding them, in the next generation, have ascribed these writings to them. We have already given several examples of these. For a full examination of this subject the reader is referred to Prof. Stowe's History of the Books of the Bible, where he will find scores of authors in the very earliest ages quoting these books and ascribing them to the different apostles whose names they now bear. Many of the writers quoted either talked with the disciples themselves, or with those who had talked with them; and thus the unbroken line of evidence descends to our age.

4. The books of the New Testament were never ascribed to any writers except the disciples of our Lord. The most boastful infidel, while professing doubt as to whether they were written by the apostles, has never been able to find any other authors for them.

5. No one else ever claimed the authorship of them. Is not this a little strange, taken from the skeptic's standpoint? Here are twenty-seven books

in the New Testament, claiming to have been written by Matthew, Mark, Luke, John, Paul, James, Peter, and Jude,—eight authors. If they did not write them, how does it happen that their authorship has always been generally conceded to them; and why have no other claims of their authorship ever been set up? Who can answer?

6. Most of these books bear the signatures of the apostles, as written by themselves, just the same as a man now, writing an important document, signs his own name with his own hand. Notice how these letters are generally commenced: "Paul, a servant of Jesus Christ,"[1] etc. "Paul, called to be an apostle of Jesus Christ."[2] James begins: "James, a servant of God," etc. And Peter thus: "Peter, an apostle of Jesus Christ."[3] Jude in a similar manner: "Jude, the servant of Jesus Christ." John also writes: "John, to the seven churches which are in Asia."[4] Finally, hear Paul himself state how very careful he was to authenticate every epistle which he wrote. "The salutation of Paul with mine own hand, which is the token in every epistle; so I write."[5] Here Paul formally, with his own hand, gives them his signature that they may be certain he is the author of this letter. Every business man will in a moment appreciate how these few lines added to the security against forgery. It is a hard thing to forge a signature; but give a business man two or three lines of any man's writing opposite the name, and he is perfectly secure against imposition. Now there were many business men in all these churches to which the apostles wrote. Is any one simple enough

---

[1] Rom. 1:1. [2] 1 Cor. 1:1. [3] 1 Pet. 1:1.
[4] Rev. 1:4. [5] 2 Thess. 3:17.

to think that the brethren among whom Paul had lived for months, and with some of them for years, could not tell the handwriting of their beloved minister, or that they would care less about the genuineness of his letter than a bank clerk would about the genuineness of a ten-dollar check? Consider the additional fact that these letters were always sent from the hand of the apostle directly to the churches by a faithful brother, a servant of the apostle, and one known to the church whither he went. This alone would secure them from imposition.

"I am not as long in this city as Paul was in Ephesus, nor one-fourth of the time that John lived there, yet I defy all the advocates of the mythical theory in Germany, and all their disciples here, to write a myth half as long as this tract, and impose it on the elders and members of my church as my writing. Let it only be presented in manuscript to the congregation,—there was no printing in Paul's days,—and in five minutes a dozen members of the church would detect the forgery, even if I should hold my peace. And were I to leave on a mission to China or India, and write letters to the church, would any of these business men, who have seen my writing, have the least hesitation in recognizing it again? Do you think anybody could forge a letter as from me, and impose it on them? What an absurdity, then, to suppose that anybody could write a gospel or an epistle, and get all the members of a large church to believe that an apostle wrote it! The first Christians, then, were absolutely certain that the documents which they received as apostolic, were really so. The church at Rome could attest the epistle to them, and the gospels of Mark and Luke written there. The church of Ephesus could attest the epistle to them, and the gospel and letters and Revelation of John written there. And so on of all the other churches; and these veritable autographs were long preserved. Says Tertullian, who was ordained A. D. 192: 'Well, if you be willing to exercise your curiosity profitably in the business of your salvation, visit the apostolical churches in which the very chairs of the apostles still preside,—in which their authentic letters themselves are recited (apud quæ *ipsæ authenticæ literæ eorum recitantur*), sounding forth the voice and representing the countenance of each one of them. Is Achaia near you, you have Corinth. If you are not far from Macedonia, you have Philippi, you have Thessalonica. If you can go to Asia, you have Ephesus; but if you are near to Italy, you have Rome.'"[6]

The original letters, then, of the apostles, with their own signatures, were still kept in the churches as late as Tertullian's time, A. D. 220. This is how it happened that everybody was so certain that the apostles wrote those letters.

7. But what settles this matter absolutely and forever, is the indisputable fact that the peculiar language and style of language in the New Testament is just that which must have been used by the apostles in that age, and by no others in their age or in any other age. Any intelligent reader knows that every language is constantly undergoing change. Compare our own language now with the same a hundred years ago, and you will find a very marked difference. Many words which were in common use then, have become obsolete now. Go back two or three hundred years, and our lan-

---

[6] Fables of Infidelity, pp. 94, 95.

guage was so very different from what it is now, that an ordinary man is puzzled to read it. The spelling was different, different words were used from those now employed to convey the same meaning, and the phraseology was different. This has always been the case with every language. Hence the moment a scholar takes up a book he can readily tell, from the language used, in what age it was written.

Again: Each section of a country speaking the same language has its peculiar idiom or dialect. Thus, in a very few minutes' conversation, a Southerner betrays his nativity by his accent and expression; a Yankee, by his New England phrases; a frontiersman, by his peculiar Western vernacular. We all remember how a little maid thus detected Peter. She said, "Thy speech betrayeth thee." He was a Galilean, and for his life he could not guard his tongue so as to hide it. Yes, reader, that same peculiarity, thus indicated, is readily seen in every line which that apostle has penned. And so of each of the apostles. The style of Paul's writing is not at all like that of Peter, nor is John's like that of James. By this we know that one man alone did not write the whole of the New Testament.

Furthermore: The style of language employed throughout the New Testament is just that which was used by the Jews in Palestine in the early part of the first century. It never was used anywhere else, by any other people, nor by the Jews themselves at any other time. We wish the reader to note this fact particularly, because it is a perfect Gibraltar to the authenticity of the New Testament, and utterly precludes the possibility of its ever having been forged in any other age or by any other people. The writers of the New Testament were Jews by birth, by education, by numerous strong attachments, and in different associations. The greater part of their writings was addressed to the Jews; hence their efforts in all their writings to remove Jewish prejudice and superstition. The religious institutions of the Jewish nation were in full establishment until after the death of all the apostles except one; hence we could not expect but that Jewish peculiarities would be found in the apostolic writings. Indeed, we would look with suspicion upon any writings which did not abound with such peculiarities.

The national polity of the Jews ended at the destruction of Jerusalem; hence we should not expect the writings of those born this side of that event to be filled with such peculiarities. The New Testament is filled with words and phrases which are known to have been peculiar to Judea, in the times of the apostles. The continual allusions to the temple-services of the Jews as then existing, and which soon passed away, and the manner of expression used in the New Testament, are such as none but Jews, brought up under the Old Testament, were accustomed to use. The New Testament abounds with quotations from the Old, and references to the types and shadows of the law, with which none but Jews were familiar, and which could not have been introduced into writings as late as the second century, without extreme awkwardness, insomuch that the forgery would have been detected.

M'Ilvaine says: "In the times of the apostles, Greek was almost a universal language. It was spread over all Palestine. The Jewish coast on the Mediterranean was occupied by cities either wholly or half Greek. On the eastern border of the land, from the Arnon upward, toward the north the cities were Greek, and toward the south in possession of the Greeks. Several cities of Judea and Galilee were either entirely or at least half peopled by Greeks. Being thus favored on all sides, this language was spread by means of traffic and intercourse, through all classes, so that the people, though with many exceptions, considered generally, understood it, although they adhered more to their own language. But the Greek thus spoken in Palestine was not like that of Attica, nor of the cities of Asia Minor; but, having become degenerated in consequence of its associations with people whose native tongue was Hebrew, by means of Chaldee and Syriac intermixtures, into western Aramean, it contained a large share of the idioms and other peculiarities belonging to its heterogeneous neighbors.

"Such was the language in which the apostles must have written. Now, if the books of the New Testament be their writings, they must contain the characteristic features of that Palestine Greek. Such is most manifestly the case. These books are in Greek, not pure and classic, such as a native and educated Grecian would have written, but in *Hebraic Greek;* in a language mixed up with the words and idioms of that peculiar dialect of the Hebrews which constituted the vernacular tongue of the inhabitants of Judea and Galilee in the age of the apostles. Had it been otherwise, were the language of the New Testament pure and classic, then the writers must have been either native and educated Grecians, or else Jews of much more Attic cultivation than the apostles of Christ. In either case a suspicion would attach to the authenticity of our sacred books. Neither case being true, the evidence of authenticity is materially confirmed. But we go farther.

"The Greek of the New Testament could not have been written by men who had learned this language after the age of the apostles. This mingling of Grecian and Aramean as it is preserved in the New Testament, ceased to be the familiar tongue of Christians in Palestine before the death of St. John. When Jerusalem, with the whole civil and religious polity of the Jews, was in the seventieth year of the Christian era entirely destroyed, and the descendants of Abraham were rooted out of the land, and foreigners came in from all quarters to take their places, the language of the country underwent such a change that, except with a scattered few who had survived the desolation of their country, the Greek of the New Testament was no more a living language. When St. John died, there was probably not a man alive who could speak or write precisely that tongue. In the second century, an attempt to compose a book in the name of the apostles, and in imitation of their Greek, would have been detected as easily as if a full-bred Frenchman, never out of France, should attempt to compose a volume in a dialect of English, and endeavor to pass it off as the work of a plain, sensible, but unpolished Yankee."[7]

These plain, undeniable facts do clearly prove that the New Testament was written in the first century by Jews living in Judea.

---

[7] M'Ilvaine's Evidences, pp. 112-114.

CHAPTER XXI.

HAS THE LANGUAGE OF THE NEW TESTAMENT BEEN CHANGED SINCE IT WAS FIRST WRITTEN?

Here, again, our infidel objector raises a great ado. He talks very knowingly about the Bible having passed through a great number of translations, handed down from generation to generation; about some fifty or a hundred thousand various readings which have been discovered; and he immediately draws the conclusion that the book is entirely unreliable. But a slight examination scatters all this dust to the four winds in a moment, and leaves the atmosphere clear and healthy.

As to the many translations which the Bible has passed through, our opponents give the impression that it was translated first from the Hebrew into the Greek, then from the Greek into the Latin, from the Latin into the French, from the French into the German, from the German into the English, and so on; thus, of course, each translation becoming more obscure and farther from the original. Be it known, then, that this is utterly false. Each translation was obtained from the original Greek and Hebrew text. That is to say, the German Bible was translated from the original Greek and Hebrew. The French Bible was not translated from the German, but directly from the Hebrew and Greek, the very source from which the German was drawn. So the English Bible was not translated from the Latin, or the German, or the French, but directly from the Greek and Hebrew. Reader, this distressing cry about the Bible passing through so many translations is thus entirely unnecessary; for it is an indisputable fact that our Bible is translated directly from the original words in which it was written by inspiration.

We will give twelve convincing arguments conclusively showing that the New Testament not only has not been, but could not be, changed since it was written.

1. The different books of the New Testament could not have been changed during the lives of their authors. No one will deny this statement. Would any one undertake to corrupt and change the writings of Paul while he himself was alive? How quick he would have exposed such an attempt!

2. They could not have been corrupted while the original letters, with the names of the apostles signed to them, remained. If such an attempt had been made, those in charge of the original letters would readily have detected the corruption. "It is well known that the original manuscripts, or autographs, of the writers, or at least some of them, were preserved for many years after their death. Ignatius appealed to them in the first century, and in the second century Tertullian affirmed that they were carefully preserved in the churches, and urged those who were curious in such matters to go and see them. And yet later than this they are appealed to by Peter, bishop of Alexandria, in the fourth century. It will, of course, be admitted that while these autographs were in existence, all corruption was of necessity prevented, because, in case any had been attempted, they would have been brought forward, and have ended the matter at once. All attempts, therefore, at corruption, must be assigned to a period posterior to, or at least to, the year 350,

which grants more than can be justly asked, that these autographs may have been destroyed immediately after the death of Peter, bishop of Alexandria."[1]

3. These books, as soon as they were written, were cherished as sacred writings by all the Christians. As soon as they were written, they were copied. Christians earnestly sought for and multiplied copies of them, carried them into distant countries, and esteemed them more sacred than the rich worldling does his deed to his large farm. "Women wore them in a volume hanging at their necks. Most persons carried it about them constantly. Some even washed their hands before they allowed themselves to take it for reading. And many have been found buried with the Gospel lying upon their breasts. Children were trained up from their infancy to repeat it by heart."[2] Why should they not? The gospels and epistles were public documents, containing the history of their Master, together with sundry commandments and ordinances, in obedience to which men were daily "mortifying the deeds of the body," enduring the scoffs, sneers, and buffetings of their neighbors, suffering trouble as evil-doers, having their property confiscated, and endangering their lives.

They contained the promises which moved them to serve God, and for the sake of which they suffered the loss of all things. They were daily read in families, expounded in religious assemblies, quoted by writers, attacked by enemies, misconstrued by heretics and "grievous wolves," and scrutinized by true Christians, lest heretics, in order to

---

[1] Thayer on Infidelity, pp. 175, 176.
[2] Id. p. 177.

escape their denunciations, should alter the sacred text. In a short time their sound went into all the earth. Copies were scattered far and near. They were translated into different languages before the close of the first century. Commentaries were written on them; catalogues of the authentic books were carefully made and circulated in order to prevent forgeries. Thus universal notoriety was given to all the books of the New Testament, almost as soon as they were written.

Now we ask, How, under the circumstances, could the Scriptures have been corrupted without detection and exposure?

4. The books of the New Testament were, at a very early period, publicly read and expounded in all the congregations of the Christians. Paul's language to the Colossians shows this plainly: "And when this epistle is read among you, cause that it be read also in the church of the Laodiceans; and that ye likewise read the epistle from Laodicea." [3]

This shows that it was a custom of the churches, when they received a letter from the apostle, to send a copy of that letter to other churches to be publicly read. These letters were recognized as Scripture. Thus Peter says of Paul's letters: "As also in all his epistles, speaking in them of these things: in which are some things hard to be understood, which they that are unlearned and unstable wrest, as they do also the other Scriptures, unto their own destruction." [4]

By this it appears that the writings of the apostles were accepted as Scripture, were familiar to all, and were read in all the churches. Justin Martyr, A. D. 140, says, "The memoirs of the

[3] Col. 4: 16. [4] 2 Pet. 3: 16.

apostles, or the writings of the apostles, are read according as the time allows; and when the reader has not time, the president makes a discourse."[5]

Copies of these writings, then, were immediately scattered everywhere; not only were they placed in the households, and in the hands of every believer, but they were read each week in the public assemblies in all the churches. This itself was sure guaranty against any change in the wording of the writings. The reader can readily see that the least alteration in such public and sacred documents would immediately have been detected by thousands.

5. The agreement of the numerous quotations from the New Testament made by the early fathers shows that they have not been corrupted. The quotations from the New Testament by the Christian writers in the first three centuries are so numerous that the whole body of the gospels and the epistles might be collected from their commentaries and other writings.

Dr. Horne says that we do not risk anything in saying that if all the ancient writings now extant in Europe were collected together, the extent of them would not be so great as that of the quotations taken from the New Testament alone. Now when we consider how exactly all these innumerable quotations from the New Testament agree in every particular, we can see how carefully Providence has guarded the exact wording of the New Testament.

6. The agreement of the different versions of the Scriptures shows that they have not been changed from the original. We possess versions

---

[5] Lardner's Works, vol. i. p. 345.

of the New Testament in various languages, reaching back to within a quarter of a century of the lives of the apostles. Scholars agree that the Syriac version called the Peshito was made before the close of the first century, while the apostles were yet living. It is known to have been in general use in the second century. "Though never brought into contact with our copies of the New Testament, because not known in Europe till the sixteenth century; though handed down by a line of tradition perfectly independent of, and unknown to, that by which our Greek Testament was received; yet when the two came to be compared, the text of the one was almost an exact version of the text of the other. The difference was altogether unimportant. So clearly and impressively has Divine Providence attested the integrity of our beloved Scriptures."[6]

The Mœso-Gothic version, discovered by Cardinal Mai in 1817, was made by Ulphilas, bishop of the Mœso-Goths, A. D. 370. This version, of which we have considerable fragments, has the same texts as ours. Other early versions, now brought to light, confirm the same fact. This furnishes the best of proof that no change has taken place.

7. The different Christian sects would guard one another from changing the Scriptures. Even during the lives of the apostles there were springing up different sects and factions of Christians, generally hostile to one another, the same as we behold to-day. Each of these sects received the Scriptures as authority for their doctrine. To them they appealed for everything. Consequently it was simply impossible for any of them to change their Scriptures to favor their own tenets without being immediately

---

[6] M'Ilvaine's Evidences, p. 123.

detected and exposed by their opponents. The reader will see that there was not the slightest chance for any man or any body of men to corrupt or falsify the Scriptures in any fundamental article, or foist into them a single expression to favor their peculiar doctrines, or erase a sentence without being detected by thousands. If one party was inclined to omit what opposed their peculiar theories, or insert what might afford them additional support, there was always some other party both willing and ready to detect the fraud. Hence no one would dare undertake it.

Suppose, for a moment, the thing were tried in our day; that the Methodists, for instance, should undertake to change some passage of Scripture to suit their doctrine. A hundred other churches would immediately cry out against it. They would point out the fraud to the world. Or suppose the Adventists should remodel some passage, or insert a text to favor their views; how quick their enemies would expose their attempt to tamper with the Scriptures. Reader, this fact alone, in every age of the world, would guard the word of God from being changed. For though one man or church might change a copy of the Scriptures which they had in their own hands, they could not change the thousands of others scattered all over the world.[7]

8. If Christians had attempted to alter the Scriptures, their heathen enemies would immediately have exposed it. Christianity has always had its bitter enemies, the same as to-day. These enemies have watched with eagle eyes, ready to make the most of any advantage. Suppose Christians now should undertake to change the Scriptures; how

---

[7] Horne's Introduction. vol. i. p. 116.

quick the infidel world would take up the circumstance, and make capital of it. Just so it would have been at any time in the history of the church. Here has been another safeguard to the integrity of the Scriptures.

9. The Jews, the bitter enemies of Christ, would have detected any such corruption. The Jews have not only possessed the Old Testament, but have always been familiar with the New Testament, and ready to find fault with it. No change in it could have been made without their notice.

10. If a change was universally made, it must have been done by Christians, heretics, or hostile opposers.

Is it credible to suppose that the enemies of Christianity, unnoticed by Christians, could have corrupted all the copies of Scripture in the world, while they were being so constantly read, revered, and affectionately protected, especially when those enemies had not, and could not get into their possession, one hundredth part of the copies then in existence?

Could any of the various sects of heretics have made the change, when in addition to being watched by Christians, they were all eagerly watching one another, anxious to sustain a charge upon which to put others down and build themselves up? Supposing true Christians could have desired an alteration in their Scriptures, could they have accomplished such a task? Heretics on the one hand, and open enemies on the other, were all wide awake and watchful, with the Scriptures in their hands, ready to grasp the least pretext against the defenders of the Christian faith.

He who believes that such a change could have

been made without detection, believes in a greater miracle than any recorded in the Bible, and that, not only without evidence, but against all evidence. David Hume thought that no testimony could prove a miracle; but if infidels prove that the Scriptures have been corrupted they prove a miracle without testimony.

Let those who think it an easy matter to change public documents without detection, undertake it. Let some Southern politician attempt to change the Declaration of Independence, or some Northern man try his hand at corrupting the Constitution of the United States, and see how far he will proceed without detection. Even if it were possible for the corruption to creep into every copy extant, thousands would detect it as soon as their eye should light upon it. Just so with the New Testament in any age of the Christian era.

Think of making a material alteration in a book translated into different languages, and transported from "sea to sea, and from the rivers to the ends of the earth,—into Britain, Germany, France, Spain, Italy, Greece, Turkey, etc.; committed to memory by thousands, and quoted by authors of the first three centuries, so that all of the New Testament, except from six to twenty-six verses, can be gathered from their writings."

No wonder that St. Augustine, after thoroughly canvassing the subject, came to the conclusion that "the integrity of the books of any one history, however eminent, cannot be so completely kept as that of the canonical Scriptures, translated into so many languages, and kept by the people of every age; and yet, some there have been who have forged writings in the names of the apostles. In vain, indeed, because that Scripture has been so esteemed, so celebrated, so known."[8]

The same writer says, in reasoning with an opposer: "If any one should charge you with having interpolated some texts alleged by you, would you not immediately answer that it is impossible for you to do such a thing in books read by all Christians; and that if any such attempt had been made by you, it would have been presently discovered and defeated by comparing the ancient copies? Well, then, for the same reason that the Scriptures cannot be corrupted by you, neither could they be corrupted by any other people."[9]

11. "It is well known that a division commenced in the fourth century, between the Eastern and Western churches, which, about the middle of the ninth century, became irreconcilable, and subsists to the present day. Now it would have been impossible to alter all the copies in the Eastern Empire; and if it had been possible in the East, the copies in the West would have detected the alteration. But, in fact, the Eastern and Western copies agree, which could not be expected if either of them was altered or falsified."[10]

12. The wonderful agreement of more than a thousand ancient manuscripts demonstrates that no important change has been made in the wording of the New Testament. Prof. C. E. Stowe, D. D., has written a critical work upon the origin and history of the books of the Bible, a volume which every student of the Bible should possess. From this I take the following facts:—

---

[8] Lardner's Works, vol. ii. p. 594.
[9] Id. vol. ii. p. 228.
[10] Horne's Introduction, vol. i. p. 117.

We have nine hundred and seventy-two entire manuscripts of the different volumes of the Greek Testament, of which forty-seven are more than one thousand years old. Let us notice five of these. 1. The Alexandrian manuscript, written in a beautiful hand, A. D. 325; 2. The Vatican manuscript, written about A. D. 300, within two hundred years of the death of St. John; 3. The Sinaitic manuscript, written as early at least as were the others; 4. The Ephraim manuscript, written about A. D. 350; and, 5. The Beza manuscript, written near A. D. 490.

"Here, then, we have accessible to us five manuscript copies of the Greek Testament, the most recent more than twelve hundred years old, and the most ancient reaching to an age of fifteen centuries. The proudest and most costly architectural structures of men have within that period either crumbled and moldered away, or become obsolete and unfit for their original use, though built of the most solid materials and put together with the utmost care; while we of this age can read the same fragile page of books which were in the hands of men forty-five and fifty generations before us."[11]

"Herodotus is the most ancient, and in many respects the most important, of the classic historians. Of his great work there are known to critics in all about fifteen manuscript copies; but most of these are of more recent date than A. D. 1450. One of the best, in the imperial library at Paris, belongs to the twelfth century; another, at the library at Florence, is as early as the tenth; and one in the library of Emmanuel College, at Cambridge, in England, may be as early as the ninth

---

[11] Stowe's Hist. of the Books of the Bible, p. 78.

century. Of the ethical writers among the classics, Plato is the most celebrated, and the most popular. The number of ancient manuscript copies of his writings is even fewer than the number of those of Herodotus, and one of the earliest, which is in the Bodleian library at Oxford, is as recent as the ninth century. . . . .

"Now let us compare with this statement the antiquity, number, and variety of the manuscript copies which we have of the historical and ethical writers of the New Testament. Of the manuscript copies of the Greek Testament, from seven hundred to one thousand of all kinds have been examined already by critics, and of these at least fifty are more than one thousand years old, and some are known to be at least fifteen hundred years old; while the oldest of the Greek classics scarcely reach the antiquity of nine hundred years, and of these the number is very small indeed, compared with those of the Greek Testament. We have manuscripts of the Greek Testament that could have been read by men who had opportunity to read the autographs of the apostles themselves; manuscripts as near to the lifetime of the apostles as we ourselves are to the lifetime of the pilgrim fathers who landed at Plymouth; and the writers of which might have themselves seen the autograph books in the churches, as we now may see the original records of the old colony in the Plymouth court-house." [12]

How good the Lord is to give us such a bright evidence of the integrity of his word! We are now as undoubtedly in possession of the genuine books of the New Testament as written by the contemporaries

---

[12] Id. pp. 59, 60.

of Jesus Christ, as if we had the autograph manuscript of its authors.

Various readings. "Over fifty thousand various readings of the New Testament!" shouts the infidel. "Who dare trust such a book as that?" It is true that uninformed persons become alarmed when they hear infidels state that among the manuscripts collated there are fifty thousand various readings; but all cause for suspicion is allayed when we learn that there are about one thousand manuscripts from which these various readings were taken; not only so, but not one in a thousand makes any important variation of meaning. They consist almost entirely of mistakes of transcribers, such as the transposition or omission of letters, the transposition of words in a sentence, or the use of certain words instead of others of a similar meaning. It is said that "the worst manuscript extant, if it were our only copy, would not change or pervert one single doctrine or precept." We also have good authority to say that the difference in the manuscripts collated is no greater than the difference in the English Bibles printed in the last two hundred years. This being true, the worst manuscripts extant neither obscure nor render doubtful a single doctrine or precept of the New Testament.

The diversity of readings is not against the integrity of the New Testament, but is decidedly in its favor; for this difference is all-sufficient proof that our present manuscripts are copied from various manuscripts of ancient times, while the fact that the difference is so small, in our present copies, shows that the difference in the original manuscripts must have been inconsiderable. This shows that our present New Testament is a faithful copy of the original.

"From the thousand manuscripts (more or less) of the Greek Testament, or parts of the Greek Testament, which have already been examined, critics have selected about fifty thousand various readings. But most of them are simple differences of orthography, as if the word *labor* were spelled in one manuscript with the u, and in another without it. Very many are simple diversities in the collocation of the words—as if one should say, *Jesus went to Jerusalem*, and another, *To Jerusalem Jesus went*. Not fifty of the fifty thousand make any change whatever in the meaning." [13]

By the untiring labors of such eminent scholars as Griesbach, Tregelles, and Tischendorf, the text of the New Testament has been brought to such perfection and accuracy as belongs to no other book ever written. Any objection upon this point now must proceed either from inexcusable ignorance or from a spirit of the most hopeless caviling. It is thus evident that we have the very words penned by the inspired disciples of the Lord. How sandy, then, is the foundation upon which infidels have built their objections to the Bible! Friend, are you risking eternity upon these grounds?

CHAPTER XXII.

THE APOCRYPHAL BOOKS.

WHAT about the apocryphal books? Were there not a large number of gospels and epistles claiming to have been written by the apostles, besides those which we now have? Was it not a long time be-

---

[13] Stowe's Hist. of the Books of the Bible, p. 81.

fore the church decided which were genuine and which were not? Did not King James decide this question? or, at least, was it not first done by Constantine? And were not some of the books now in the Bible almost rejected, and only voted in by one or two majority? It makes one indignant to hear infidels promulgating such falsehoods as these, when every scholar of any reading knows better.

King James of England, about two hundred and fifty years ago, selected fifty-four learned Christian men to translate the Holy Scriptures out of the original Hebrew and Greek into English, though translations had several times, and many years before, been made by others. These translators had nothing to do in voting on what books should be received as the genuine books of the Bible, or what should not. No such question came before them. They simply translated the books of the Bible just as they found them in the original, and as they had always stood, and been received since the days of the apostles. Neither did Constantine, his council, nor any other council, vote on the books of the Bible, receiving this book, rejecting that book, and disputing over another. Unscrupulous infidels have started these theories and kept them going. But they are utterly false.

The facts in the case are simply these:—

1. "Besides our gospels and the Acts of the Apostles, no Christian history claiming to be written by an apostle or apostolical man is quoted within three hundred years after the birth of Christ, by any writer now extant or known; or if quoted, is quoted with marks of censure and rejection."[1]

"The four gospels which we have, and these

---

[1] Paley's Evidences, p. 124.

only, have always been acknowledged and quoted by Christians and heretics, Jews and pagans, as authoritative books of the Christian church. . . . It has never been pretended that the Christian church has acknowledged any other gospels as canonical."[2]

2. There is no evidence that any spurious or apocryphal books whatever existed in the first century of the Christian era, in which century all our historical books are proved to have been extant. There are no quotations from any such books by the apostolical fathers for the first one hundred years.

3. In after generations, when these apocryphal books began to appear, they were never read in the Christian churches, as the books of the New Testament were always read.

4. They were never admitted into the volume with those which we now have.

5. They never appear in the catalogues given by early writers, with the books of the true Scriptures. Indeed, when the catalogues of the true books are given, these spurious ones are frequently mentioned as existing, but as being spurious. Thus Eusebius, in his Ecclesiastical History, written A. D. 315, after giving the genuine books, says: "Among the spurious must be numbered both the books called the Acts of Paul and that called Pastor and the Revelation of Peter, besides those books called the Epistle of Barnabas,"[3] etc. This is only a sample of how carefully the distinction was always made.

"This species of evidence comes later than the rest, as it was not natural that catalogues of any

---

[2] Stowe's Hist. of the Books of the Bible, p. 141.
[3] Eusebius' Eccl. Hist. chap. xxv. p. 110.

particular class of books should be put forth, until Christian writings became numerous, or until some writings showed themselves, claiming titles which did not belong to them, and thereby rendering it necessary to separate books of authority from others. But when it does appear, it is extremely satisfactory; the catalogues, though numerous, and made in countries at a wide distance from one another, differing very little, differing in nothing which is material, and all containing the four gospels. To this last article there is no exception.

"I. In the writings of Origen which remain, and in some extracts preserved by Eusebius, from works of his which are now lost, there are enumerations of the books of Scripture, in which the four gospels and the Acts of the Apostles are distinctly and honorably specified, and in which no books appear besides what are now received. The reader, by this time, will easily recollect that the date of Origen's work is A. D. 230.

"II. Athanasius, about a century afterward, delivered a catalogue of the books of the New Testament in form, containing our Scriptures and no others; of which he says, 'In these alone the doctrine of religion is taught; let no man add to them, or take anything from them.'

"III. About twenty years after Athanasius, Cyril, bishop of Jerusalem, set forth a catalogue of the books of Scripture publicly read at that time.

"IV. And, fifteen years after Cyril, the Council of Laodicea delivered an authoritative catalogue of canonical Scripture, like Cyril's

"V. Catalogues now become frequent. Within thirty years from the last date, that is, from the year 363 to near the conclusion of the fourth century, we have catalogues by Epiphanius, by Gregory Nazianzen, by Philaster, bishop of Brescia in Italy, by Amphilochius, bishop of Iconium, all, as they are sometimes called, clean catalogues (that is, they admit no books into the number besides what we now receive), and all, for every purpose of historic evidence, the same as ours.

"VI. Within the same period, Jerome, the most learned Christian writer of his age, delivered a catalogue of the books of the New Testament, recognizing every book now received, with the intimation of a doubt concerning the epistle to the Hebrews alone, and taking not the least notice of any book which is not now received.

"VII. Contemporary with Jerome, who lived in Palestine, was St. Augustine in Africa, who published likewise a catalogue, without joining to the Scriptures, as books of authority, any other ecclesiastical writing whatever, and without omitting one which we at this day acknowledge.

"VIII. And with these concurs another contemporary writer, Rusin, a presbyter of Aquileia, whose catalogue, like theirs, is perfect and unmixed, and concludes with these remarkable words: 'These are the volumes which the fathers have included in the canon, and out of which they would have us prove the doctrine of our faith.'"[4]

As the book of Revelation has been particularly assailed, we deem it proper to say a few words about it. We often hear it asserted that it was never known till long after the time of the apostles, and that it was finally admitted into the Bible, after a great struggle, by a vote of one majority. This story has been repeated so confidently

---

[4] Paley's Evidences, pp. 123, 124.

that uninformed persons have really come to believe it; but it is all a wicked falsehood.

On this subject a learned writer truthfully remarks: "The testimony of the early and contemporary witnesses is unanimous and uncontradicted in favor of the book. Though well known and extensively used in the churches, not a breath of suspicion was ever blown upon its reputation, until nearly one hundred and fifty years after the death of the apostle to whom it is ascribed; and then not confidently, but doubtingly; not on any critical grounds alleged or pretended, but solely on account of the supposed difficulty of its interpretation, the bad use which had been made of it, and a dislike to the doctrines which it was imagined to contain."[5]

The occasion on which the genuineness of this book was first questioned was the following: About A. D. 230, Nepos, a certain bishop from Egypt, began to advocate the notion of a thousand years' personal reign of Christ upon the earth. He was very zealous in propagating this false theory. He drew his argument principally from the book of Revelation. At first, a large number in Africa fell into the heresy. But a few years afterward, Dionysius, bishop of Alexandria, so thoroughly refuted this theory that it was quite generally abandoned. This occurred A. D. 255. As the Apocalypse was the source from which the heretics had drawn their false doctrine, the bishop began to question that book itself, though he could bring nothing against it. He acknowledged that he could not understand the book, yet would not on that account reject it. He allowed that it was

---

[5] Stowe's Hist. of the Books of the Bible, p. 470.

written by a man named John, who was a holy and inspired man. He did not attempt to bring any evidence against the genuineness or authenticity of the book itself.

This was the first open attack ever made on the genuineness of the Apocalypse, and it is plain, from the bishop's own evidence, that he could bring no respectable authority against it. It is also plain that he had no historical ground for his conjectures; but that the testimony of history was all against him; that he himself was not at all confident about the doubtfulness of the book; and that his wish to get rid of its authority arose entirely from his apprehension of its obscurity, and its influence on the millennial controversy. This controversy continued to prevail through several centuries; and during that time its opposers felt an anxiety to rid themselves of the authority of the Apocalypse, and their efforts in this direction only served to keep up the dispute. All who were induced to reject the book, did so, not on historical testimony against it, nor for a want of such testimony in its favor, but simply on doctrinal grounds. But the absurdity and false doctrines ascribed to this book belong to the interpreters, and not to the book itself.

That this book was unanimously received by the entire Christian church, immediately after the death of St. John, is abundantly shown by Dr. Stowe in his able work, History of the Books of the Bible, chapter twelve. Here the reader will find a list of more than a score of the most noted Christian writers of the first three centuries, beginning with the immediate successors of St. John,—persons who were personally acquainted with him,—and extending down through a period of over two hundred years, all indorsing the book of Revelation as holy

Scripture, written by St. John. Who could ask better testimony than this? It was included in the catalogues of the New-Testament books composed at that time by different fathers. No book of the New Testament stands better authenticated than this book.

6. The apocryphal writings were never noticed by the adversaries of the Christians, were never quoted or referred to by them, while they frequently quoted books of the New Testament.

7. They were never alleged by the different parties in theological controversies. This shows that they were considered of no authority. But every book of the New Testament was frequently thus quoted.

8. No commentaries were ever written on these apocryphal books. They were never translated into other languages. In short, little or no notice is taken of them in any age, at least until we come down into the Dark Ages, after the canon of the New-Testament Scriptures had been fairly and unanimously settled. Finally, besides the silence of two centuries, they were with one consent universally repudiated by Christian writers of succeeding ages.

One thing is noticeable in all these apocryphal writings; viz., that they proceed upon the same fundamental history of Christ and his apostles as that which is set forth in the New Testament. The bare events and relations of the gospels are confirmed in these writings. They neither deny nor contradict any of them. They simply claim to give additional facts. But these writings are of no authority, and were never received as Scripture by the church in any age.

The difference between a genuine and a spurious

book is easily proved. A book may be regarded as presumably spurious, 1. When doubts have been entertained from the first that it was the work of the reputed author; 2. When his intimate friends have denied that it was his work; 3. When a great number of years has elapsed since the death of the reputed author, during which time the book was entirely unknown or unheard of; 4. When the style is very different from that of the author whom it claims; 5. When events are recorded in it which are known to have occurred since the death of the pretended author; 6. When doctrines are taught which are contrary to the teachings of the pretended author.[6]

Now every one of these evidences of the spuriousness of a work is true of these apocryphal books, while they are not true in a single case with regard to any other books of the New Testament. Whoever will take the trouble to read the apocryphal books, and to compare them with the New Testament, will have his mind set at rest immediately. The last observation shows them to be entirely dissimilar. They are in every way inferior, gross, low, and silly. A late critical author truly says of them:—

"The impugners of the New-Testament gospels appeal to the fact, that there are gospels acknowledged to be apocryphal, as a proof of their theory that our recognized gospels are also myths or forgeries. Any one who candidly examines these spurious gospels, and compares them with the New Testament, will find in them, not a refutation of our sacred writers, but a most convincing testimony to their intelligence, honesty, and supernatural in-

---

[6] Michælis' Introduction to the New Testament, vol. i. p. 25.

spiration. So totally diverse are they from the genuine gospels, in conception, in spirit, in execution, in their whole impression, in all respects so entirely unlike, so immeasurably inferior, that the New Testament only shines the brighter by the contrast. They have scarcely so much resemblance to the genuine gospels as the monkey has to a man."[7]

Here, then, we stand with the blessed New Testament in our hands, feeling perfectly certain that it is the genuine uncorrupted writings of the apostles and their companions. Thank God that the evidence is so clear and so abundant!

CHAPTER XXIII.

THE OLD TESTAMENT, WHEN WAS IT WRITTEN, AND BY WHOM?

WE have in our hands to-day the Holy Scriptures of the Old Testament. They are scattered by the million all over the world, and believed in by four hundred million people. They claim to have been written by a people called the Jews, who at that time lived in the land of Palestine. Is this claim well founded? What evidence have we that it is true? Much every way.

1. There is a numerous people to-day called the Jews. Their native land is Judea, the very place where this book was written. Their native tongue

---

[7] Stowe's Hist. of the Bible, p. 203.

is Hebrew, the very language in which this book was written. And what is more, they unanimously acknowledge that it was written by their ancestors. Indeed, they believe it so thoroughly that many of them have died for their faith. They everywhere claim to regulate their lives by its precepts. This, in the absence of any proof to the contrary, is evidence that they are the authors of it.

2. These books have been handed down, generation after generation, from father to son, as the writings of the very men whose names they bear at the present time. Those who lived at the time when these books were written, and were acquainted with the men who wrote them, received them as their writings, and handed them down to their children as such. This is another strong proof that they were the genuine writings of the prophets.

3. The authorship of these books is never ascribed to anybody else but the ancient prophets and Jewish teachers whose names they bear. The most critical infidel has never been able to find any other authors for them.

4. No one else ever claimed the authorship of them. If they are not the works of their reputed authors, then opponents should be able to show who did write them, and to give some proof of it. But no; they can never do this. They simply raise objections, throw out doubts, make insinuations, and leave the matter there.

5. The names of their authors are still signed to most of these books. Read a few:—

"The words of the Preacher, the son of David, king in Jerusalem." [1]

---

[1] Eccl. 1: 1.

Who dare say, then, that this was not written by the son of David? Again:—

"The Song of songs, which is Solomon's."[2]

Where is the man who can deny this, and say it was not Solomon's? Once more:—

"The vision of Isaiah, the son of Amoz, which he saw concerning Judah and Jerusalem in the days of Uzziah, Jotham, Ahaz, and Hezekiah, kings of Judah."[3]

Skeptic, do you say that Isaiah did not write this? What proof can you bring to the contrary? Take one more example:—

"The words of Jeremiah, the son of Hilkiah, of the priests that were in Anathoth in the land of Benjamin."[4]

If you assume that this was not written by Jeremiah, nor in the line of Benjamin, but by some Catholic monk in the Dark Ages, you should produce proof to support that assertion. This is impossible; we therefore prefer the direct and reliable testimony of the man whose name is signed to it, rather than any vague surmising unsupported by the least evidence.

6. The language and style of writing in these books prove them to have been written by Jews in Asia, thousands of years ago. That they are not all composed by one writer, any scholar knows who has examined them at all. The style of each author is different. The book of Isaiah is not at all of the style of Jeremiah; nor is the style of Ezekiel like that of Daniel. Each shows a different author. Moreover, the style of language in all the Old Testament is distinctly oriental. No such language

---

[2] Song of Solomon, chap. 1:1.
[3] Isaiah 1:1. [4] Jer. 1:1.

was ever used in America, nor in Europe; but it is just the style of language which was in vogue in the East a thousand years before Christ's time.

It is admitted by all that none but Jews could have written the Old Testament. Therefore, if it is a forgery, it must be the work of a Jew. But did the Jews forge it? Let us see. If a person were brought before a court of justice to answer to the charge of forgery, and no evidence were produced against him, he would, of course, be acquitted. But suppose the crime of forgery to be totally inconsistent with the character of the accused, would it not require very conclusive evidence to convince you of his guilt? The case of the Jew, as connected with the Old Testament, is an instance in point.

It certainly must have required a very powerful motive to influence a Jew to so bold and daring an undertaking. What could it have been? It could not have been national pride; for the books of which we speak do not flatter the Jewish nation, but, on the other hand, abound in declarations like the following: "Ye rebelled against my word;" "Behold, it is a stiff-necked people;" "The Lord thy God giveth thee not this good land to possess it for thy righteousness, for thou art a stiff-necked people;" "I know thy rebellion and thy stiff neck; behold, while I am yet alive with you this day, ye have been rebellious against the Lord."[5] The pentateuch abounds no more in such declarations than do the prophets. "Behold," said Jeremiah, "ye trust in *lying* words that cannot profit; will ye *steal, murder*, and commit *adultery*, and *swear falsely*, and *burn incense unto Baal*, and *walk aft-*

---

[5] Ex. 32: 9; 33: 3–5; Deut. 9: 6, 13, 14; 31: 27.

er other gods whom ye know not?[6] Turn to almost any page of the Old Testament, and you will find it abounding in such declarations as those above quoted.

The love of fame could not have prompted a Jew to forge the books of which we speak; for that passion would have led him also to flatter and extol the national character of the Jews. Besides, so far from securing personal fame, the crime, if detected, would have been punished by death. Nor could the love of wealth have led to such an act; for no wealth was to be gained by the undertaking. We ask again, What motive could stimulate the forger of the Bible to his thankless task? No one would perpetrate so great a forgery without a prospect of some benefit to be derived from it; an insane man only would indite falsehoods, knowing that they would only bring punishments upon his own head.

"These books are not such as any person would forge to gain popularity or make money by. There is nothing in them to bribe the good opinion of influential people, or catch the favor of the multitude. On the contrary, their stern severity and unsparing denunciation of popular vice and profitable sin must have secured their rejection by the Jewish people, had they not been constrained by undeniable evidence to acknowledge their divine authority. They set out with the assertion of the divine authority of the law of Moses, and everywhere sharply reprove princes, priests, and people, for breaking it. The prophets, so far from seeking popularity, are foolhardy enough to denounce the bonnets, hoops, and flounces of the ladies, and to cry Woe! against the regular business of the most respectable note-

---

[6] Jer. 7: 8, 9.

shavers—to croak against the march of intellect, and shake public confidence in the prosperity of their great country—to ally themselves with fanatical abolitionists, and introduce agitating political questions into the pulpit; crying, *Woe to him that useth his neighbor's service without wages, and giveth him not for his work.* To crown all, they organized abolition clubs to procure immediate emancipation, and published incendiary proclamations in the cities of slave-holders; and, strange to say, they were allowed to escape with their lives; and their writings were held sacred by the children of those very men and women they so unsparingly denounced,—a conclusive proof that the calamities they predicted had compelled them to acknowledge these prophets as the heralds of God. The proof must have been conclusive indeed which compelled the Jews to acknowledge the writings of the prophets as sacred."[7]

Whether the Old Testament was a forgery or not, it is evident that the Jews received it as genuine and authoritative; yea, and regulated all the business of their lives by it. It must have been read and revered by all. "The reader of the Old Testament will speedily find that these writings are not merely a connected history of the nation, of great general interest, like Bancroft's or Macaulay's, but of no such special interest to any individual as to force him, by a sense of self-interest, or the danger of loss of liberty or property, to correct their errors. On the contrary, every farmer in Palestine was deeply concerned in the truth and accuracy of the Bible; for it contained not only the general boundaries of the country, and of the par-

---

[7] Fables of Infidelity, p. 172.

ticular tribes, like the survey of the Maine boundary, or of Mason and Dixon's line; but it delineated particular estates also, and was, in fact, the Report of the Surveyor-General deposited in the county court for reference, in case of any litigation about sale or inheritance of property.

"The genealogies of the tribes and families were also preserved in these writings; and on the authenticity and correctness of these records every farm in the land depended; for as no lease ran more than fifty years, every farm returned to the heirs of the original settler, at the year of jubilee. Thus every Jewish farmer had a direct interest in these sacred records; and it would be just as hard to forge records for the county courts of Ohio, and pass them off upon the citizens as genuine, and plead them in the courts as valid, as to impose at first, or falsify afterward, the records of the commonwealth of Israel. This will appear more clearly, when we consider that they contained also the laws of the land,—the Constitution of the United States of Israel, with the statutes at large,—according to which every house and farm and garden in the whole country was possessed, every court of justice was guided, every election was held,—from the election of a petty constable to that of a governor of the State,—and the militia enrolled, mustered, officered, and called out to the field of battle.

"These laws prescribed the way in which every house must be built, regulated the weaver in weaving his cloth, the tailor in making it, and the cooking of every breakfast, dinner, and supper eaten by any Israelite over the world, from that day to this. Now let any one who thinks it would be an easy matter to forge such a series of documents, and get people to receive and obey them, try his hand in making a volume of Acts of Assembly, and passing it off upon the people of Ohio for genuine. Let him bring an action into one of the courts, and persuade the judges to give a decision in his favor, upon the strength of his forged or falsified statutes, and then he may hope to convince us that the laws of Moses are simply a collection of religious tracts which came to be held sacred through lapse of time, nobody knows how or why."[8]

7. The Hebrew, the language in which the Old Testament was written, is overwhelming proof as to who wrote this book, and when it was written. No people except the ancient Hebrews ever wrote that language. Nor was it written by them later than five hundred years before Christ. Hence the Old Testament must have been written by the Hebrews, as early, at least, as five hundred years before Christ.

"It is an undeniable fact that Hebrew ceased to be the living language of the Jews soon after the Babylonish captivity, and that the Jewish productions after that period were in general either in Chaldee or Greek. The Jews of Palestine, some ages before the appearance of our Saviour, were unable to comprehend the Hebrew original without the assistance of a Chaldee paraphrase, and it was necessary to undertake a Greek translation, because that language alone was known to the Jews of Alexandria. It necessarily follows, therefore, that every book which is written in *pure* Hebrew, was composed either before or about the time of the Babylonish captivity. This being admitted, we may advance a step farther, and contend that the period which elapsed between the composition of the most

---

[8] Fables of Infidelity, pp. 173, 174.

ancient and the most modern book of the Old Testament was very considerable; or, in other words, the most ancient books of the Old Testament were written a length of ages prior to the Babylonish captivity. No language continues during many centuries in the same state of cultivation, and the Hebrew, like other tongues, passed through the several stages of infancy, youth, manhood, and old age. If, therefore, as we have already remarked, on comparison the several parts of the Hebrew Bible are found to differ, not only in regard to style, but also in regard to character and cultivation of language,—if one discovers the golden, another the silver, a third the brazen, a fourth the iron age,—we have strong internal marks of their having been composed at different and distant periods.

"No classical scholar, independently of the Grecian history, would believe that the poems ascribed to Homer were written in the age of Demosthenes, the orations of Demosthenes in the time of Origen, or the commentaries of Origen in the days of Lascaris and Chrysoloras. For the very same reason it is certain that the five books which are ascribed to Moses were not written in the time of David, the Psalms of David in the age of Isaiah, nor the prophecies of Isaiah in the time of Malachi. But it appears from what has been said above, in regard to the extinction of the Hebrew language, that the book of Malachi could not have been written much later than the Babylonish captivity; before that period, therefore, were written the prophecies of Isaiah, still earlier the Psalms of David, and much earlier than these the books which are ascribed to Moses. There is no presumption therefore, whatsoever, *a priori*, that Moses was not the author or compiler of the pentateuch. And the ignorance of the assertion which has lately been made,—that the Hebrew language is a compound of the Syriac, Arabic, and Chaldee languages, and a distortion of each of them with other provincial dialects and languages that were spoken by adjoining nations, by whom the Jews had at various times been subdued and led captive,—is only surpassed by its falsehood and its absurdity."[9]

This point we consider entirely unanswerable. It never has been and never will be answered.

8. In the providence of God we are furnished with another strong proof as to when the Bible was written, and by whom. Seven hundred and thirty years before Christ, the ten tribes were carried into captivity, and heathen sent to Samaria to fill their place. From this mixture of the heathen and the apostate Jews grew up the Samaritans.[10] From this date the Samaritans and Jews were not only entirely separated, but were bitter enemies of each other. The Samaritans retain the five books of Moses, written in the oldest Hebrew characters, and preserve them sacredly. These books are still in their possession, and they read from them in Palestine to-day.

That no spurious production has ever been substituted for the original composition of Moses is evident from this fact: These Samaritan Scriptures agree with the Hebrew, except in some trifling variations, to which every work is exposed by length of time. It is absolutely certain that the five books, which we now ascribe to Moses, are the very same as those which both Jews and Samaritans had

---

[9] Horne's Introduction, vol. i. pp. 50, 51. [10] 2 Kings 17.

nearly twenty-six hundred years ago.[11] Here again we have a nail in a sure place.

9. The Lord has furnished us another good evidence upon this question. About the year 282 B. C., the Old Testament was translated from the Hebrew into the Greek language. This Greek translation, commonly called the Septuagint, was made in Alexandria, in Egypt. It was used by the Jews everywhere, and was the very one from which Christ and the apostles quoted. This translation we now have, and the books are the same as in our Bibles. From this fact it is evident that we still have the identical books which the most ancient Jews declared to be genuine. No ancient profane book whatever has such a testimony in its favor.[12] How carefully the Lord has guarded the preservation of his word.

10. We have unquestionable testimony to the genuineness of the Old Testament in the fact that its canon was fixed some centuries before the birth of Christ. The author of the book of Ecclesiasticus refers to the prophecies of Isaiah, Jeremiah, and Ezekiel by name. He speaks also of the twelve minor prophets. He also mentions the law and the prophets. According to the best chronology, the book of Ecclesiasticus was written two hundred and thirty-two years before the Christian era, and was translated into Greek for the use of the Alexandrian Jews. Jesus, son of Sirach, states that these books were studied by his grandfather; hence they existed at that time.[13]

11. That the pentateuch, or five books of Moses, existed first of all the books of the Bible, and

---

[11] Horne's Introduction, vol. i. p. 60.
[12] Id. vol. i. p. 46.   [13] Id. vol. i. pp. 45, 46.

many hundred years before the later books, is established by the testimony of every book which follows it.

"Every book of the Old Testament implies the previous existence of the pentateuch; in many of them it is expressly mentioned, allusion is made to it in some, and it is quoted in others. These contain a series of external evidence in its favor which is hardly to be confuted; and when the several links of this argument are put together, they will form a chain which it would require more than ordinary abilities to break. In the first place, no one will deny that the pentateuch existed in the time of Christ and his apostles, for they not only mention it, but quote it. 'This we admit,' reply the advocates of the hypothesis which it is our object to confute, 'but you cannot, therefore, conclude that Moses was the author, for there is reason to believe that it was composed by Ezra.' Now, unfortunately for men of this persuasion, Ezra himself is evidence against them; for, instead of assuming to himself the honor which they so liberally confer on him, he expressly ascribes the book of the law to Moses—'and they set the priests in their divisions, and the Levites in their courses, for the service of God, which is in Jerusalem, as it is written *in the book of Moses.*' [Ezra 6 : 18.]

"Further: The pentateuch existed before the time of Ezra, for it is expressly mentioned during the captivity in Babylon, by Daniel (9 : 11–13), B. C. 537 or 538. Long before that event it was extant in the time of Josiah (2 Chron. 34 : 15), B. C. 624, and was then of such acknowledged authority that the perusal of it occasioned an immediate reformation of the religious usages, which had not been observed according to the 'word of the

Lord, to do after all that is written in this book' (2 Chron. 34:21). It was extant in the time of Hoshea, king of Israel, B. C. 678, since a captive Israelitish priest was sent back from Babylon (2 Kings 17:27) to instruct the new colonists of Samaria in the religion which it teaches. By these Samaritans the book of the law was received as genuine, and was preserved and handed down to their posterity, as it also was by the Jews, as the basis of the civil and religious institutions of both nations. It was extant in the time of Jehoshaphat, king of Judah, B. C. 912 (2 Chron. 17:9), who employed public instructors for its promulgation. And, since the pentateuch was received as the book of the law, both by the ten tribes, and also by the two tribes, it follows as a necessary consequence that they each received it *before* they became divided into two kingdoms; for if it had been forged in a later age among the Jews, the perpetual enmity that subsisted between them and the Israelites would have utterly prevented it from being adopted by the Samaritans; and had it been a spurious production of the Samaritans, it would never have been received by the Jews. There remains, therefore, only one resource to those who contend that Moses was not the author, namely, that it was written in the period which elapsed between the age of Joshua and that of Solomon

"But the whole Jewish history from the time of their settlement in Canaan to the building of the temple at Jerusalem, presupposes that the book of the law was written by Moses. The whole of the temple service and worship was regulated by Solomon, B. C. 1004, according to the law contained in the pentateuch, as the tabernacle service and worship had previously been by David, B. C. 1042.

Could Solomon indeed have persuaded his subjects that, for more than five hundred years, the worship and polity prescribed by the pentateuch had been religiously observed by their ancestors, if it had not been observed? Could he have imposed upon them concerning the antiquity of the Sabbath, of circumcision, and of their three great festivals? In fact, it is morally impossible that any forgery could have been executed by or in the time of Solomon. Moreover, that the pentateuch was extant in the time of David is evident from the very numerous allusions made in his Psalms to its contents; but it could not have been drawn up by him, since the law contained in the pentateuch forbids many practices of which David was guilty. Samuel (who judged Israel about the years B. C. 1100–1060 or 1061) could not have acquired the knowledge of Egypt which the pentateuch implies."[14]

In the book of Joshua, which, though reduced to its present form in later times, was undoubtedly composed, in respect to its essential parts, at a very early period, frequent references may be found to the book of the law. For instance, Joshua is commanded to do "all which the law of Moses' commanded;" and it is enjoined upon him that "this book of the law should not depart out of his mouth." Joshua, in taking leave of the people of Israel, exhorts them to do all which is written in the book of the law of Moses; and he recites on this occasion many things contained in it. When the same distinguished leader had taken his final farewell of the tribes, he wrote the words of his address in the book of the law of God. In like manner it is said that Joshua built an altar on Mount Ebal as it is written in the book of the law of Moses, and that

---

[14] Horne's Introduction, vol. i. chap. ii. sect. 1, pp. 53-55.

"he read all the words of the law, the blessings and the cursings, according to all that is written in the book of the law." [15] The pentateuch, therefore, was extant in the time of Joshua.

12. Still another testimony: "About fifty years before the time of Christ, were written the Targums of Onkelos on the Pentateuch, and of Jonathan Ben-Uzziel on the Prophets (according to the Jewish classification of the books of the Old Testament); which are evidence of the genuineness of those books at that time." [16]

13. It is an undisputed fact that the Old Testament was translated into the Greek language, and placed in the Alexandrian library as early as B. C. 282. But to the one who accepts the evidence in favor of the New Testament, educed in a previous chapter, it is enough to know that Christ and the apostles quoted the Old Testament as possessing supreme authority. Christ never hints that the Jews, Pharisees, and lawyers, had made or corrupted the Scriptures, to which they pretended to adhere; but he censures them for neglecting to obey the law of God, and accuses them of making it of none effect by their traditions. He treats the Scriptures as an infallible standard. His admonition to the Jews is, "*Search the Scriptures.*" His reproof to the Sadducees is, "Ye do err, *not knowing the Scriptures.*" He proves his doctrine by *the Scriptures*, which cannot be broken. Yea, he goes farther; he asserts that "all things must be fulfilled which were written in the law of Moses, and in the prophets, and in the Psalms, concerning me." [17]

---

[15] Joshua 1:7, 8; 23:6; 24:26; 8:30-34.
[16] Horne's Introducton, vol. i. p. 45.
[17] Matt. 15:6; John 5:39; Matt 22:29; John 10:35; Luke 24:44.

If we turn from Christ to his apostles, we find them using similar language. Paul declares, "All Scripture is given by inspiration of God." He speaks of the oracles of God having been committed to the Jews, and calls the Old Testament "the word of God." And Peter says, "Prophecy came not in old time by the will of man, but holy men of God spake as they were moved by the Holy Ghost."[18] The New Testament everywhere indorses the Old.

Having already proved beyond contradiction that the New Testament was written eighteen hundred years ago, these numerous quotations from and references to the Old Testament show that it existed in the time of Christ. All but five of the lesser books of the Old Testament are quoted in the New; and these quotations given, number no less than eight hundred and eighty-eight! What a testimony not only to the existence, but to the value of the Old Testament at that time!

14. We have another important witness,—Josephus. He was a Jewish priest, and contemporary with the apostles. Examine his testimony to the existence of the Old Testament in his time. It will be remembered that at a very early period the Old Testament was divided into the law, the prophets, and the Psalms. In his treatise against Apion he says: "We have not thousands of books, discordant, and contradicting one another; but we have only *twenty-two*, which comprehend the history of all former ages, and are justly regarded as divine. Five of them proceed from Moses; they include as well the *laws*, as an account of the creation of man, extending to the time of his [Moses']

---

[18] 2 Tim. 3:16; Rom. 3:2; 9:6; 2 Pet. 1:21.

death. This period comprehends nearly three thousand years. From the death of Moses to that of Artaxerxes, who was king of Persia after Xerxes, the *prophets*, who succeeded Moses, committed to writing, in thirteen books, what was done in their days. The remaining four books contain *hymns* to God [the Psalms] and instructions of life for man."[19] So we have the best of evidence that the Old Testament existed at that time.

15. We have the testimony of profane writers to the same effect: "Thus, Manetho, Eupolemus, Artapanus, Tacitus, Diodorus Siculus, Strabo, Justin the abbreviator of Trogus, and Juvenal, besides many other ancient writers, *all* testify that Moses was the leader of the Jews and the founder of their laws."[20] Had we the space we would give quotations from these authors. We have not presented a hundredth part of the testimony which might be given, yet if that which has been given does not satisfy the reader that the Old Testament was written by the ancient Hebrews many hundred years before Christ's time, it is simply because evidence has no weight with him.

CHAPTER XXIV.

HAS THE OLD TESTAMENT BEEN CORRUPTED?

Has the Old Testament been corrupted since it was written by Moses and the prophets? We unhesitatingly answer, No; for we have the best of

---

[19] Lib. i. sect. 8. p. 441. ed. Havercamp.
[20] Horne's Introduction, vol. i. chap. ii. sect. 1, p. 58.

evidence that its integrity has been strictly maintained, and that we have the words of the inspired penmen just as they were written. In proof of this we offer the following evidences:—

1. There is no proof whatever of any such alteration. The sharp-eyed enemies of the Bible, with all their searching, have never been able to show any such change. This fact alone is sufficient evidence that the Old Testament has never been corrupted. We cannot reasonably be required to prove a thing unchanged, until our enemies first show some evidence that it has been changed. This they never have done and never can do.

2. Consider how carefully the Lord has guarded the preservation of his word. The book of the law, first written by Moses, was placed in the side of the ark, in the most holy place, as we learn from Deut. 31; 24-26. No one but the high priest ever entered the most holy place, and he only once a year. Here, then, was a standard copy, from the pen of Moses himself, which was sacredly kept for reference through all coming generations. How could it be changed?

3. The tribe of Levi was set apart, by the order of God himself, for the express purpose of teaching this law, preserving copies of it, and seeing that it was obeyed. Here was another safeguard against its being either lost or corrupted. How different has it ever been with books written by profane authors; they have been left to shift for themselves. Each man might take care of his own book; there was no public interest to guard any of them. But it was the special duty of one whole tribe to look after the book of God, and to teach it to the people. Besides, every action of their daily

life was regulated by its precepts. There was no chance to change such a book under such circumstances.

4. These books, from the very time they were written, were received as the sacred word of the living God. The whole nation looked upon them with the deepest reverence and awe; much greater than even pious men do now. The Jewish historian, Josephus, in the following testimony shows how sacredly these books were regarded: "What trust we put in these our writings is manifest by our deeds. Though so long time has elapsed, no one has ever dared to add to, or take from them, or make any change in them whatever. It is as it were inborn with every Jew, from the very first origin of the nation, to consider these books as the doctrines of God, to stand by them constantly, and, if need be, cheerfully to die for them. It is no new thing to see the captives of our nation, many of them in number, and at many different times, endure tortures and deaths of all kinds in the public theaters, rather than utter a word against our laws, or the records which contain them."[1]

See how careful they had to be to treasure up these sacred words. Thus the Lord instructed them:—

"And these words, which I command thee this day, shall be in thine heart; and thou shalt teach them diligently unto thy children, and shalt talk of them when thou sittest in thine house, and when thou walkest by the way, and when thou liest down, and when thou risest up. And thou shalt bind them for a sign upon thine hand, and they shall be as frontlets between thine eyes. And thou shalt

---

[1] Against Apion, lib. i; sect. 8; Stowe's Hist. p. 566.

write them upon the posts of thy house, and on thy gates." [2]

They were to diligently teach them to their children. They must write them on their door-posts. They must put them on their garments, and learn them by heart. The people who were to teach their children must have had copies of the Sacred Scriptures; the priests and Levites and the magistrates must have had copies of them, as being the laws of the land. The king was required to write a copy of this law in a book, and read therein all the days of his life.[3] There was a severe prohibition against making any alteration in the words of the law.[4]

Remember that the land was not then flooded with books, as now. When the larger part of the Old Testament was written, there was only one book in the whole world, and that was these very Scriptures. Even when the last book in the Old Testament was written, it is not probable that the Jews had any other book than this; though they must have had many copies of this one book, as has been already shown. This contained their whole literature. It was the A B C book for the children, the reader for the youth, the statute law-book for the business man, and the geography for the traveler. In short, it was all the book they had, and was read publicly among the people every Sabbath day.[5] It is absurd to talk about changing such a book under such circumstances. It would have been an impossibility. My friend, you know in your heart that the thing is unreasonable.

5. If, before the time of Christ, the books of the

---

[2] Deut. 6: 6–9.
[4] Deut. 4: 2.
[3] Deut. 17: 18, 19
[5] Acts 13: 27.

Old Testament had been willfully corrupted, the prophets who flourished during that time, and who were neither slow nor timid in reproving the sins of both people and rulers, would not have passed by such a heinous offense in silence. But they do not intimate that a corruption had been attempted. This is proof that it never was undertaken.

6. Nine hundred and seventy-five years before Christ, the nation was divided into two kingdoms,—Judah and Israel. Both nations retained the same book of the law. The rivalry that existed between the two kingdoms prevented either of them from altering or adding to the law. After the Israelites were carried captive into Assyria, other nations were placed in the cities of Samaria, and mingled with the remnant of the Israelites left in the land. These Samaritans received the pentateuch; hence "the Samaritans had the pentateuch as well as the Jews; but with this difference, that the Samaritan pentateuch was in the old Hebrew or Phenician characters, in which it remains to this day; whereas the Jewish copy was changed into Chaldee characters, in which it also remains to this day, which were fairer and clearer than the Hebrew, the Jews having learned the Chaldee language during their seventy years' abode at Babylon. The jealousy and hatred which subsisted between the Jews and the Samaritans, made it impracticable for either nation to corrupt or alter the text in anything of consequence without certain discovery; and the general agreement between the Hebrew and Samaritan copies of the pentateuch, which are now extant, is such as plainly demonstrates that the copies were originally the same. Nor can any better evidence be desired, that the Jewish Bibles have not been corrupted or interpolated, than this very book

of the Samaritans; which, after more than two thousand years' discord between the two nations, varies as little from the other as any classic author in less tract of time has disagreed from itself by the unavoidable slips and mistakes of so many transcribers."⁶

7. The Old Testament was translated into the Greek B. C. 282. This is called the Septuagint. Here was another guard against any alteration.

8. Long before the time of Christ, the Jews were divided into various sects, as Pharisees, Sadducees, etc. Each party watched the others with jealous eyes, ready to find fault with them on the least occasion; hence if one party had undertaken to change their Scriptures, another would have exposed them. Thus there was no chance for the slightest change to take place.

9. If the Jews had changed any part of their Scriptures after the coming of Christ, they would have altered those plain prophecies concerning Christ; but this has never been done. Those prophecies still remain in the Hebrew Bible just as clear and unaltered as of old. If the Old-Testament Scriptures had been corrupted in any manner, Christ and his apostles would have pointed out the corruption, and would have rebuked the Jews for it, as they rebuked them so sharply and frequently for other sins. But neither Christ nor the apostles ever intimated such a thing. Indeed, as we have before shown, they constantly made lengthy quotations from the Old Testament, always indorsing it, and never intimating that it had been corrupted in any manner.

10. If the Old Testament was ever altered or

---

*Horne's Introduction, vol. i. pp. 112, 113.

corrupted, the work must have been done either by one person or by many. It cannot be conceived as possible that one man would have been able to alter all the copies in the hands of so many people. Such a thing would have been a miracle indeed. Nor is it reasonable to believe that the whole nation would have unanimously agreed to alter their holy Scriptures, without any protest from any party or individual. Reader, we feel almost ashamed to argue a case which is so plain.

11. After the establishment of Christianity, the Jews and the Christians were at enmity with each other, which made any material corruption by either party impossible. Had such an attempt been made by the Jews, the Christians would have immediately detected it; and so, if the Christians had attempted it, the Jews would have very quickly pointed it out. But nothing of the kind ever occurred.

12. From the rise of Christianity to the present time, the very books which now compose the Old Testament have always been regarded as constituting the whole of the Old-Testament Scriptures. The catalogues of these books made in the early centuries by many eminent men, such as "the author of the synopsis attributed to Athanasius, by Epiphanius, and Jerome (toward the close of the fourth century), by Origen (in the middle of the third century), and Melito, bishop of Sardis (toward the close of the second century), all agree with the above enumeration. To these we may add the testimonies of the Greek translators of the Old Testament, Aquila, Theodotion, and Symmachus, who lived toward the close of the second century, and that of the Peshito, or old Syriac version, executed very early in the second, if not at the close of the first, century of the Christian era. Here

the Jewish testimonies join us."[7] All these testimonies confirm the fact that our books of the Old Testament are just the same that the ancients had.

13. "The *agreement of all the manuscripts* of the Old Testament (amounting to nearly eleven hundred and fifty) which are known to be extant, is a clear proof of its uncorrupted preservation. These manuscripts indeed are not all entire; some contain one part and some another. But it is absolutely impossible that *every* manuscript, whether in the original Hebrew or in any ancient version or paraphrase, should or could be designedly altered or falsified in the same passages, without detection either by Jews or Christians."[8] This fact alone proves that we have the Old Testament uncorrupted.

14. And, finally, all the evidences we have given in a previous chapter, showing that the New Testament has been preserved unchanged, prove also the preservation of the Old Testament. It was received by the Christians as the word of God the same as the New Testament. These are both bound together and read together. Reader, we think the evidences upon this point are conclusive.

CHAPTER XXV.

WHY WE REJECT THE APOCRYPHA.

The question is frequently asked why the books of the apocrypha are not accepted as a part of the Sacred Scriptures. There are many and good reasons why they are rejected.

---

[7] Horne's Introduction, vol. i. p. 44. [8] Id. p. 114.

1. These books were never sanctioned by Christ and his apostles, nor by any of the other writers of the New Testament. Both Jesus and his apostles, in all their speaking and writing, were constantly making, not only frequent references to the books of the Old Testament, but numerous quotations from them. They seemed to be ever in their minds. Everything they said or did was with reference to the teachings of that book,—the law and the prophets, the Psalms, etc. They often mention them by name. In the small volume of the New Testament there are nearly nine hundred quotations from the Old Testament; but not a single quotation from, nor even an allusion to, any of the books of the apocrypha, though there are many places where instances in the apocryphal writings would be directly in point, and although it is quite probable that the writers of the New Testament were acquainted with the books of the apocrypha. Hence they must have designedly abstained from alluding to them in their writings, from the fact that they considered them of no authority. This alone is sufficient evidence on which to reject them.

2. They formed no part of the original Hebrew books contained in the Hebrew canon, and were not written till after the catalogue of the inspired books had been made up. Not one of the books of the apocrypha was ever written in Hebrew or Chaldee, as were the books of the Old Testament. They were never received by the Jews as sacred books. On this point we have the direct testimony of Josephus, in his work against Apion, Book I. sect. 8. He there gives an account of all the books held sacred by the Hebrews. This testimony is copied and indorsed by Eusebius, the celebrated Christian historian. "In the first of these works

he gives us the number of the canonical books of the Scriptures called the Old Testament, such as are of undoubted authority among the Hebrews, setting them forth, as handed down by ancient tradition, in the following words:—

"'We have not, therefore, among us innumerable books that disagree and contradict one another, but only two and twenty, embracing the record of all history, and which are justly considered divine compositions. Of these, five are the books of Moses, comprehending both the laws and the tradition respecting the origin of man, down to his own death. This time comprehends a space of nearly three thousand years. But from Moses until the death of Artaxerxes, who reigned after Xerxes, king of Persia, the prophets after Moses wrote the events of their day in thirteen books. The remaining four comprehend hymns to the praise of God, and precepts for the regulation of human life. From Artaxerxes until our own times, the events are all recorded, but they are not deemed of authority equal with those before them, because that there was not an exact succession of the prophets.'"[2]

Comparing these statements of Josephus with his numerous quotations from the Old Testament in his historical writings, we clearly see that he recognized just the same number of books that we have now, and no others. The Jews reckon these books thus:—

THE FIVE BOOKS OF MOSES.

1. Genesis.
2. Exodus.
3. Leviticus.
4. Numbers.
5. Deuteronomy.

---

[2] Eusebius' Eccl. Hist. book iii. chap. x. p. 97.

THE THIRTEEN PROPHETIC BOOKS.

1. Joshua.
2. Judges and Ruth (one.)
3. Two books of Samuel.
4. Two books of Kings.
5. Two books of Chronicles.
6. Ezra and Nehemiah (one).
7. Esther.
8. Isaiah.
9. Jeremiah.
10. Ezekiel.
11. Daniel.
12. Twelve minor prophets.
13. Job.

THE FOUR BOOKS OF HYMNS AND PRECEPTS.

1. Psalms.
2. Proverbs.
3. Ecclesiastes.
4. Canticles.

This is according to the Jewish arrangement.[3] This makes just twenty-two books, one for each letter of their alphabet. It will be noticed that Josephus plainly recognized the existence of the apocryphal books, and expressly excluded them from the inspired writings. This again is sufficient evidence upon which to reject them from the catalogue of the inspired books.

3. They were unanimously rejected for several centuries by the early Christian churches, and by the most learned scholars of the Christian fathers. Of this fact there is the most abundant proof. The evidence is so great that in our limited space we can scarcely more than refer to it. Take a few examples: Melito, after the apostles, was a distinguished bishop of Sardis, an able writer, and a man of great influence among the early Christians. He traveled into Palestine for the express purpose of ascertaining exactly the canon of the Old Testa-

---

[3] Stowe's Hist. of the Books of the Bible, pp. 566, 567.

ment, and gave the result of his researches in the following letter, which we find in Eusebius:[4]—

"I accordingly went to the East, and, coming to the very place where these things were preached and transacted, I have accurately learned the books of the Old Testament. Their names are as follows: Five books of Moses; to wit, Genesis, Exodus, Leviticus, Numbers, Deuteronomy. Joshua Nave [of Nun], Judges, Ruth. Four books of Kings, [two of Samuel and two of Kings]. Two of Paralipomena (Chronicles), the Psalms of David, the Proverbs of Solomon (which is also Wisdom), Ecclesiastes, the Song of Songs, Job. Of the prophets, Isaiah, Jeremiah. Of the twelve prophets, one book. Daniel, Ezekiel, Esdras [Ezra, including also Nehemiah, and perhaps Esther]."[5]

Where are the books of the apocrypha? Not one of them is referred to. The book of Ezra, which he does not mention, was frequently included under the name of Esdras, as it was generally supposed that book was written by Ezra.

Next we have the testimony of Origen, the great Biblical scholar of the Eastern Church, A. D. 200, who rejects all of the apocryphal books. His testimony is found in Eusebius, Book VI. chapter 25.

The great Athanasius, the renowned champion of the trinity, A. D. 330, rejects all of them, except the book of Baruch.

Hilary, the celebrated bishop of Poitiers, A. D. 350, rejects them all. And so we might mention the names of the best Christian scholars of antiquity, all of whom reject them.

"From the preceding exhibition it is as plain as

---

[4] Eusebius' Eccl. Hist. book iv. chap xxvi.
[5] Stowe's Hist. of the Books of the Bible, p. 568.

daylight can make anything plain, that the Romish Church, in receiving the apocryphal books as a part of Scripture, has not only set at naught all historical truth, but acted in direct violation of its own fundamental principle. The *unanimous consent of the fathers* is what she requires for the establishment of a doctrine ; but on this subject, instead of a *unanimous consent*, for the first four centuries she is met with an all but *unanimous dissent.*"[6]

4. The books of the apocrypha were first declared canonical by the Roman Catholic Council at Trent, A. D. 1546, only a little over three hundred years ago. This, it will be noticed, was after the rise of Luther. They did this to condemn him, because, like a sensible man, he rejected these books, as all scholars before him had done. But many of the ablest Roman Catholics were bitterly opposed to receiving these books ; and it was only after a fierce struggle, and through the overwhelming majority of ignorant priests who composed the council, that their acceptance was carried. But being once made, as Rome never errs, the decision had to stand. Hence these books were incorporated in the Catholic Bible from that day forward, but not into our Bible.

5. These books are to be received simply as historical works. They are valuable in that respect, but in no other.

---

[6] Stowe's Hist. of the Books of the Bible, p. 582.

CHAPTER XXVI.

CAN WE BELIEVE THE BIBLE?

In our investigation thus far, we have learned that the Bible was written in the land of Palestine; the Old Testament by the ancient prophets of the Jews, and the New Testament by the disciples of Jesus. We now inquire whether these Scriptures are reliable, whether we can believe what they say. Does the New Testament contain a true history of the life, ministry, death, resurrection, and ascension of the Lord Jesus Christ, and the subsequent life and ministry of his immediate disciples, so that we may receive as historically correct whatever is related therein?

We prove the credibility of the New Testament just as we do that of any other book. The fact that this book relates the actions of a divine Saviour and his apostles, and other ancient books relate the actions of wicked men, does not change the nature of the evidence in this case from what it would be in others.

We have proved that the books of which the New Testament is composed were written in the first century of the Christian era, by the original disciples of Christ. This should be considered as strong presumptive evidence that the main events recorded in them are true.

The question now is this: Were the writers of the Bible able to tell correctly the facts about which they wrote? Was there any possibility of their being deceived about them? We maintain that this is utterly impossible. They did not receive their statements second-hand, nor from hearsay, nor even from a written book. They were themselves cognizant of those facts. They looked on with their own eyes while the events they have related were being enacted. They heard Jesus with their own ears, and saw him with their own eyes, not once or twice, but many times,—not in the performance of some complicated trickery, but in the simplest affairs of life.

Take the most ordinary cases in the gospel narratives. The apostles all state that they were acquainted with a certain man called Jesus Christ; that they knew him personally; that they were with him, traveled with him, ate with him, and conversed with him, for more than three years. They state that they were with him in the city of Jerusalem; that they saw him arrested by soldiers; they were present when he was tried by the priests; they heard him condemned; they saw him taken out of the city by the soldiers, and nailed to the cross, etc. It is to just such facts as these that they testify over and over again. Now, is it possible that twelve men, for the period of over three years, under such circumstances, could be deceived, so as to believe that these things occurred when they did not occur? Such a supposition is too absurd. Then we maintain that these witnesses, who have written the life of Christ, could not have been deceived, at least as to the main facts which they relate. If, then, they were not the most deliberate liars, there did exist in that place, and at that time, such a man as Jesus Christ; and he did the works they have recorded of him, and spoke the words which they have reported him to have spoken.

If the writers of the New Testament had sufficient opportunity to become acquainted with the

CAN WE BELIEVE IT? 191

facts which they relate, they are certainly competent witnesses. We do not think it necessary to bring a great array of facts upon this point. The writers of the New Testament were eye-witnesses of the most of the facts which they relate.[1] Others had a perfect understanding of all that Jesus began both to do and to teach.[2] It does not require a great amount of knowledge to be able to write the gospel history. It is contained in a small space. Thirty pages of a common family Bible contain the whole of what any one of the Evangelists has written, and there are no perplexed questions in these writings. They are simply a plain, straightforward history of events as they transpired, without any painting, gilding, notes of explanation, or criticisms.

Now when we consider that Matthew and John were both companions of Jesus Christ, that they accompanied him in all his journeyings, and sat at his feet to receive instruction from him in his retired moments, we must conclude that they were competent witnesses. Consider also that the book of Mark was revised and corrected by Peter, another eye-witness of the works of Christ; that Luke's narrative was written under the supervision of the apostle Paul, who had also seen Christ; and that Mark and Luke harmonize with Matthew and John, the gospel of the latter not having been written until after the books of Mark and Luke were in circulation, and we must conclude that in no other series of events recorded in ancient history have we such ample security against fraud and deception.

In addition to the four systematic memoirs of

---

[1] Luke 1:2; 1 John 1:1–4.
[2] Luke 1:3; Acts 1:1.

Christ to which we have referred, we have a collection of letters written by four others, in which reference is continually made to the events related in these memoirs. These eight persons, separated from one another by a wide extent of territory, give us their separate and independent statement of things which they deemed worthy of record, in the life of Christ, and the sayings and doings of many of his friends and enemies.

These witnesses, being scattered and persecuted as they were, could not possibly confederate together, nor copy their statements from one another, without detection and immediate exposure. Yet when their books were brought together and compared, their agreement was such that every one must conclude that they are all competent witnesses. A crooked stick will not tally with a straight one;—so in this case, if any one of these writers is incompetent to bear witness to the truth, a discrepancy between his testimony and that of others will manifest itself. While, if none of the writers are capable of telling the truth, we shall not expect harmony between any of them. But there is a perfect harmony, yea, an undesigned coincidence, in their separate testimonies.

Suppose a number of the friends of Napoleon Bonaparte—members of his staff—had written each of them a book professing to be a biography of their general, had vouched in every way for the truth of their statements, and had staked their reputation upon the accuracy of what they had written; and that, too, in the midst of a generation familiar with the life and actions of their subject. Now suppose that all of these books agree precisely in their statements, would it not be reasonable to infer that, in point of historical facts, these books are correct? Would not any sane man know that an untruth, of any magnitude, incorporated in such a biography could not escape detection? The fact that these books were published in the midst of the generation and nation where Bonaparte lived, and circulated among those who were acquainted with his history; that, notwithstanding their notoriety, their accuracy was not called in question and their statements refuted when first published; and that the authors expected these books to be received as correct biographies of this great general, is a sufficient warrant for the accuracy of the general features of the books, though they might differ in some of the minute details.

This statement is especially applicable to the books of the New Testament. They were published in the age in which the principal events narrated are said to have occurred, and among the people where they are said to have occurred. Not only so, but the people where the New Testament was first circulated were on the alert, and anxious to take advantage of the smallest misstatement, as their acquaintance with the facts which it records would enable them at a glance to do. The authors of the New Testament must have been acquainted with these facts. They must have known that their adversaries possessed an advantage which nothing but truth could overcome. Hence, whether they were honest or not, their statements must have been true, as nothing could have stopped the mouths of their enemies but the knowledge of the facts related.

It is impossible that a number of contemporary books, recording the same events, and written in the age in which these events occurred, should be received as true by the people of that age, many of whom were familiar with the facts on record, unless they were literally correct.

Now, "it is an extraordinary and singular fact, that no history since the commencement of the world has been written by so great a number of the companions and friends of an illustrious person as that of our Saviour. One contemporary history is a rarity; two is a coincidence scarcely known; four is, so far as appears, unparalleled. We have therefore an unequaled opportunity of coming at the truth."[3] "Now this unfailing agreement of four several, independent, and contemporaneous historians, each so circumstantial, each so full of allusions to the events and institutions and customs of the times, and none contradicted by any evidence whatever, is as convincing an evidence of the honest accuracy of all, as any mind should require. Were the gospel history untrue, such evidence would have been morally impossible. It is peculiar to that history. No other can plead it to any similar extent."[4]

We now come to the second point; viz., Have we reason to rely with implicit confidence upon the honesty of the writers of the New Testament? The proof presented of the competency of these writers, is also a proof of their honesty. When we take up the book concerning which we make our present inquiry, we find it teaching a pure system of morals, one particular of which is, "Lie not one to another." This book also informs us that "all liars shall have their part in the lake that burneth with fire and brimstone, which is the second death." Now the question is, Can we credit the testimony

---

[3] M'Ilvaine's Evidences, p. 150. [4] Id. p. 151.

of those who said, "Lie not"? or are they themselves such notorious liars that they lied publicly and repeatedly? that it was the continual business of their lives to lie? and that they died with a lie in their mouths, when they, for the word of their testimony, were put to death?

We begin the argument by asking what motive could have prompted the writers of the New Testament to write what they did, except the consciousness of its truth. It is contrary to nature for men to undertake anything without a motive. So that if no human inducement was held before them to publish what was not true, perhaps a higher one stimulated them to tell the truth.

The apostles did preach and publish that Jesus died and rose again. If they had been seeking popularity, they would certainly have taken some other course. Infidels acknowledge that the apostles preached a pure morality; hence it could not have been to obtain license for lust that they confederated together to circulate a falsehood. It must have been to advance themselves in wealth, honor, or power.

But their new religion made no provision for any of these. Peter and John were so poor that when asked by a beggar for alms, Peter answered, "Silver and gold have I none." And though the friends of Christianity sold their possessions, and brought the money and laid it at the apostles' feet, so that they could have made themselves independently rich, had they chosen so to do, instead of managing the money matters themselves they elected seven deacons to attend to it, and gave themselves continually to the ministry of the word and prayer. And after the apostles had labored more than a score of years in the propagation of

Christianity, with almost unlimited success, they could appeal to the churches in language like this: "I have coveted no man's silver, or gold, or apparel." "Yea," says Paul, "ye yourselves know, that these hands have ministered unto my necessities, and to them that were with me."[5] Those to whom the apostle made this appeal were well acquainted with the fact that while Paul was preaching for a year and a half from Sabbath to Sabbath, in Corinth, he spent the six working days of every week laboring in the tent factory of Aquila and company. The same apostle, subsequently, in writing to his brethren at Corinth, could say in behalf of the apostles, "Even unto this present hour we both hunger, and thirst, and are naked, and are buffeted, and have no certain dwelling-place; and labor, working with our hands; being reviled, we bless; being persecuted, we suffer it; being defamed, we entreat; we are made as the filth of the world, and are the offscouring of all things unto this day."[6] The author of the Christian religion was born in a manger, and was so poor through his life that he had not where to lay his head. And one of the last writers of the New Testament writes from a dungeon in Rome to his brother Timothy, to bring his old cloak, and "do his diligence to come before winter."[7] Thus we discover that whether the apostles were popular or not, they were penniless.

But have they gained honor by propagating this falsehood, if indeed it be a falsehood? Let us see. The very first thing which their enemies did when they commenced to tell their story was to command them to "speak no more in this name." The next

---

[5] Acts 20:34.   [6] 1 Cor. 4:11–13.   [7] 2 Tim. 4:21.

was to imprison and beat them. After that a general persecution ensued, in which Stephen was put to death, and from this time the witnesses were scattered. Persecution drove them from place to place. Saul, a young and popular lawyer, carried the documents in his pocket which authorized him to put the saints to death. Thus he persecuted from city to city until he was arrested and made an apostle of this new religion. And behold the prospect placed before him. Says Jesus, "I will show him how great things he must suffer for my name's sake." And he says himself, "And now, behold, I go bound in the spirit unto Jerusalem, not knowing the things that shall befall me there, save that the Holy Ghost witnesseth in every city, saying that bonds and afflictions abide me."[8] Hear him give the proofs of his calling of God to the ministry:—

"Are they ministers of Christ? (I speak as a fool) I am more; in labors more abundant, in stripes above measure, in prisons more frequent, in deaths oft. Of the Jews five times received I forty stripes save one. Thrice was I beaten with rods, once was I stoned, thrice I suffered shipwreck, a night and a day I have been in the deep; in journeyings often, in perils of waters, in perils of robbers, in perils by mine own countrymen, in perils by the heathen, in perils in the city, in perils in the wilderness, in perils in the sea, in perils among false brethren; in weariness and painfulness, in watchings often, in hunger and thirst, in fastings often, in cold and nakedness."[9]

Now, if this is merely a contrivance of the writers of the New Testament, is it not strange that they

---

[8] Acts 20:22 23. [9] 2 Cor. 11:23-27.

adhered to it as they did? It bitterly opposed all the habits, prejudices, and dispositions of the people, insomuch that all manner of suffering was heaped upon them. They submitted to misery and contempt, took joyfully the spoiling of their goods, willingly endured to be counted fools and the offscouring of all things, and rejoiced that they were counted worthy to suffer shame, to fight with wild beasts at Ephesus, and at last to die in attestation of the truth of their affirmations, when at any time they could have renounced their religion and retrieved their worldly losses. Yes, this is strange conduct. But, strange as it is, seven of these witnesses were put to death, and one of them banished for the word of his testimony; and yet not a word of confession was ever extorted from one of them.

As there could have been no inducement for the writers of the New Testament to give publicity to a falsehood, we now proceed to give evidence that they wrote the truth. The manner in which these writers published their testimony to the world, bears every mark of truthfulness. Their statements are in a high degree circumstantial. False witnesses will not introduce many particulars into their narratives; while "he that doeth truth cometh to the light." Falsehood does not deal much in dates, times, and places of easy reference; it rather fears and avoids them. It is said that "generality is the cloak of fiction; while minuteness is the mantle of truth."

When the writers of the New Testament recorded a miracle, they always went into a detail of circumstances, which rendered the whole matter easy of reference, and, if false, of exposure. The miracles of Jesus Christ were not done in a corner. They were all wrought in public places, and in a public manner; so that if a mistake should have been made in recording one of them, thousands of witnesses who were present at the time the miracle was performed could have corrected it. The Evangelists record the astonishing miracle of feeding five thousand men upon five barley loaves and two small fishes; they tell the time of the year when, and the place where, it was done, and many other circumstances connected with it. Thus they put it into the power of these five thousand men, and myriads of their contemporaries, to have exposed the fraud if it had been one.

Again: When John records the resurrection of a dead man, he does not simply state that Christ raised a man from the dead, but he says that his name was Lazarus, that he resided in the village of Bethany, about fifteen furlongs from Jerusalem, that he was laid in a cave with a stone rolled to its mouth; he tells the length of time that he had been dead; how he came out of the sepulcher; names several prominent individuals that were present, gives the impression which it made upon the Jews, gives the history of the calling of the council to decide what should be done with the man who had raised the dead, tells how they were divided in opinion with regard to it, gives the language of Caiaphas the high priest, and the subsequent treatment which Lazarus received from the Jews. Surely nothing but truth would dare to deal in such circumstantialities. It looks as if this writer was not afraid of anything that the people of Bethany, or their descendants, might do. This one circumstance is enough to prove that this book was written in all the confidence of truth.

Notice, further, that the author of the Christian religion did not live away back in some fabulous age, like the author of the Hindoo religion, or of the Chinese religious system. No; Jesus Christ lived in one of the most celebrated ages of the world,—the time of the Cæsars. Neither did he live in an unfrequented country, back in the desert or in the wilderness, where he could have been seen by only a few. No; he not only made his appearance in Judea, a well-known country, but much of his life was passed in Jerusalem, the capital of the nation, and even in the temple, where all the people congregated. His deeds were not done simply before the ignorant, but before lawyers, scribes, and the rulers. Nor did his disciples, like the Mormons of our day, flee into the desert, and colonize there; but, on the contrary, they planted their churches in the most celebrated cities of the world, such as Rome, Athens, and Antioch. These facts show that they were not afraid of the light. Everything was done openly and publicly, just as men always do when they are conscious that they have the right and the truth.

Would an impostor of the third or fourth century, if he were going to write a book to impose upon the people as an apostolic document, commence it as follows? "Now in the fifteenth year of the reign of Tiberius Cæsar, Pontius Pilate being governor of Judea, and Herod being tetrarch of Galilee, and his brother Philip tetrarch of Iturea and of the region of Trachonitis, and Lysanias the tetrarch of Abilene, Annas and Caiaphas being the high priests, the word of God came unto John, the son of Zacharias, in the wilderness, and he came into all the country about Jordan, preaching the baptism of repentance for the remission of sins."[10]

---

[10] Luke 3: 1–3.

Here, in one sentence, are twenty-three historical, geographical, political, and genealogical references; every one of which can be confirmed by reference to secular history. The combined efforts of the enemies of Christianity have never been able to disprove one out of hundreds of such statements as the above. Such statements show where, and when, the New Testament was written.

"As a specimen of the argument, let us confine our observations to the history of our Saviour's trial, execution, and burial. They brought him to Pontius Pilate. We know, both from Tacitus and Josephus, that he was at that time governor of Judea. A sentence from him was necessary before they could proceed to the execution of Jesus; and we know that the power of life and death was usually vested in the Roman governor. Our Saviour was treated with derision; and this we know to have been a customary practice at that time, previous to the execution of criminals, and during the time of it. Pilate scourged Jesus before he gave him up to be crucified. We know from ancient authors that this was a very usual practice among the Romans. The account of an execution generally ran in this form: He was stripped, whipped, and beheaded, or executed. According to the Evangelists, his accusation was written on the top of the cross; and we learn from Suetonius and others that the crime of the person to be executed was affixed to the instrument of his punishment. According to the Evangelists, this accusation was written in three different languages; and we know from Josephus that it was quite common in Jerusalem to have all public advertisements written in this manner. According to the Evangelists, Jesus had to bear his cross; and we know from other sources of information that this was the constant practice of those times. According to the Evangelists, the body of Jesus was given up to be buried at the request of friends. We know that, unless the criminal was infamous, this was the law, or the custom, with all Roman governors.

"These and a few more particulars of the same kind, occur within the compass of a single page of the evangelical history. The circumstantial manner of the history affords a presumption in its favor, antecedent to all examination into the truth of the circumstances themselves. But it makes a strong addition to the evidence, when we find that in all the subordinate parts of the main story, the Evangelists maintain so great a consistency with the testimony of other authors, and with all that we can collect from other sources of information; as to the manners and institutions of that period. It is difficult to conceive, in the first instance, how the inventor of a fabricated story would hazard such a number of circumstances, each of them supplying a point of comparison with other authors, and giving to the inquirer an additional chance of detecting the imposition. And it is still more difficult to believe that truth should have been so artfully blended with falsehood in the composition of this narrative, particularly as we perceive nothing like a forced introduction of any one circumstance. There appears to be nothing out of place, nothing thrust in with the view of imparting an air of probability to the history. The circumstances upon which we bring the Evangelists into comparison with profane authors, are often not intimated in a direct form, but in the form of a slight or distant allusion. There is not the most remote appearance of its being fetched or sought for. It is brought in accidentally, and flows in the most natural and undesigned manner out of the progress of the narrative."[11]

No one ever ventured in any publication to deny the statements of the Evangelists. If the facts recorded in the New Testament are untrue, many of them can be easily disproved; such as the summoning of the chief priests and scribes, and demanding of them where Christ should be born; the destruction of the male children of Bethlehem; the preaching of John in the wilderness; the number baptized; the beheading of John by the intrigues of Herodias; the miraculous feeding of five thousand men; the resurrection of Lazarus; the crucifixion of Christ; the supernatural darkening of the sun for the space of three hours; the rending of the vail of the temple from top to bottom; the quaking of the earth; the resurrection of Christ and many saints, who went into the city and appeared to many; the speaking with foreign tongues on the day of Pentecost; the healing of a well-known public beggar; the circumstance of Paul being detained a prisoner by Felix; the conduct of the Philippian magistrates; the sending of Paul to Cæsar; and a hundred other things the most easy of detection and exposure; yet no ancient writer has ever contradicted one of these statements. Unquestionably they would have done so, had they been able to support their contradiction. The fact that enemies permitted these accounts to go out uncontradicted, is a testimony from them in their behalf.

"If you reject the testimony of Christ and his apostles as false, and say you cannot believe them in matters of fact, how can you respect their mo-

---

[11] Campbell's Debate with Owen, pp. 285, 286.

rality? Of all the absurdities of modern infidelity, the respectful language generally used by its advocates in speaking of Christ and his apostles, is the most inconsistent. He claimed to be a divine person, and professed to work miracles. The infidel says he was not a divine person, and wrought no miracles. The consequence is unavoidable,—such a pretender is a blasphemous impostor. And yet they speak of him as 'a model man,' an 'exemplar of every virtue.' What! an impostor a model man? A blasphemer and liar an exemplar of every virtue? Is that the infidel's notion of virtue? Why, the devils were more consistent in their commendations of his character, 'We know thee who thou art, THE HOLY ONE OF GOD!' Let our modern enemies of Christ learn consistency from their ancient allies."[12]

Just so of the apostles; either they were true, honest, God-fearing men, and told the exact truth, or else they were the most arrant hypocrites and willing deceivers the world has ever seen.

"How can we accept their code of morals if we refuse to believe them when they speak of matters of fact? Is it possible to respect men as moral teachers whom we have convicted of forging stories of miracles that never occurred, and confederating together to impose a lying superstition on the world? For this is plainly the very point and center of the question about the truth of the Bible, and I am anxious you should see it clearly. A fair statement of this question is half the argument. The question, then, is simply this: Was Jesus really the divine person he claimed to be, or was he a blasphemous impostor? When

---

[12] Fables of Infidelity, p. 116.

the apostles unitedly and solemnly testified that they had seen him after he was risen from the dead, that they ate and drank with him, that their hands had handled his body, that they conversed with him for forty days, and saw him go up to Heaven, did they tell the truth, or were they a confederated band of liars? There is no reason for any other supposition. They could not possibly be deceived themselves in the matters they relate. They knew perfectly whether their statements were true or not. We are not talking about matters of dogma, about which there might be room for difference of opinion, but about matters of fact,—about what men say they saw, and heard, and felt,—about which no man of common sense could possibly be mistaken."[13]

One of the most convincing proofs that the writers of the Bible are candid, truthful, and reliable in their statements, is found in the fact that they seek to conceal nothing. "There is nothing like flattery or reserve in their narrations or their addresses. 'Their own frailties and follies, and the misconduct of their greatest heroes and sovereigns, are recorded with singular and unexampled fidelity. They offer no palliation of their conduct, they conceal nothing, they alter nothing,' however disgraceful to the Hebrew worthies and to the Hebrew nation. No candid reader can peruse their writings attentively, without observing that this is a just, though imperfect representation of their character; nor can any one suppose that men of such a character would wish to deceive their readers."[14]

They record the drunkenness of Noah, the prevarication of Abraham, the deception of Jacob, the

---

[13] Id. p. 117. [14] Horne's Introduction, vol. i. p. 189.

adultery of David, the apostasy of Peter, the quarrel between Paul and Barnabas, and many other like sins of their most noted and prominent men. They do not stop to palliate them, nor excuse them. They state the naked facts, and leave the matter there. Would hypocrites and deceivers take such a course? No, indeed. The stamp of truth is on every page of the Bible. It speaks as God alone speaks, telling the truth and nothing but the truth. Reader, it is safe to risk our souls upon the statements of such a book.

We have already noticed that the Bible abounds in geographical, historical, and other references. The value of these as evidences of its authenticity is well illustrated in the following anecdote:—

In a village in Yorkshire, England, lived two men who were cloth manufacturers. One was named Walsh, the other Stetson. Walsh was an unbeliever. It was a favorite opinion of his that the Bible "was all made up." He could never believe that it was written where it professed to have been, and by the men said to have written it. But Stetson was an earnest Christian.

Walsh was part owner of a factory, and one year he had set his heart on making a very large and fine piece of cloth. He took great pains with the carding, spinning, dyeing, weaving, and finishing of it. In the process of manufacture it was one day stretched on tenter-hooks to dry. It made a fine show, and he felt very proud of it. The next morning he arose early to work at it; to his amazement it was gone. Some one had stolen it during the night.

After weeks of anxiety and expense, a piece of cloth answering the description was stopped at Manchester, awaiting the owner and proof. Away to Manchester went Walsh, as fast as the express train could carry him. There he found many rolls of cloth which had been stolen. They were very much alike. He selected one which he felt satisfied was his. But how could he prove it? In doubt and perplexity, he called on his neighbor Stetson.

"Friend Stetson," said he, "I have found a piece of cloth which I am sure is the one which was stolen from me. But how to prove it is the question. Can you tell me how?"

"You don't want it unless it is really yours?"

"Certainly not."

"And you want proof that is plain, simple, and such as will satisfy yourself and everybody else?"

"Precisely so."

"Well, then, take Bible proof."

"Bible proof! Pray, what is that?"

"Take your cloth to the tenter-hooks on which it was stretched, and if it be yours every hook will just fit the hole through which it passed before being taken down. There will be scores of such hooks, and if the hooks and the holes just come together right, no other proof will be wanted that the cloth is yours."

"True. Why didn't I think of this before?"

Away he went, and sure enough, every hook came to its little hole, and the cloth was proved to be his. The tenter-hooks were the very best evidence that could be had.

Some days after this, Walsh met his friend again.

"Stetson," said he, "what did you mean the other day by calling the tenter-hooks 'Bible proof'? I'm sure if I had as good evidence for the Bible as I had for my cloth, I never should doubt it again."

"You have the same, only better, for the Bible."

"How so?"

"Put it on the tenter-hooks. Take the Bible and travel with it; go to the place where it was made. There you will find the Red Sea, the Jordan, the Lake of Galilee, Mount Lebanon, Hermon, Carmel, Tabor, and Gerizim; there you will find the cities of Damascus, Hebron, Tyre, Sidon, and Jerusalem. Every mountain, every river, every sheet of water mentioned in the Bible is there, just as the Bible speaks of it. Sinai, and the Desert, and the Dead Sea are there. The holes and the hooks come together exactly. The best guide-book through that country is the Bible. It must have been written there on the spot, just as your cloth must have been stretched on your tenter-hooks. That land is the mold in which the Bible was cast, and when you bring the land and the book together, they fit to perfection."

Walsh felt the force of this argument, and he gave up his infidelity, and began to read the Bible with an interest he never had felt in it before.

CHAPTER XXVII.

DID CHRIST DIE?

In a previous chapter we have abundantly proved that there did once live in Judea such a person as Jesus Christ. We now propose to show that this man was actually raised from the dead. But let us first inquire if he really died. What evidence have we of this? Much every way.

1. The prophets had foretold that he should die. Isaiah said of him, "He is brought as a lamb to the slaughter;" "he hath poured out his soul unto death;" "he made his grave with the wicked and with the rich in his death."[1] Daniel, in his great prophecy concerning the Messiah, said, "And after threescore and two weeks shall Messiah be cut off, but not for himself."[2] These are plain predictions that the Messiah should die.

2. When Jesus came, and while as yet there was no prospect of his being crucified, he repeatedly affirmed that he was to be put to death by his enemies. "From that time forth began Jesus to show unto his disciples, how that he must go unto Jerusalem, and suffer many things from the elders and chief priests and scribes, and be killed, and be raised again the third day."[3]

Of all the religions the world has ever known, the Christian religion is the only one based upon the death of its author. Is it not strange that an impostor, who was seeking nothing but worldly aggrandizement, as must have been the case with Jesus of Nazareth if he was not the Messiah, should found the truth of all he says upon his death,—upon his dying in a certain manner, remaining dead a certain length of time, and then rising a majestic and triumphant conqueror?

All other religions have made provision for the wealth, ease, honor, and popularity of their founders; but the Christian religion made no such provision. Its Author was proclaimed as being "despised and rejected of men," "a man of sorrows and acquainted with grief," "esteemed not," "bear-

---

[1] Isa. 53: 7, 12, 9.   [2] Dan. 9: 26.   [3] Matt. 16: 21.

ing the sins of many," "being numbered with transgressors," and finally as "pouring out his soul unto death."[4] He himself knew that he must die the most shameful of all deaths, and there was no possibility of his having "the joy that was set before him," in anticipation of which he endured all he did, without first dying.

3. The Jews then acknowledged, and have always acknowledged, that Jesus was really put to death. He was not crucified by his disciples, but by the Romans and the Jews; and they were in very good earnest. There was no chance for a make-believe death in this case.

Whether it be a fact or not, it was a universal belief among the Jews, as well as the Christians, that Christ was dead. They never thought of accounting for his exit from the tomb by the claim that he was not dead when placed there. Festus, in declaring the matter to Agrippa, states the true ground of difference between Christians and all others of his time: "Against whom, when the accusers stood up, they brought none accusation of such things as I supposed; but had certain questions against him of their own superstition, and of one Jesus which was dead, whom Paul affirmed to be alive."[5] In the days of the apostles the question was not, Did he die? but, Did he rise?

Everybody knows that the Jews were the bitterest enemies of Christ and Christianity. Now if there never was such a man as Jesus, if he never lived and never died, if the New Testament is simply a fable, gotten up long after it claims to have been, how does it happen that the Jews came to acknowledge the principal fact in the whole record;

---

[4] Isa. 53. [5] Acts 25: 18, 19.

viz., the life and death of Jesus? Let the infidel account for this if he can.

4. Profane history states that Christ died. Tacitus was the most celebrated Roman historian. He lived but a few years after Christ. Writing of the Christians, he says, "The author of that name was Christ, who, in the reign of Tiberius, was put to death as a criminal under the procurator Pontius Pilate."[6] This is very definite. The death of Christ, then, was never denied in those days by either Jews or Gentiles.

5. All the New-Testament writers affirm most positively that he died. Thus testifies Peter, who was an eye-witness, who stood by the cross and saw him die. In addressing the Jews concerning Jesus of Nazareth, he says, "Him, being delivered by the determinate counsel and foreknowledge of God, ye have taken, and by wicked hands have crucified and slain."[7] If this declaration had not been notoriously true, Peter would not have dared to make it in the presence of more than three thousand of the Jews, who had just crucified the Saviour, and had the disposition to serve the apostle in the same way.

All nature, at the time when Christ expired, bore testimony, not only to his death, but to his superhuman nature. The vail of the temple was rent in twain from top to bottom. The earth quaked to her center. Rocks were rent asunder. All nature was dressed in mourning. The sun became black as sackcloth, and the centurion, as he gazed upon the scene, said, "Truly this was the Son of God," so firmly was he convinced that the Lord of glory had expired. Dionysius, the Areop-

---

[6] Lardner's Works, p. 611.   [7] Acts 2:23

agite, although eight hundred miles distant, as he beheld the sun hide its face, witnessed the bursting of rocks, and felt the earth tremble under his feet, exclaimed, "Either the Author of nature is suffering, or the universe is falling apart."

6. The gospel of Matthew was written about six or eight years after the death of Christ. It was written especially for the Jews, and was circulated in Jerusalem and all through Judea, within less than ten years from the time when it is said that Christ was crucified. Matthew states that there was a supernatural darkness and an earthquake, that the vail of the temple was rent, graves were opened, etc., at the hour when Christ died. Now suppose that none of these things really occurred; what would have been the result of such a statement? Every Jew he met would have stared him in the face, and told him that he was a liar and an impostor. Suppose a man should try a similar course to-day. He writes a book in which he asserts that in the city of Chicago, ten years ago, a noted man was arrested, brought before the highest tribunal in the city, condemned, and publicly hanged, thousands beholding it. He states that at his death the sun was darkened; that there was an earthquake; that dead men arose and came into the city, etc. Reader, how far would such a book go before it would be exposed, particularly if the book and its author were attracting special attention? How soon the falsity of the thing would be exposed. Statements denying his assertions, with thousands of reliable names attached, would immediately be scattered everywhere. That would end the matter.

Now, why did not the Jews do this? Why did they not get up a contrary statement, denying his assertions? The reason is evident. They could not do it. Jesus did actually die, and that in the most public manner, and everybody knew it.

7. Notice how public his death is said to have been. Had Jesus been an impostor, had his death been merely a farce, or had the disciples contrived the story of it afterward, the scene would have been laid in some unfrequented place, in the wilderness or in the desert, where there were but few people; it would have been among the ignorant, who could have been easily deceived. But how different are the facts in this case. The trial, condemnation, and death of Jesus took place in the most public manner, at Jerusalem, the metropolis of the nation. It was also on a high feast day, when thousands were present from every quarter of the land. Notice the characters connected with it. There were Herod and Pilate, with the high priest and the dignitaries of the nation, men who were accustomed to public affairs, and to observe things sharply. The Roman soldiers, also, were eye-witnesses of the event. Could all of these persons have been deceived? Then, too, the manner of his death, by crucifixion, prevented any deception being practiced. There was not the least possibility of a farce in the whole transaction.

The apostle John says that he himself stood by the cross and saw Jesus die: "When Jesus therefore saw his mother, and the disciple standing by, whom he loved, he saith unto his mother, Woman, behold thy son! Then saith he to the disciple, Behold thy mother! And from that hour that disciple took her unto his own home." "And he that saw it bare record, and his record is true; and he knoweth that he saith true, that ye might believe."[8] John saw the nails driven into the Saviour's hands and through his feet. He saw the Roman spear thrust into his heart, and he saw his Master after he was dead. Was he not competent, then, to bear testimony?

As it was not lawful to let executed criminals hang on the cross over the Sabbath day, the Roman soldiers were sent to break their legs and take them down. They went to the thieves and brake their legs, "but when they came to Jesus and saw that he was dead already, they brake not his legs." Let the reader take notice. This is not simply the statement of Matthew, Mark, Luke, John, or Paul. It is the statement of the soldiers who would have broken his legs had he been alive. It would not do to leave this matter here; his death must be placed beyond dispute; so the soldier puts a spear into his side, and makes a wound from whence issues blood and water. Anatomists tell us that the water came from the pericardium, or casement around the heart. It is enough: even Pilate must now cease to "marvel that he is already dead:" his heart has been pierced by the soldier's spear.

The Jews who hated Jesus knew that he had promised to rise from the dead on the third day; hence they came to Pilate, "saying, Sir, we remember that that deceiver said, while he was yet alive, After three days I will rise again. Command therefore that the sepulcher be made sure until the third day, lest his disciples come by night, and steal him away, and say unto the people, He is risen from the dead; so the last error shall be worse than the first. Pilate said unto them, Ye have a watch; go your way, make it as sure as ye

---

[8] John 19: 26, 27, 35,

can. So they went, and made the sepulcher sure, sealing the stone, and setting a watch."[9]

Now as these men were specially anxious to prove Jesus to be an impostor, and as they were so particular to set a guard over his tomb, we may be certain that they were sure that he was really dead before they left him; hence if the death of any man was ever made sure beyond a peradventure, it was that of Jesus Christ.

8. The centurion made an official report to Pilate, stating that Jesus was certainly dead: "And Pilate marveled if he were already dead; and calling unto him the centurion, he asked him whether he had been any while dead. And when he knew it of the centurion, he gave the body to Joseph."[10] Here, then, we have the certificate of a government officer affirming the fact of Jesus' death. No wonder, then, that a fact so thoroughly confirmed as this, and put beyond all question, was so universally believed by the Jews, Christians, and heathen, in the early ages, as we know this fact to have been. Christ died; there is no doubt about that. But the great question now is, Did he rise from the dead?

CHAPTER XXVIII.

DID CHRIST RISE FROM THE DEAD?

THE resurrection of our Lord Jesus Christ may be claimed as the chief corner-stone of Christianity. On it the New-Testament writers predicate his claims to the Messiahship.[1] With it the Christian

---

[9] Matt. 27: 63-66. [10] Mark 15: 44, 45.
[1] Acts 17: 31; Rom. 1: 4.

religion stands; without it, it falls. "But as I am brought forward to this most wonderful of all events, the resurrection of Jesus Christ, which is, too, the capital item in the apostolic testimony, and the fact on which the whole religion and hopes of Christianity depend and terminate, I feel strongly disposed to show that this is the best attested fact in the annals of the world. For I wish to have it placed upon record, and to be known as far as this work ever shall extend, either in time or place, that in our view the shortest and best, because the most irrefragable way, to prove the whole truth and absolute certainty of the Christian religion, is to prove the resurrection of Jesus Christ from the dead. This proved, and deism, atheism, and skepticism of every name fall prostrate to the ground. The atheist will himself say, Let this be proved, that Jesus Christ rose from the dead, walked upon this earth, ate, drank, and talked with men for forty days afterward, and, in the presence of many witnesses, ascended up into Heaven, and after his ascent thither, sent down infallible proofs that he was well received in the heavenly world, and I will believe." [2]

Yes; prove the resurrection of Jesus, and you have forever settled the truthfulness of the Christian religion. Plato argued about the immortality of the soul; but Paul declares that Christ brought life and immortality to our bodies. The question in dispute among the Jews was not, Is the soul immortal? but, Shall the dead ever come to life again? [3] This was what the Sadducees questioned, and what Jesus affirmed.[4] This is the central pillar of the Christian's hope.

---

[2] Campbell's Debate with Owen, p. 290.
[3] Job 14: 14.   Matt. 22: 23–33.

RESURRECTION OF CHRIST. 217

The resurrection of Christ is so essential to Christianity that one of its ablest advocates once said, "And if Christ be not risen, then is our preaching vain, and your faith is also vain."[5] Then this apostle proceeds to argue the question by stating that "Christ died for our sins according to the Scriptures, and that he was buried, and that he rose again the third day."[6] He asks the Corinthians to believe these facts, and promises them salvation upon the ground that they keep them in memory. But he does not require them to believe without evidence; hence he proceeds to state his evidence:—

1. "He was seen of Cephas." What better testimony could be required? Here is the testimony of a living witness; not to an opinion, but to a fact, to what *he had seen*. He had seen Christ after he had risen, and therefore knew what it was to which he was bearing testimony.

2. "He was seen of the twelve." Here, then, are twelve witnesses, all bearing testimony that they had seen Christ alive after he was deposited in the tomb. Certainly this is sufficient. "In the mouth of two or three witnesses every word shall be established." It seems that the Lord is determined to leave the infidel without excuse, by encompassing this subject with such a "cloud of witnesses" that no sophistry can evade it. Hence,

3. "He was seen of above five hundred brethren at once."[7] Paul does not tell us how many more than five hundred brethren there were, but informs us that there were "above" that number. But the infidel shall have the advantage of all the odd numbers. We will therefore suppose there were

---

[5] 1 Cor. 15: 14.   [6] 1 Cor. 15: 3, 4.   [7] Verse 6.

just five hundred, to which add the twelve, and we have five hundred and twelve. This is enough to prove any point that can be proved by human testimony. But this is not all.

4. "He was seen of James, then of all the apostles."[8]

5. "And last of all, he was seen of me also."[9]

Here, then, are at least five hundred and thirteen witnesses enumerated by Paul, who testify that Christ had been raised. All of them saw him, and some of them talked with him.[10] And some ate and drank with him after his resurrection.[11] Certainly no one can question the competency of the witnesses.

After Paul states the number of witnesses, he appeals to the majority of them as still living, and refers the Epicureans to them. This he would not have ventured to do, had he not been conscious of the truth of his statement; for he must have known that those sagacious Grecian philosophers would have exposed him. They had the disposition to do so, and, if the witnesses he mentions could not have been found, they had the ability to do it. The fact that they did not expose this great apostle to be in error, is a mighty evidence in favor of the resurrection of Christ. Paul, having now stated who his witnesses are, opens the case, and begins to argue as follows:—

1. He tells them that upon this testimony they had once believed. "So we preach, and so ye believed." Next, he says,

2. "And if Christ be not risen, then is our preaching vain, and your faith is also vain."[12]

---

[8] 1 Cor. 15:7. [9] Verse 8. [10] John 21.
[11] Acts 10:41. [12] 1 Cor. 15:14.

What motive could stimulate us to preach the resurrection of Christ, if it be not true? Let the infidel think of this. Paul says, "He was seen of me also." What, except the truth, could have prompted Paul to make such a statement? It was not his education, nor the circumstances which had hitherto surrounded him. He was born a Jew, and all his anticipations and prospects were Jewish. His ancestors were Jews. His preceptor was a Jew. His associates were Jews. He was raised in the metropolis of Judea, at the feet of Gamaliel, and was intimately acquainted with the whole Jewish Sanhedrim. Not only so, but he was brought up in the greatest antipathy against Jesus and his followers.

As soon as his education was finished, he proceeded to persecute the Christians, and even went to strange cities in pursuit of them, and seized them, male and female, and cast them into prison, compelled them to blaspheme, and actually gave his voice against them when they were put to death.

But now he is preaching the resurrection of Christ, and confounding both Jew and Greek. We ask again, What has caused this great change? Paul answers the question: "He was seen of me also." And now, without any earthly motive or worldly prospect, except the one which Jesus sets before him, namely, "I will show him how great things he must suffer for my name's sake," [13] he begins to preach a risen Saviour. Certainly, if it had not been a fact that Christ was raised, his preaching was vain; for there was no compensation for it in this world, and there could be none in the world to come.

---

[13] Acts 9: 16,

3. "We are found false witnesses of God, because we have testified of God that he raised up Christ; whom he raised not up, if so be that the dead rise not."[14]

The Epicurean philosopher could only deny the resurrection of the dead by denying that Christ was raised; and that would impeach over five hundred witnesses; hence they must adopt the conclusion that nearly six hundred men had been bribed, and employed to testify to, and circulate, a falsehood. To believe this, would require more credulity than to believe that Christ was raised.

4. "If in this life only we have hope in Christ, we are of all men most miserable."[15] How true! They gained nothing in this life by publishing his resurrection, but stripes, reproaches, and dangers, and could gain nothing in the next, if he was not risen; for death would be an eternal sleep.

5. "If I have fought with beasts at Ephesus, what advantageth it me, if the dead rise not? Let us eat and drink, for to-morrow we die."[16] This statement is made as a proof of Paul's sincerity in proclaiming the doctrine of the resurrection by virtue of the resurrection of Christ; a point upon which he could not possibly have been mistaken.

Paul did not fight with beasts simply to amuse the crowd that were looking on; but his belief in the resurrection of Christ, and consequently the resurrection of all the dead, was so firm that rather than renounce it he would consent to enter the arena and fight for his life with the ferocious beasts of the forest. "I die daily," said he. Is not this a proof of his honesty and sincerity, as well as of the importance of the subject? What could in-

---

[14] 1 Cor. 15:15.   [15] Verse 19.   [16] Verse 32.

duce him thus to do,—to die every day, *i. e.*, to daily expose himself to death, and suffer as much as the pains of death, rather than renounce his belief that Christ had been raised?

Again we ask, What but Paul's belief of the fact could have induced him to preach the resurrection of Christ, and, as a consequence, the resurrection of the dead? What could have induced him not only to endanger his life, but to be accounted the offscouring of the earth and the filth of all things, to suffer hunger, nakedness, stripes, imprisonment, and death, for promulgating a falsehood? Can the infidel show that the like has ever occurred? If Paul was a deceiver he was knowingly and designedly such; hence he must have willingly preferred foes to friends, pain to pleasure, misery to happiness, bonds to freedom, and death to life. Can the infidel believe all this?

"If weak thy faith, why choose the harder side?"

Infidels do not deny that the writers of the New Testament believed that Christ was raised. But they say, "There was a mistake somewhere; for the resurrection of Christ was a miracle, and no testimony can prove a miracle." As to where the mistake is, they are not agreed. Some do not pretend to know. Some are very certain that he did not die. Others are quite as sure he died but did not rise. How to account for the disappearance of the body they do not know. Some suppose that it may have been miraculously resolved back to its primitive elements, thus getting up one miracle to get rid of another. Others claim that the disciples stole him, and others that the guard stole him. One infidel, not long since, took all the above positions in a conversation of not an hour's length with the writer. If the patient reader will follow us, he shall soon see the fallacy of all these positions.

1. *Did the disciples steal him out of the sepulcher?* Jesus had plainly declared that he would rise the third day, and both the disciples and the Jews well knew of it. The fact that he thus publicly gave notice of his future resurrection, so that his keenest enemies were fully apprised of it, carries with it the strongest mark of sincere dealing. An impostor would not have done this. The Jews, knowing that Jesus had said he would rise the third day, took every possible precaution to make certain that the body was not taken from the grave by any one. Who, then, can believe that the disciples stole the body? Some, however, seem to think they did. In three days from the time he was put into the sepulcher the great stone which was placed at its mouth was rolled away, and the body of Jesus was missing. What had become of it? Great precaution had been taken, and every possible means used to keep the body entombed. The sepulcher was sealed with the Roman signet, thus endangering the life of any one who should meddle with it. In addition to this, a watch was placed there to guard the sepulcher, to keep the disciples from removing the body of their Master.

Is it possible that the soldiers could all have fallen asleep at once, and slept so soundly that they were not awakened by the rolling away of the stone, and the removal of the body of Jesus from the sepulcher, when the penalty of death was attached to the law which forbade their sleeping? A dead body is not to be removed by sleight of hand. It requires a number of hands to move it. The great stone could not have been moved by men walking on tiptoe to prevent discovery. So if the guard were really asleep, the noise of moving the stone, lifting the body, and the hurry of carrying it away, must have awakened them. And is it not strange that the disciples should have happened to know the exact time at which this miraculous sleep was to come simultaneously over every member of the guard, and be on hand to take the body of Jesus away? Then remember how cowardly these same disciples were only the day before. When Jesus was arrested, most of them ran and hid themselves. Peter, the boldest of them all, was cowed before a little maid, and denied that he ever knew Jesus. Where there was comparatively little danger they fastened the doors, while they timidly ate their supper at home.[17] Is it not strange that these trembling disciples should all at once have waxed so bold as to venture upon stealing the body of Jesus, and hiding it for the sake of preaching a risen Saviour, and that without the remotest prospect of any reward, either in this world, or in the world to come? The one who believes all these absurdities need not laugh at the credulity of Christians.

But suppose it were all true; suppose the guard did thus miraculously go to sleep, and the disciples did succeed in getting the body of Jesus, and hiding it so effectually that it has never been found from that day to this,—who knows that it is so? Who can testify to it, or assert it as a fact? Who saw the disciples steal the body of Jesus? No one. The members of the guard, being asleep, could not testify that the disciples stole it. All they could say, was, "The body was there when we went to sleep, but when we awoke, it was not there." For aught they or any one else knew, he arose from

---

[17] John 20: 19; Mark 16: 14.

the dead. When the infidel asks us to believe that the disciples stole the body of Jesus, he asks us not only to believe without testimony, but to believe contrary to all testimony.

2. *Did the guard steal the body from the tomb?* Some infidels say, Yes. We say, No. Infidels do not pretend to have any evidence that the guard stole Jesus. But when they deny his resurrection they are compelled to account somehow for the disappearance of his body; and the idea that the disciples stole it is so inconsistent that many of them cannot adopt it. Their only subterfuge is to affirm that the guard stole it. A little examination will convince the reader of the absurdity of this position.

The sealing of the stone placed at the door of the sepulcher forbade the guard to remove it, as positively as it did the disciples. The guard were there to secure the body in the tomb, and their guilt would have been the same, whether they removed it or permitted some one else to remove it. Is it reasonable to suppose they would hide that body, and thus expose themselves to death? Suppose we for a few moments reject all common sense, and adopt the position that the guard removed the body for the purpose of utterly confounding the disciples when the proper time should arrive. Suppose the disciples were as credulous, enthusiastic, and fanatical, as infidels claim that they were. Mary, on the morning of the first day of the week, goes to the sepulcher, and finds the stone rolled away and the body gone. "There," cries she, "he is risen, just as I expected. I will go and tell the disciples;" and away she goes, saying, "He is risen! he is risen!" The disciples respond, "Certainly, we expected him to rise this morning."

The guard can hardly keep the secret of what they have done. "It is too good to keep." But they impatiently await the arrival of the fiftieth day. The time comes. Pentecost is here. The Jews are assembled from every quarter, and Peter begins to preach. Hear him:—

"Ye men of Israel, hear these words: Jesus of Nazareth, a man approved of God among you, by miracles and wonders and signs, which God did by him in the midst of you, as ye yourselves also know; him, being delivered by the determinate counsel and foreknowledge of God, ye have taken, and by wicked hands have crucified and slain; whom God hath raised up, having loosed the pains of death; because it was not possible that he should be holden of it."[18]

And then he proceeds, like all other fanatics, to quote Scripture to prove his doctrine. "Therefore let all the house of Israel know assuredly that God hath made that same Jesus, whom ye have crucified, both Lord and Christ."[19]

But just then a stir is heard in the audience; all eyes are turned toward the door; and what do they behold? A band of Roman soldiers carrying a dead man. They lay him before Peter, and as they uncover his face we hear them say, "Peter, here is your Prince of life; here is the one that you say is alive." What a quietus this must have put on Peter's preaching!

This would be a beautiful theory for the skeptic. It lacks only one essential element, and that is truth. They did not present the body of Jesus before Peter, for the very good reason that they did

---

[18] Acts 2: 22–24.   [19] Acts 2: 36.

not have it. Nor did anybody ever afterward find the body, or any trace of it. No; they knew he had risen, hence they cried out, "What shall we do?" Peter told them to repent and be baptized; and, strange to tell, *three thousand of the murderers of Jesus were baptized in his name before night.* Is it possible that they were baptized in the name of a dead man, and one whom living they had despised and killed? Believe it who can; we cannot. So far from the body of Jesus being stolen by the guard, they, enemies as they were, were the first witnesses of his resurrection.

Notwithstanding every effort to keep the Messiah in the grave, on the third morning "the angel of the Lord descended from Heaven, and came and rolled back the stone from the door, and sat upon it. His countenance was like lightning, and his raiment white as snow; and for fear of him the keepers did shake, and became as dead men. And the angel answered and said unto the women, Fear not ye; for I know that ye seek Jesus, which was crucified. He is not here; for he is risen, as he said. Come, see the place where the Lord lay."[20] "Some of the watch came into the city, and showed unto the chief priests all the things that were done. And when they were assembled with the elders, and had taken counsel, they gave large money unto the soldiers, saying, Say ye, His disciples came by night and stole him away while we slept. And if this come to the governor's ears, we will persuade him, and secure you. So they took the money, and did as they were taught. And this saying is commonly reported among the Jews until this day."[21]

---

[20] Matt. 28 : 2-6.   [21] Matt. 28 : 11-15.

The watch bore testimony to the resurrection of Christ, and this made it necessary to call an especial assembly of the priests and elders, who decided that it would not do to let it be known that Christ had risen; hence they bribed the watch, paying them large sums of money, and instructed them to say, "His disciples came by night, and stole him away while we slept." Infidel, do you want the testimony of this watch after they have been thus bribed? We do not; especially when they contradict their own word for the sake of "filthy lucre." We choose to receive the testimony which they gave before they met with the council of priests.

Matthew boldly states that it was commonly reported among the Jews that the disciples stole the body of Jesus. "Suppose the whole history here mere fiction,—the resurrection itself, the earthquake, the fright of the soldiers, and the story they were hired to tell,—suppose none of these ever happened. Now the gospels, whenever they were published, whether ten, fifty, or five hundred years after the time at which these things are said to have taken place, state that a story was then, at the time of their publication, commonly reported among the Jews, that the body of Jesus was stolen by his disciples. But if there was no resurrection, of course no such story could have been reported among the Jews; and the falsehood of the gospels would have been demonstrated on the spot. And how stupid must these writers have been, if impostors, to make a statement which everybody knew was false, and which must so plainly seal the condemnation of their histories. Can any man bring himself to believe that he who had ingenuity enough to invent the gospel history, would have been so blind as not to see the bearing of this observation?"[22]

Having now remōved the main objection to the truth of the resurrection of Christ, we will proceed to offer additional arguments in its favor. A strong argument may be predicated upon the fact that the disciples did not expect him to arise, nor were they, after the resurrection, willing to believe that he had risen. Listen to the disciples as they journeyed from Jerusalem to Emmaus: "We trusted that it had been He which should have redeemed Israel."[23] This expression implies that they had lost all hope. Their preparation for the embalming of the Saviour, also proves their incredulity about his resurrection, and the fact that they did not expect him to rise. When Jesus was buried, the last lingering hope of the disciples was buried with him.

On the third morning the women went to embalm their Lord. As they hastened toward the place, they said among themselves, "Who shall roll us away the stone?" But when they reached the sepulcher, to their utter astonishment the stone was rolled away. They looked into the sepulcher, but their Lord was not there. They did not yet suspect that he had risen. Hear them saying, with aching hearts and tearful eyes, "They have taken away the Lord out of the sepulcher, and we know not where they have laid him." After this the other women appear to have left the sepulcher, "but Mary stood without at the sepulcher, weeping." Looking up, she saw Jesus, but did not recognize him. "She, supposing him to be the gardener, saith unto him, Sir, if thou have borne him

---

[22] Christianity vs. Infidelity, pp. 237. 238.
[23] Luke 24 : 21.

hence, tell me where thou hast laid him, and I will take him away." [24] She had not yet learned that the Lord had risen. But Jesus now removes her suspense; he said unto her, Mary; she turned and joyfully recognized him as her Master. In obedience to his command, she went with her companions, and told the apostles that she had seen the Lord. "And their words seemed to them as idle tales, and they believed them not."

In order to settle the question, and to relieve the disciples of suspense, as well as to convince the women of their mental hallucination, Peter and John resolved themselves into a committee to investigate the matter. So they ran to the sepulcher. John, being the swiftest of foot, got there first. He stooped down and looked into the sepulcher, and saw the linen clothes, but saw not the Lord. Meanwhile Peter arrived, and, being naturally impulsive, immediately went into the sepulcher, and, as he moved the linen clothes about, in order to be sure that he was not mistaken, he became convinced that the Lord was not there. Yet he did not believe that he had risen until with his own eyes he gazed upon his resurrected Lord. [25]

The disciples were not yet willing to believe; hence, as before remarked, two of them, as they journeyed from Jerusalem to Emmaus, reasoned together very doubtingly about the events which had taken place. Said they, "We trusted that it had been He which should have redeemed Israel." Then they added, with a little ray of hope, that certain women had astonished them by reporting that an angel had appeared to them saying that Jesus was alive. But they had little faith in this report.[26]

---

[24] John 20:15 [25] Luke 24:1-12. [26] Luke 24:13-34.

Dear reader, are you astonished that Jesus should upbraid them, saying, "O fools, and slow of heart to believe all that the prophets have spoken; ought not Christ to have suffered these things, and to enter into his glory?"[27]

Next he appeared to the eleven as they sat at meat. One would think that they were prepared to believe, especially if they could see him with their own eyes; yet they were not. "But they were terrified and affrighted, and supposed that they had seen a spirit. And he said unto them, Why are ye troubled? and why do thoughts arise in your hearts? Behold my hands and my feet, that it is I myself: handle me and see; for a spirit hath not flesh and bones, as ye see me have. And when he had thus spoken, he showed them his hands and his feet. And while they yet believed not for joy, and wondered, he said unto them, Have ye here any meat? And they gave him a piece of a broiled fish, and of a honey-comb. And he took it, and did eat before them."[28]

Certainly all room for deception was gone. When they supposed they had seen a *phantasma*, they had the privilege of undeceiving themselves on that point by handling him, and knowing that it was Jesus himself; that he really had flesh and bones. So determined was the Saviour to bar against unbelief that he called for food, and ate before them. They were now fully convinced. But Thomas happened not to be of the number present. The other disciples, eager to convince him of the resurrection of Christ, "said unto him, We have seen the Lord. But he said unto them, Except I shall see in his hands the print of the nails, and put my

---

[27] Luke 24: 25, 26.   [28] Verses 37–43.

finger into the print of the nails, and thrust my hand into his side, I will not believe." [29]

We may wonder whether Thomas will be gratified; whether that most convincing of all tests will be given. Yes; Thomas must be convinced, though it is done by thrusting his hand into the wounded side of the Saviour. When Jesus met him with the other disciples, "then saith he to Thomas, Reach hither thy finger, and behold my hands, and reach hither thy hand, and thrust it into my side; and be not faithless, but believing. And Thomas answered and said unto him, My Lord and my God. Jesus saith unto him, Thomas, because thou hast seen me, thou hast believed; blessed are they that have not seen, and yet have believed." [30]

Certainly no further testimony can be required. Luke fully expressed the true state of the case when he said that Jesus "showed himself alive after his passion by many *infallible* proofs, being seen of them [the disciples] forty days, and speaking of the things pertaining to the kingdom of God." [31]

Reader, never was any fact more abundantly proved than the fact that Jesus Christ did rise from the dead. Consider what has been proved. Consider how very carefully the Jews guarded that sepulcher; that it was death for the soldiers to sleep on guard; that those soldiers had no motive for removing the body themselves, or that if they had removed it they would afterward have produced it when the disciples were creating such an excitement by affirming that Jesus was alive. Why did not some of those sharp-eyed enemies hunt up the body and bring it forward to refute the statement of the disciples? Nay, the soldiers themselves, at

---

[29] John 20:25.   [30] Verses 27-29.   [31] Acts 1:3.

the risk of their lives for being off the post of duty, left the grave in fear, and told the truth,—that Jesus was risen. We have seen that the disciples were too timid to undertake so bold a thing as to rob that grave with the armed guard about it. Their persistent unbelief concerning his resurrection, after he had risen, demonstrates that they never conceived the idea of asserting his resurrection till the facts compelled them to do so. They saw him with their own eyes; they saw the wounds in his hands and feet and side; they saw him eat honey and fish; they heard his words; they handled him with their own hands.[32] They were with him as familiar friends,[33] not merely once or twice, but many times, for forty days after his resurrection. Now, under these circumstances, when a dozen men all affirm that they positively knew these things to be facts, we must either certainly believe what they affirm, or believe that they all deliberately lie in the most blasphemous manner. But no one familiar with the lives of the apostles will believe them to have been such hardened wretches and arrant hypocrites. They suffered everything for their faith, and finally gave their lives to prove their sincerity.

"Now we all admit that a man may be sincerely wrong in his *opinions*, and so misled as to die for them rather than to retract. But if, in matters of *fact*, such as the assassination of Julius Cæsar, the death of Napoleon, or the battle of Bunker Hill, where the fact is submitted to all the senses, our senses could not be relied on, there would be an end to all certainty in the world. Now when a person is so fully persuaded of such facts as to die

---

[32] 1 John 1:1.   [33] Acts 10:41.

in attestation of them, the death of such a person is not only a proof of his sincerity, but of the fact, because it is an object of sensible proof in which there was no possibility of deception.

"The martyr to an opinion, in dying, says, *I sincerely think*. But the martyr to a fact, in dying, says, *I most assuredly saw*, or *I certainly heard*. Now the possibility of thinking wrong, even after having thought for years, is quite conceivable; but the possibility of seeing or hearing wrong, or not seeing or hearing at all, when opportunities have been frequent, and every way favorable; is inconceivable." [34]

The resurrection of Jesus, then, is a fact; one of the most carefully guarded and well-attested facts that was ever recorded. And if Christ was raised from death, then Christianity is true; the Bible is true; and infidels are the open enemies of Jesus Christ. Beware how you reject such overwhelming evidence as this, and risk the salvation of your soul against it. Unbeliever, are you prepared to meet Christ, and to prove him an impostor?

CHAPTER XXIX.

THE INSPIRATION OF THE BIBLE PROVED BY PROPHECY.

ONE of the strongest evidences of the truth of the Bible is the fulfillment of its prophecies. It contains numerous predictions of events which lie entirely beyond the ken of human wisdom. Human

---

[34] Campbell's Debate with Owen, p. 297.

sagacity could never have foreseen and foretold the numerous remarkable events which the history of the world records as exact fulfillments of the predictions of the ancient seers of God.

The evidences of prophecy are so extensive that it cannot be expected they will all be exhibited in one short chapter. "We are like the man who stands by an immense magazine of wheat. He may take a handful and hold it out to view; but he cannot exhibit each grain in the mass to the eye of any purchaser; it would be a task endless and painful."[1] We can do no more than bring a handful of the fruit from the good land, and exhibit it as a specimen of what the reader may find if he will go into the labor of research.

The evidences of prophecy are of a superior kind. They have advantages over every other kind of evidence. For the proof of miracles we must have recourse to ancient history; and the argument on the authenticity and integrity of the Bible is handed down from generation to generation without increasing in strength. But the fulfillment of prophecy may come under our own observation, or be conveyed to us by living witnesses. Also, this class of evidence is daily gaining strength. Prophecy is, and has been, fulfilling throughout the earth since the uttering of the first prediction, and will continue thus to do until " all things which God hath spoken by the mouth of all his holy prophets since the world began," shall have met their accomplishment.

The mere publication of a prediction is no proof that it is a revelation from God; but any one prediction which has been fulfilled, is of itself an evi-

---

[1] Nelson on Infidelity, p. 34.

dence of a supernatural revelation, or, more properly speaking, is a revelation. For surely no one but God himself can foretell distant future events, which depend entirely upon Him " who worketh all things after the counsel of his own will."

If, then, one instance of the undoubted accomplishment of prophecy can be produced, we have established the position that a revelation has been given to man. And if the prophets have faithfully foretold the *first* advent of the Messiah, they may have been as faithful in foretelling his *second* advent. If they have prophesied truly concerning Nineveh, Babylon, Tyre, Rabbah, and Jerusalem, the prophecies concerning the time when " the cities of the nations " shall fall, and great Babylon come in remembrance before God, may also prove true. If they have been correct in foretelling the state of the Jews, the Egyptians, and other nations, they may not mistake when they foretell the whirlwind that shall go forth from nation to nation, the result of which will be that " the slain of the Lord shall be at that day from one end of the earth even unto the other end of the earth."

The remark has often been made that most of the prophecies are obscure, and some of them so highly symbolical that they cannot be understood. We admit that there are obscurities and symbols in prophecy; so there are in other important writings; but who thinks of rejecting any of the sciences because of obscurity? And as far as the symbols are concerned, we know of not one which is given without a rule by which it can be interpreted. God has manifested great wisdom in the use of symbols, for in so doing he has hidden his mysteries from the wise and prudent, and revealed them unto babes.

All Protestants agree that the little horn, brought

to view in Dan. 7, which was to wear out the saints of the Most High, etc., is the papal power. Indeed, every specification of that prophecy has been fulfilled in that power. Now suppose that, instead of clothing this prophecy in symbolic language, the Lord had ordained that it should read as follows: "And the Pope of Rome shall come up and shall destroy three of the ten kingdoms, namely, the Heruli, the Vandals, and the Ostrogoths, and shall wear out the saints, and put seventy-five millions of them to death, and abolish the second and change the fourth commandment," would not the prophecy written in this manner preclude the possibility of its own fulfillment? If it had read so, the Bishop of Rome could have understood it as well as any one, the result of which would have been, he never would have taken the name of Pope; or, if he had, he would have had that part of Daniel's prophecy expunged from the Bible, so that we should have been deprived of it.

It is strange that infidels allow all other writers and speakers to deal in symbols and figures of speech, and yet do not allow the authors of the Bible the same privilege.

Our public speakers talk of the American Eagle, of its spreading its pinions from the Atlantic to the Pacific, of its wings being bathed in blood, etc., etc. Infidels never object to this, nor do they have any trouble in understanding such expressions when used by political orators. Why will they not also allow the God of the Bible the privilege of symbolism? "When, therefore, the skeptic insists that prophecy be given literally in the style of history written in advance, he simply requires that God would make it utterly unintelligible. We can gather clear and definite ideas from the significant hieroglyphics of symbolic language, but the literalities of history written in advance would be worse to decipher than the arrow-headed inscriptions of Nineveh. Just imagine to yourself Alexander the Great reading Guizot, instead of Daniel; or Hildreth, as being less mysterious than Ezekiel; and meeting, for instance, such a record as this: 'In the year of Christ, 1847, the United States conquered Mexico, and annexed California.' 'In the year of Christ—what new Olympiad may that be?' he would say. 'The United States, of course, means the States of the Achæan League, but on what shore of the Euxine may Mexico and California be found?' What information could Aristotle gather from the record that 'in 1857 the trans-Atlantic telegraph was in operation'? Could all the augurs in the seven-hilled city have expounded to Julius Cæsar the famous dispatch, if intercepted in prophetic vision, 'Sevastopol was evacuated last night, after enduring for three days an infernal fire of shot and shell'? Nay, to diminish the vista to even two or three centuries, what could Oliver Cromwell, aided by the whole Westminster Assembly, have made of a prophetic vision of a single newspaper paragraph of history written in advance, to inform him that 'three companies of dragoons came down last night from Berwick to Southampton by a special train, traveling $54\frac{1}{2}$ miles an hour, including stoppages, and embarked immediately on arrival. The fleet put to sea at noon, in the face of a full gale from the S. W.'? Why, the intelligible part of this single paragraph would seem to them more impossible, and the unintelligible part more absurd, than all the mysterious symbols of the Apocalypse."[2]

---

[2] Fables of Infidelity, pp. 132, 133.

But for the gratification of infidels we propose to confine ourselves to those prophecies which are not clothed in symbolic language, and the specifications of which are so numerous that no human sagacity could have pointed them out.

1. *The dispersion of the Jews.* Take the prophecies concerning the Jews. Read them and mark their fulfillment, though it should astonish you. We can select only a very few, those plainly foretelling their dispersion among all nations. Moses, their great prophet, fifteen hundred years before Christ, thus strikingly foretold what should happen to that nation:—

"The Lord shall cause thee to be smitten before thine enemies. Thou shalt go out one way against them, and flee seven ways before them; and shalt be removed into all the kingdoms of the earth." "And thou shalt become an astonishment, a proverb, and a byword, among all nations whither the Lord shall lead thee." "And the Lord shall scatter thee among all people, from the one end of the earth even unto the other; and there thou shalt serve other gods, which neither thou nor thy fathers have known, even wood and stone. And among these nations shalt thou find no ease, neither shall the sole of thy foot have rest; but the Lord shall give thee there a trembling heart, and failing of eyes, and sorrow of mind. And thy life shall hang in doubt before thee; and thou shalt fear day and night, and shalt have none assurance of thy life."[3]

The remarkable preservation of the Jews as a distinct people, though scattered among all nations, is thus forcibly stated: "Lo, the people shall

---

[3] Deut. 28: 25, 37, 64–66.

dwell alone, and shall not be reckoned among the nations."[4] Another prophet declares, "My God will cast them away, because they did not hearken unto him; and they shall be wanderers among the nations."[5]

Thus they were to become wanderers among the nations. Now, reader, look at these prophecies candidly. They were written by Moses thirty-three hundred years ago, before Israel had entered the promised land, thousands of years before any of our modern nations had been born. These prophecies were written out in the old Hebrew language, and have been read every day since by the very nation to whom they refer,—the Jews. Now note the remarkable fulfillment of these predictions. For nearly four thousand years the Jews have been a distinct people. They went down into Egypt and dwelt in the midst of a powerful nation; but they came out as distinct a race as they went in. In the land of Palestine they were surrounded on every side by other nations, with whom they dwelt and even intermarried more or less; but yet they preserved their distinct identity.

They went into captivity in Babylon, and were dispersed among the heathen; but they came back as distinctly and peculiarly Jewish as they went away. They were under the rod of the Romans; but they remained Jews still. After the destruction of the temple, A. D. 70, they began to be scattered among all nations, and for eighteen hundred years they have been scattering more and more widely, till now you can go to no climate, or country, or people, where Jews are not. You may find them in Asia, Europe, Africa, and America; but

[4] Num. 23:9.   [5] Hosea 9:17.

they are Jews everywhere and always. They are dispersed among the Armenians, the French, the English, the Spanish, the Americans,—everywhere; but they are Jews still. They dwell, a few in this village, a hundred in that, and a thousand in another, mingled among the people; and yet they are not of them; they are Jews.

How shall we account for this singular phenomenon? The history of the world presents nothing else like it. Other nations rise up, continue distinct for a while, then go down, and are entirely lost in the great mass. Look at our own country. Thousands from all nations are pouring in here; French, Germans, Danes, and all other nationalities, are represented among us. For two or three generations their nationality is preserved; but after that it is entirely lost. They mingle with the people about them, and their genealogy and nationality are lost. But not so with the Jews, though they have been resident here for two hundred years,— longer than the representatives of most other nations; yet they are Jews, as distinct from all the rest of us as was the first Jew that landed on our shores. This is a remarkable fact, with which every intelligent person is acquainted. The Jews are dispersed everywhere, yet they are citizens nowhere.

The Jew is an astonishment. Go into almost any clothing-store in our large cities, and you will see a phenomenon for which you never can account except from the Scriptures. There is the Jew, preserving all the peculiarities possessed by his nation eighteen hundred years ago. How does it happen that for so long a period he has resisted all the customs of society, all the powers of persecution, and all other almost irresistible influences driving him toward amalgamation with other nations?

"In the face of the power of the Chinese Empire, in spite of the tortures of the Spanish Inquisition, amid the chaos of African nationalities and the fusion of American democracy, in the plains of Australia and in the streets of San Francisco, the religion, customs, and physiognomy of the children of Israel are as distinct this day as they were three thousand years ago, when Moses wrote them in the pentateuch, and Shishak painted them on the tombs of Medinet Abou. How does the infidel account for it? It will not do to allege the favorite story about purity of blood and Caucasian race; for the question is, How does it happen that this people, and this people alone, have kept the blood pure, while all other races are so mingled that no other race can be found pure on earth? Besides, lest any should suppose such a cause sufficient for their preservation, another nation, descended from the same father and the same mother,—the children of Jacob's twin brother,—have utterly perished, and there are not any remaining of the house of Esau.

"Human sagacity, with all the facts before its face, cannot give any rational account of the causes of this anomaly. It cannot tell to-day why this people exists separate from, and scattered through, all nations, from Kamtchatka to New Zealand; how, then, could it foretell, three thousand years ago, this singular exception to all the laws of national existence? While the sun and moon endure, the nation of Israel shall exist as God's witness to God's word,—an undeniable proof that the mouth of the Lord hath spoken it."[6]

But the Jew is not only an astonishment, but is

---

[6] Fables of Infidelity, pp. 149, 150.

actually a proverb and byword among all nations. How often we hear of a person being as "rich as a Jew," "swearing like a Jew," "lying like a Jew," etc. It is so among all nations. "Moses foretold that they should be removed into all the kingdoms of the earth, scattered among all people, from one end of the earth even unto the other,—find no ease or rest,—be oppressed and crushed always,—be left few in number among the heathen,—pine away in their iniquity in their enemies' land,—and become an astonishment, a proverb, and a byword unto all nations. These predictions were literally fulfilled during their subjection to the Chaldeans and Romans; and, in later times, in all nations where they have been dispersed. Moses foretold that their enemies would besiege and take their cities; and this prophecy was fulfilled by Shishak, king of Egypt, Shalmaneser, king of Assyria, Nebuchadnezzar, Antiochus Epiphanes, Sosius, and Herod, and finally by Titus."[7]

Though they have been so widely dispersed among all nations, they have remained distinct from them all; and, notwithstanding the various oppressions and persecutions to which they have in every age been exposed in different parts of the world, "there is not a country on the face of the earth where the Jews are unknown. They are found alike in Europe, Asia, America, and Africa. They are citizens of the world, without a country. Neither mountains, nor rivers, nor deserts, nor oceans, which are the boundaries of other nations, have terminated their wanderings. They abound in Poland, in Holland, in Russia, and in Turkey. In Germany, Spain, Italy, France, and Britain,

---

[7] Horne's Introduction, vol. i. p. 324.

they are more thinly scattered. In Persia, China, and India,—on the east and west of the Ganges,—they are few in number among the heathen. They have trodden the snows of Siberia, and the sands of the burning desert; and the European traveler hears of their existence in the regions which he cannot reach, even in the very interior of Africa, south of Timbuctoo. From Moscow to Lisbon, from Japan to Britain, from Borneo to Archangel, from Hindostan to Honduras, no inhabitant of any nation upon earth would be known in all the intervening regions but a Jew alone."

"What a marvelous thing is this," says Bishop Newton, "that after so many wars, battles, and sieges; after so many rebellions, massacres, and persecutions; after so many years of captivity, slavery, and misery, they are not destroyed utterly, and though scattered among all people, yet subsist a distinct people by themselves! Where is anything like this to be found in all the histories, and in all the nations, under the sun?"

Again the same writer says: "What nation hath subsisted as a distinct people in their own country so long as these have done in their dispersion into all countries? And what a standing miracle is this, exhibited to the view and observation of the whole world! Here are instances of prophecies delivered above three thousand years ago, and yet, as we see, fulfilling in the world at this very time; and what stronger proof can we desire of the divine legation of Moses? How these instances may affect others, I know not; but as for myself, I must acknowledge they not only convince, but amaze and astonish me beyond expression."

Contrast a moment the wonderful preservation of this peculiar nation, with the overthrow and extinction of many nations with whom they were once contemporary. Take the Amalekites, for instance. Of them, God said in the days of Moses, " I will utterly put out the remembrance of Amalek from under heaven." [8] The Amalekites were at that time a powerful nation; and long afterward they were strong enough to subdue the Jews and rule over them. Why should they not have been the nation to continue forever, and the Jews the ones to be soon exterminated? But no; the prophecy ordained the reverse of this, and so it came to pass. Where is Amalek now? Utterly blotted out from the face of the earth thousands of years ago. Not a descendant of Amalek walks the earth, while the Jews to-day number six millions. What has become of the Philistines? where are the Moabites? and who could find a Canaanite to-day? Not one of all these nations exists.

" Where are the Assyrians and Chaldeans? Their name is almost forgotten. Their existence is known only to history. Where is the empire of the Egyptians? The Macedonians destroyed it, and a descendant of its ancient race cannot be distinguished among the strangers that have ever since possessed its territory. Where are they of Macedon? The Roman sword subdued their kingdom; and their posterity are mingled inseparably among the confused population of Greece and Turkey. Where is the nation of ancient Rome, the last conquerors of the Jews, and the proud destroyers of Jerusalem? The Goths rolled their flood over its pride. Another nation inhabits the ancient city. Even the language of her former people is dead. The Goths, where are they? The Jews, where are

---

[8] Ex. 17: 14.

they not? They witnessed the glory of Egypt, and of Babylon, and of Nineveh; they were in mature age at the birth of Macedon and of Rome; mighty kingdoms have risen and perished since they began to be scattered and enslaved; and now they traverse the ruins of all, the same people as when they left Judea, preserving in themselves a monument of the days of Moses and the Pharaohs, as unchanged as the pyramids of Memphis, which they are reputed to have built. You may call upon the ends of the earth, and will call in vain for one living representative of those powerful nations of antiquity by whom the people of Israel were successively oppressed; but should the voice to gather that people out of all lands be now heard from Mount Zion, calling for the children of Abraham, no less than six millions would instantly answer to the name, each bearing in himself unquestionable proofs of that noble lineage.

"What is this but a miracle? Connected with the prophecy which it fulfills, it is a double miracle. Whether testimony can ever establish the credibility of a miracle, is of no importance here. This one is obvious to every man's senses. All nations are its eye-witnesses."[9]

Look a moment at the prophecy concerning the desolation of their land, which was once so rich and fertile, a land flowing with milk and honey: "And I will make your cities waste. . . .
"And I will bring the land into desolation; and your enemies which dwell therein shall be astonished at it."[10] Judea was once a perfect garden, rich, fruitful, and thriving. It supported millions

---

[9] M'Ilvaine's Evidences, pp. 264, 265.
[10] Lev. 26:31, 32.

of people. All over its hills roamed great flocks of sheep and herds of cattle. There were thousands of farms under good cultivation, thriving villages, large cities, fine palaces, gold and silver in abundance. But alas! all this has passed away. To-day the whole land is desolate; her temples are burned down; her palaces have been reduced to mere hovels; her villages are no more; her teeming millions are gone. The land is sterile and uncultivated; its fruit is small and poor, and there is no pasture on the hills. How literally the word of God has been fulfilled! Let the infidel Volney, after visiting that land, tell of its appearance. He thus writes of it:—

"Here, said I, here once flourished an opulent city; here was the seat of a powerful empire. Yes! these places, now so desert, were once animated by a living multitude; a busy crowd circulated in these streets, now so solitary. Within these walls, where a mournful silence reigns, the noise of the arts, and shouts of joy and festivity, incessantly resounded. These piles of marble were regular palaces; these prostrate pillars adorned the majesty of temples; these ruined galleries surrounded public places. Here a numerous people assembled for the sacred duties of religion, or the anxious cares of their subsistence. Here industry, parent of enjoyment, collected the riches of all climates, and the purple of Tyre was exchanged for the precious thread of Sercia; the soft tissues of Cachemire, for the sumptuous tapestry of Lydia; the amber of the Baltic, for the pearls and perfumes of Arabia; the gold of Ophir, for the tin of Thule. And now a mournful skeleton is all that subsists of this powerful city! Naught remains of its vast domination, but a doubtful and empty remembrance! To the tumultuous throng which crowded under these porticoes has succeeded the solitude of death. The silence of the tomb is substituted for the bustle of public places. The opulence of a commercial city is changed into hideous poverty. The palaces of kings are become a den of wild beasts; flocks fold on the area of the temple, and unclean reptiles inhabit the sanctuary of the gods. Ah! how has so much glory been eclipsed? How have so many labors been annihilated? Thus perish the works of men, and thus do empires and nations disappear!"

"Alas! I have passed over this desolate land! I have visited the palaces, once the theater of so much splendor, and I beheld nothing but solitude and desolation. I sought the ancient inhabitants and their works, and could find only a faint trace, like that of the foot of a traveler over the sand. The temples are fallen, the palaces overthrown, the ports filled up, the cities destroyed, and the earth, stripped of inhabitants, seems a dreary burying place. Great God! whence proceed such fatal revolutions? What causes have so altered the fortunes of these countries? Why are so many cities destroyed? Why has not this ancient population been reproduced and perpetuated? Thus absorbed in contemplation, a crowd of new reflections continually poured in upon my mind. Everything, continued I, confounds my reason, and fills my heart with trouble and uncertainty."[11]

This prophecy, then, has been fulfilled, infidels themselves being witnesses.

2. *The destruction of Jerusalem.* No prophecy of the New Testament is plainer than that given

---

[11] Volney's Ruins, book i.

by Jesus himself concerning the destruction of Jerusalem. When the disciples called his attention to the wonderful glory of the temple, he answered them thus:—

"As for these things which ye behold, the days will come, in the which there shall not be left one stone upon another, that shall not be thrown down." "There shall be great distress in the land, and wrath upon this people. And they shall fall by the edge of the sword, and shall be led away captive into all nations; and Jerusalem shall be trodden down of the Gentiles, until the times of the Gentiles be fulfilled." [12]

As every intelligent reader knows, this prophecy was fulfilled in the destruction of Jerusalem by the Roman army, A. D. 70, about forty years after it was foretold by Jesus. The event is renowned in history as being one of the most awful scenes of bloodshed, misery, and destruction that the world has ever witnessed. The city was entirely leveled with the dust, and its beautiful temple was wholly destroyed. The very ground upon which it stood was plowed as a field. The Jews to this day remember with hatred the name of the Roman soldier, Rufus, who plowed up the foundations of their city and temple.

The Jews were taken into captivity and dispersed in every direction. About sixty years after this, Jerusalem was partially rebuilt by the Emperor Adrian. A Roman colony was settled there, and the Jews were forbidden to enter the city upon the pain of death. Soon after this the Jews made a desperate effort to recover their city, but they entirely failed in their attempt. About three hun-

---

[12] Luke 21: 6, 23, 24.

dred years after Christ, in the time of Constantine the Great, they made another effort to regain their city, but again failed.

Soon after this, Julian the apostate came to the throne of the Roman Empire. Having renounced Christianity, he became a powerful opponent of the faith. He was a learned and talented man, and had all the resources of the empire at his command. As paganism was not yet dead, all its votaries rallied around him. He determined to overthrow Christianity, and prove Jesus to have been a liar; for he had said that Jerusalem should remain trodden down by the Gentiles. This mighty emperor vowed that he would prove this a falsehood; Jerusalem should be rebuilt, the Jews should be gathered back, and their temple should rise again. All the Jews throughout the world were exultant. They were all ready to second the effort of the emperor, and return to their beloved city. At his call they came from all the provinces of the empire, and assembled in triumph on the hills of Zion. The Roman army was on the ground. Everything that was needed was furnished in abundance by the Roman emperor. The zeal of the Jews knew no bounds. Their wealth, their strength, their time, even the labor of their most delicate females, was devoted with the utmost enthusiasm to the preparation of the ground, covered then with rubbish and ruins. They had as their leader one who sat on Cæsar's throne, who nodded and the nations trembled. Certainly the prospect looked fair for the prophecy of Jesus soon to be proved false.

" The Emperor Julian was an accomplished warrior. He ruled over the land shown to Abraham, and ten times as much. He hated the Saviour as bitterly as did those who crucified him. He had been educated under the sound of the gospel, and knew the words of Christ. He was familiar with the writings of the Evangelists. He resolved that Jerusalem should be trodden under foot of the Israelites, instead of the Gentiles. The reader is invited to examine the account of this as given by one whose hatred of the gospel equaled that of Julian himself. The author of the 'Decline and Fall of the Roman Empire' was under the necessity of stating some facts concerning this effort to defeat the words of Christ, made by the mighty and the wise. At the invitation of the emperor, the children of Judah assembled to rebuild their temple, and to claim the inheritance of their fathers. Their enthusiasm was wonderful. Even their delicate females were seen carrying off rubbish in their silver vails. Their joyful companies labored, cheered on by the sound of instruments of music and animating voices. But the emperor did not trust this undertaking to the Israelites alone. Wealthy as they were, devoted as they were, he resolved to make this matter more certain still. He could aid by his proclamations, his royal decrees, or his treasures, but it was not a trifle he had at heart; to show the gazing earth that the Jewish worship *should* be restored where the Lord had said the Gentiles should continue to tread, was no ordinary achievement. He went himself to their aid with those cohorts and those legions that had crossed rivers, hills, and deserts, that had elevated or dethroned monarchs, and before whom it was hard indeed to stand. Here, then, was to be a trial of the strength of Heaven and the strength of earth, in determined contest and fairly balanced opposition. Jews and Romans, Christians and heathen, gazed to see whether the emperor could or could not go

EVIDENCES FROM PROPHECY. 251

contrary to the declaration uttered by the Man of sorrows, who had not where to lay his head."[13]

"Was the temple rebuilt? The foundations were not entirely laid. Why? Was force deficient; or zeal, or wealth, or perseverance, when Roman power and Jewish desperation were associated? Nothing was lacking. 'Yet,' says Gibbon, 'the joint efforts of power and enthusiasm were unsuccessful, and the ground of the Jewish temple still continued to exhibit the same edifying spectacle of ruin and desolation.' There was an unseen hand, which neither Jews nor emperors could overcome. The simple account of the defeat of this threatening enterprise of infidelity is thus given by a heathen historian of the day, a soldier in the service, and a philosopher in the principles of Julian :—

"'While Alypius, assisted by the governor of the province, urged with vigor and diligence the execution of the work, horrible balls of fire breaking out near the foundation, with frequent and reiterated attacks, rendered the place from time to time inaccessible to the scorched and blasted workmen; and the victorious element continuing in this manner obstinately and resolutely bent, as it were, to drive them to a distance, the undertaking was abandoned.' 'Such authority should satisfy a believing, and must astonish an incredulous mind,' acknowledges even the skeptical Gibbon. He cannot but own that 'an earthquake, a whirlwind, and a fiery eruption, which overturned and scattered the new foundations of the temple, are attested with some variations, by contemporary and respectable evidence.'

"One writer, who published an account of this

---

[13] Nelson on Infidelity, pp. 62-64.

wonderful catastrophe in the very year of its occurrence, boldly declared, says Gibbon, *that its preternatural character was not disputed, even by the infidels of the day*. Another speaks of it thus: 'We are witnesses of it, for it happened in our time, not long ago. And now, if you should go to Jerusalem, you may see the foundations open; and if you inquire the reason, you will hear no other than that just mentioned.'

"Whether this attempt of Julian was defeated by miraculous interposition, is a question which our present object does not require us to argue. Two things are certain: First, that the power and wealth of the Gentiles were united with the devoted enthusiasm of the Jews, to defeat the prophecy of Christ, by rebuilding the temple, by re-establishing its ritual, and by reorganizing a Jewish population as possessors of Jerusalem; secondly, that contrary to all expectation, when nothing was lacking for the work, and none in the world lifted a finger against it, it was suddenly abandoned on account of sundry alarming and singular phenomena bursting from the original site of the temple, by which even the fanaticism of the Jews was deterred, and the enmity of Julian to the gospel defeated. These undeniable facts are sufficient to show, with impressive evidence, the hand of God protecting the prophetic character of our Lord.

"When, in connection with these, you consider the great anxiety so universally felt among the Jews of all centuries, to enjoy the privilege of living and dying in Jerusalem; that no risk of life, or sacrifice of property, would be thought too great for the purpose of once more setting up the gates and altars of the holy city; that the nation is now as numerous as at any period of its ancient glory;

and yet, that during almost the whole period since the destruction of Jerusalem, so entirely have Jews been prevented from living on her foundations that they have had to purchase dearly the permission to come within sight of her hills, and to this day are taxed and oppressed to the dust, as the cost of being allowed to walk her streets and look at a distance upon her Mount Moriah,—you will acknowledge that the prediction of our Saviour in reference to their exclusion from Jerusalem, has been not only most strikingly fulfilled, but fulfilled in spite of the most powerful causes and efforts for its defeat."[14]

Here we have a visible evidence, a standing proof, of the fulfillment of this remarkable prophecy. There lies Jerusalem to-day, trodden under foot of the Gentiles. For the last eighteen hundred years it has been in this condition. The Romans first colonized it; and the temple to Jupiter was erected over the sepulcher of Jesus. Next, the Mohammedans put their feet upon it. The Arabians, the Turks, and sometimes rulers from Egypt, continued to trample it under their feet for hundreds of years. Again and again has Jerusalem been captured and recaptured; but never have the Jews taken it.

The Jerusalem of sacred history is a fact no more. Not a vestige remains of the capitol of David and Solomon; not a monument of Jewish times is standing. There lies the old city, groaning under the oppression of the Gentiles. Reader, think of it a moment. Six millions of Jews to-day,—the wealthiest people in the world! Why do they not return to their native land? Why do they not rebuild their beloved city, re-erect their temple, and thus

---

[14] M'Ilvaine's Evidences, pp. 309–312.

prove this prophecy a failure? How the infidels would lift their heads and rejoice should this be done! What a grand evidence it would furnish them that Jesus was a false prophet! For eighteen centuries his prophecy concerning Jerusalem has been pointed to by Christians as proof of his divine character. Why have not all the host of infidels, Jews, and pagans, long ere this risen up and defeated this prophecy? Let them answer if they can. Reader, God has spoken, and his word must be fulfilled.

3. *The spread of the gospel.* "And this gospel of the kingdom shall be preached in all the world for a witness unto all nations; and then shall the end come."[15]

Here is another prophecy of our divine Saviour. He declared in plain terms to his little handful of disciples, that the gospel which he was there beginning in so humble a manner should at length be preached in all the world for a witness to all nations. It should be presented to every nation on the earth. How little prospect there seemed to be of this when he made that declaration! Jesus was a poor young man of Judea. He was hated by his own countrymen. He had neither education, wealth, connections, nor means of his own. His disciples were all poor and uneducated. He was known only a few miles around. To all human appearance, his gospel would soon go out in obscurity; but right there he foretold its wonderful spread, as we have seen. Now, reader, has this prophecy failed, or has it been accomplished? Eighteen centuries have rolled by, and where is there a nation to-day that has not heard the gospel?

---

[15] Matt. 24:14.

Where is there a nook or corner of the earth where it is unknown? These words of Jesus have been translated into nearly three hundred different languages, comprising all the principal languages of the world. Missionaries of the cross have gone by thousands and tens of thousands in every direction, until they have penetrated to all the dark corners of the earth. Listen to the following testimonies:—

"Now, having looked at the forces which are at work for the spread of Christianity, let us look a little at the field in which it has been carried. The whole world has been ransacked and explored; there is not a corner on the globe where Christianity is unknown. And the missionaries that have been, now for more than half a century, at work, have leavened almost every quarter of the globe."
"At this moment, over China, Japan, Persia, Hindostan, Turkey, East, South, West, and North Africa, Madagascar, Greenland, and the hundreds of Pacific isles, are thirty-one thousand Christian laborers."[16]

"Three-fourths of the earth's surface is under Christian government and influence, including the probable great future centers of the world's population. The whole heathen world is dotted with missions, each reproducing in miniature the same processes that have marked the general church."[17]

At a union meeting in the Baptist church, Stockton, California, Rev. J. Thompson, district secretary and agent of the California Bible Society, stated that the Bible is now printed in between two hundred and sixty and three hundred languages

---

[16] *Christian Union.*
[17] *Phrenological Journal*, Oct., 1871.

and dialects, and that there is not a nation in the world where it is not known.

Infidel reader, that prophecy is fully and exactly accomplished, which proves that Jesus did know the future. He also said he would come at last to judge the world. Are you ready?

4. *Egypt.* Some six hundred years before Christ, the prophet Ezekiel thus foretold what was to be the future condition of Egypt:—

"And I will bring again the captivity of Egypt, and will cause them to return into the land of Pathros, into the land of their habitation; and they shall be there a base kingdom. It shall be the basest of the kingdoms; neither shall it exalt itself any more above the nations: for I will diminish them, that they shall no more rule over the nations."[18] "And I will make the rivers dry, and sell the land into the hand of the wicked; and I will make the land waste, and all that is therein, by the hand of strangers: I the Lord have spoken it. Thus saith the Lord God: I will also destroy the idols, and I will cause their images to cease out of Noph; and there shall be no more a prince of the land of Egypt; and I will put a fear in the land of Egypt."[19]

Egypt was one of the most ancient and powerful kingdoms of the world. At the time this prophecy was uttered, nothing could seem more improbable than its accomplishment. Egypt contained eighteen thousand cities and seventeen million inhabitants. It was the most fertile country in the world. It was protected by the Mediterranean on one side, the Red Sea on another, and an impassable desert on the other. For hundreds of years, Egypt had

---

[18] Eze. 29: 14, 15.   [19] Eze. 30: 12, 13.

been the center of learning, and mighty monarchs had ruled over it. But God had spoken. He said it should become a base kingdom, even the basest of kingdoms; it should no more exalt itself above the nations; strangers should rule over it, and there should be no more a prince of the land of Egypt. It is now more than twenty-four centuries since these prophecies against Egypt were delivered. Have they been fulfilled? Yes, in every particular; and there lies prostrate Egypt to-day, a mournful witness to the truthfulness of God's holy prophets.

"Invaded and subdued by Nebuchadnezzar, king of Babylon, according to the word of the Lord, both by Jeremiah (46:13), and by Ezekiel (30:10), subjected afterward by the Persians under Cambyses, and to the Macedonians by Alexander the Great (Isa. 19:1-13), Egypt was, after his death, governed for nearly three centuries by the Ptolemies, the descendants of one of his generals, at which time it was an opulent kingdom, till, about thirty years before the Christian era, it came under the Roman yoke; and Saracens, Mamelukes, and Turks have since successively ruled over it. Its history shows the completion of the prophecies concerning it." [20]

Now let the infidel Volney once more bear testimony to the truth:—

"Such is the state of Egypt. Deprived twenty-three centuries ago of her natural proprietors, she has seen her fertile fields successively a prey to the Persians, the Macedonians, the Romans, the Greeks and Arabs, the Georgians, and, at length, the race of Tartars, distinguished by the name of

---

[20] Keith on Prophecy, p. 116, abridged ed.

Ottoman Turks. The Mamelukes, purchased as slaves, and introduced as soldiers, soon usurped the power and elected a leader. If their first establishment was a singular event, their continuance is not less extraordinary. They are replaced by slaves brought from their original country. The system of oppression is methodical. Everything the traveler sees or hears reminds him that he is in the country of slavery and tyranny. In Egypt there is no middle class, neither nobility, clergy, merchants, nor land-holders. Ignorance, diffused through every class, extends its effects to every species of moral and physical knowledge." [21]

Gibbon, another infidel, says: "A more unjust and absurd constitution cannot be devised than that which condemns the natives of a country to perpetual servitude under the arbitrary dominion of strangers and slaves. Yet such has been the state of Egypt above five hundred years. The most illustrious sultans of the Baharite and Borgite dynasties were themselves promoted from the Tartar and Circassian bands; and the four-and-twenty beys, or military chiefs, have ever been succeeded, not by their sons, but by their servants." [22]

Says Mr. Patterson: "Mehemet Ali cut off the Mamelukes, but still Egypt is ruled by the Turks, and the present ruler (Ibrahim Pasha) is a foreigner. It is needless to remind the reader that the idols are cut off. Neither the nominal Christians of Egypt, nor the iconoclastic Moslems, allow images to appear among them. The rivers, too, are drying up. In one day's travel, forty dry water-courses will be crossed in the Delta; and water-skins are needed now around the ruined cit-

---

[21] Volney's Travels, vol. i. pp. 74, 108, 110, 198.
[22] Decline and Fall, vol. vi. pp. 109, 110, Dublin ed. 1789.

ies whose walls were blockaded by Greek and Roman navies."[23]

Again, after quoting Eze. 29:15, he says: "Every traveler will attest the truth of this prediction. The wretched peasantry are rejoiced to labor for any who will pay them five cents a day, and eager to hide the treasure in the ground from the rapacious tax-gatherer. I have seen British horses refuse to eat the meal ground from the mixture of wheat, barley, oats, lentiles, millet, and a hundred unknown seeds of weeds and collections of filth which form the produce of their fields. For poverty, vermin, and disease, Egypt is proverbial."[24]

Unbeliever, have you not been surprised as you have compared the prophecies concerning Egypt with the last twenty-four centuries of its history? Or have you taken no pains to compare them? If not, are you not justly censurable for your unbelief? Is it not strange that among all the nations of the earth, only one answers to this prediction of the prophet, and that the very one that the prophet calls by name in his prophecy?

5. *Babylon.* The prophets are no less definite in giving the future history of particular cities, than in that of the nations concerning which we have been inquiring. Especially is the reader's attention called to the prophecies concerning the ancient city of Babylon. But before quoting these prophecies it may be necessary to give a brief description of "the beauty of the Chaldees' excellency."

Alexander Keith says: "The walls of Babylon, before their height was reduced to seventy-five feet

---

[23] Fables of Infidelity, p. 141.   [24] Id. p. 142.

by Darius Hystaspes, were above three hundred feet high; they were eighty-seven feet broad, and forty-eight miles in compass. The temple of Belus, six hundred feet in height; the artificial hanging gardens, which, piled in successive terraces, towered as high as the walls; the embankment which restrained the Euphrates; the hundred brazen gates; the palace built by Nebuchadnezzar, surrounded by three walls, forty-eight miles in compass; and the adjoining artificial lake, the circumference of which was far more than a hundred miles, and its depth, by the lowest account, thirty-five feet,—all displayed many of the mightiest works of mortals, concentrated in a single spot. This great Babylon was the glory of kingdoms, and the beauty of the Chaldees' excellency, the golden city, the lady of kingdoms, and the praise of the whole earth. The Scriptures, which thus describe it, mark minutely every stage of its fall, till it should become what now it is,—a complete desolation. And every feature of its present aspect is delineated in the prophecies, with all the precision with which they could be drawn by the traveler who looks on fallen Babylon itself."[25]

Isaiah thus predicts the doom of this great city: "And Babylon, the glory of kingdoms, the beauty of the Chaldees' excellency, shall be as when God overthrew Sodom and Gomorrah. It shall never be inhabited, neither shall it be dwelt in from generation to generation; neither shall the Arabian pitch tent there; neither shall the shepherds make their fold there. But wild beasts of the desert shall lie there; and their houses shall be full of doleful creatures; and owls shall dwell there, and satyrs

---

[25] Keith on Prophecy, p. 101, abridged ed.

shall dance there. And the wild beasts of the islands shall cry in their desolate houses, and dragons in their pleasant palaces; and her time is near to come, and her days shall not be prolonged." "I will also make it a possession for the bittern, and pools of water; and I will sweep it with the besom of destruction, saith the Lord of hosts."[26]

This prediction was uttered before Babylon arrived at the height of its glory. Nebuchadnezzar had not yet said, "Is not this great Babylon which I have built?" The walls were thought to be impregnable, and twenty years' provisions were stored up within their inclosure, so that in case of a siege the inhabitants could not be starved out. Certainly Isaiah must have been considered insane when he uttered such predictions. "Babylon," said he, "shall be as when God overthrew Sodom and Gomorrah." Not destroyed as suddenly, but as effectually.

After the destruction of Babylon by Cyrus, Alexander attempted to restore it to its former glory, and make it the metropolis of a universal empire. He set ten thousand men to work at it; but he died, and the undertaking was abandoned. The glory of Babylon kept diminishing. At the commencement of the Christian era, Babylon was only partially inhabited. Peter dated his first epistle from that place. But the fiat had gone forth, "It shall be as Sodom and Gomorrah." So it kept going down, until, in the fourth century, its walls formed an inclosure for wild beasts, and the "golden city" was converted into a hunting ground. The name of Babylon was cut off from the history of the world. A long interval succeeded without any history con-

---

[26] Isa. 13: 19-22; 14: 23.

cerning it, or even its site being known. So literally has the language, "It shall be as when God overthrew Sodom and Gomorrah," been fulfilled.

The prophet goes on to state that it shall never be inhabited, neither shall it be dwelt in from generation to generation, neither shall the Arabian pitch tent there, neither shall the shepherds make their folds there.

Every one who has visited the spot attests the fulfillment of this wonderful prediction. Mignon declares Babylon to be "a tenantless and desolate metropolis." Sixteen centuries have passed since it was inhabited by a single human being. Another writer says: "The name and remnant are cut off from Babylon. There the Arabian pitches not his tents; there the shepherds make not their folds; but wild beasts of the desert lie there, and their houses are full of doleful creatures. It is a possession for the bittern, and a dwelling-place for dragons; a wilderness, a dry land, and a desert; a burnt mountain, empty, wholly desolate, pools of water, heaps, and utterly destroyed; a land where no man dwelleth; every one that goeth by it is astonished."

The dread of evil spirits prevents the Arab from pitching his tent there. Mignon declares that though he was fully armed and attended by six Arabs he could not induce them by any reward to spend the night among the ruins of Babylon, from their apprehension of evil spirits, so completely is the prophecy fulfilled,—"The Arabian shall not pitch tent there."

Sir Robert K. Porter saw two majestic lions in the ruins of a palace, and Mr. Fraser says: "There were dens of wild beasts in various places; and Mr. Rich perceived in some a strong smell like that of a lion. Bones of sheep and other animals were seen in the cavities, with numbers of bats and owls." [27]

These testimonies prove the fulfillment of that part of the prophecy which reads: "Wild beasts of the desert shall lie there; and their houses shall be full of doleful creatures; and owls shall dwell there, and satyrs shall dance there. And the wild beasts of the islands shall cry in their desolate houses, and dragons in their pleasant palaces; and her time is near to come, and her days shall not be prolonged."

But the same prophet has declared that it should be made a possession for the bittern, a water-fowl, and that it should be pools of water; while another prophet has said that it should become heaps, a dwelling-place for dragons; and in another place, that it should become a burnt mountain. [28]

How can such contradictions be true? inquires the infidel. But it is really true that while the lion in one part of Babylon is howling his testimony to the truth of God's word, the bittern in a pool in another part, and the "doleful creatures" in another, and the heaps and burnt mountains in still others, are warning the traveler over its ruins to "take heed" to the "sure word of prophecy."

Mignon says: "Morasses and ponds tracked the ground in various places. For a long time after the subsiding of the Euphrates, a great part of this place is little better than a swamp; at another season it is 'a dry waste and burning plain.' Even at the same period, 'one part on the western side is low and marshy, and the other an arid desert.'" [29]

Mr. Alexander quotes Mignon as saying: "The whole view was particularly solemn. The majestic

---

[27] Fables of Infidelity, p. 144. [28] Jer. 51: 35-38, 25.
[29] Fables of Infidelity, p. 145.

stream of the Euphrates, wandering in solitude, like a pilgrim monarch, through the silent ruins of his devastated kingdom, still appeared a noble river, under all the disadvantages of its desert-tracked course. Its banks were hoary with reeds, and the gray osier willows were yet there, on which the captives of Israel hung up their harps, and, while Jerusalem was not, refused to be comforted. But how is the rest of the scene changed since then! At that time those broken hills were palaces—those long undulating mounds, streets—this vast solitude, filled with the busy subjects of the proud daughter of the East. Now, wasted with misery, her habitations are not to be found, and for herself, a worm is spread over her."[30]

6. *Tyre.* The Lord ordered the prophet Ezekiel hus to utter the doom of that renowned city:—

"And they shall destroy the walls of Tyrus, and break down her towers. I will also scrape her dust from her, and make her like the top of a rock. It shall be a place for the spreading of nets in the midst of the sea; for I have spoken it, saith the Lord God; and it shall become a spoil to the nations."[31]

Tyre was the New York of Asia, and at the time the prophet uttered these predictions it was the commercial metropolis of the world. All nations traded in its streets. The ships from every country anchored in its harbor. It flourished like a green bay-tree; and its wise men were renowned throughout all the world. Why should it not stand forever? But no, the prophet had spoken; his words must be fulfilled. It was not to become as Baby-

---

[30] Alexander's Evidences, p. 152.
[31] Eze. 26: 4, 5.

lon,—"desolate, without an inhabitant;" nor as Rabbah,—"a couching place for flocks;" nor yet as Damascus,—"a ruinous heap;" but its dust was to be scraped off, its timbers and stones thrown into the sea. It was to become a scraped rock, whereon fishers were to dry their nets.

The prophecy of Ezekiel has been so literally fulfilled that even Volney quotes it as a vulnerable fragment of antiquity, and applies it to Tyre. He says the vicissitudes of time, or rather the barbarism of the Greeks of the lower empire, and the Mohammedans, have accomplished the prediction.[32]

Passing over the destruction of Tyre by Nebuchadnezzar, prophesied of in Isa. 23, and also its destruction by Alexander, when its stones, timbers, and dust were thrown into the sea, to make a bridge to New Tyre, let us notice its present situation. The whole village of Tyre, says Volney, "contains only fifty or sixty poor families, who live obscurely on a trifling fishery." "The port of Tyre," says Dr. Shaw, "is choked up with sand and rubbish to that degree that the boats of those fishermen who now and then visit this once renowned emporium, and dry their nets upon its rocks and ruins, can, with great difficulty only, be admitted."

Infidel reader, sail down the coast of the Mediterranean to-day; look up the site of the ancient Tyre, and there you will find another interesting testimony to the truthfulness of God's prophecies. You will find but a few fishermen's huts, a few bare rocks where these fishermen dry their nets and mend their sails. Put this down in your diary, lay it up in your heart; for the God who foretold the ruin of that great city, has also foretold a day of fearful

---

[32] Volney's Travels, vol. ii. pp. 210-212.

Judgment for the ungodly, and you had better prepare for it.

7. *The four great kingdoms of the world.* One of the plainest prophecies of the Bible is to be found in the second and seventh chapters of Daniel, pointing out the rise and fall of the four great kingdoms of the world. Every school-boy is familiar with the fact that in the history of our world there have been, in succession, four great and mighty kingdoms, which have ruled over the nations of the earth. The first of these was Babylon, founded by Nimrod, the great-grandson of Noah.[33] This ancient kingdom gradually grew stronger and more extensive, until about six hundred years before Christ, when Nebuchadnezzar became its king. Under him it arrived at the height of its glory. It was then the grand, overshadowing kingdom of the world. All others were powerless before it. But in the year 538 B. C. this mighty kingdom was overthrown by the Medo-Persians, under Cyrus the Great. From that time, for about two hundred years, Persia was the most renowned kingdom in the world. It was opulent and powerful. All nations trembled before it.[34]

About three hundred years before Christ, Alexander the Great arose as king of the Greeks, and in a remarkably short time utterly overthrew the Persian Empire, conquered nearly all the known world, and founded the third great power in the earth,—the Greek Empire. Greece, then, was the third great kingdom of the world. But about a hundred and fifty years before Christ, Greece began gradually to decline, and Rome as steadily came up, until

---

[33] Gen. 10: 10.
[34] The above facts, with regard to Babylon and Medo-Persia, are treated of at great length in Rollin's Ancient History.

finally, in the year B. C. 30, she conquered the last division of the Grecian Empire, and succeeded in becoming the mistress of the world. All other kingdoms had to bow to Rome. Its empire became more extensive than any other kingdom had previously been. Gibbon says it was so extensive that the world became a safe and dreary prison to any man fleeing from the power of the empire. Its authority extended everywhere,—not a kingdom but that owned her superiority. Rome was the fourth kingdom of the world. It ruled not only in Africa and Asia, but also over all of Europe. About three or four hundred years after Christ, however, this mighty empire began to break up, and continued to decline until it was finally divided into ten kingdoms. These kingdoms were formed from the old empire, and most of them exist to-day in the kingdoms of modern Europe.

The above is an outline of the history of the great empires of our world, as every reading person knows.[35] Now turn to one of the prophets of the Lord, who wrote six hundred years before Christ, while Babylon was still at the height of its glory, and there we have these very empires most plainly pointed out in prophecy.

God gave Nebuchadnezzar a wonderful dream, and then sent his prophet Daniel to interpret it. Thus we read:—

"Thou, O king, sawest, and behold a great image. This great image, whose brightness was excellent, stood before thee; and the form thereof was terrible. This image's head was of fine gold, his breast and his arms of silver, his belly and his thighs of brass, his legs of iron, his feet part of iron and part

---

[35] See Rollin, Gibbon, Goldsmith, Goodrich, and other historians.

or clay. Thou sawest till that a stone was cut out without hands, which smote the image upon his feet that were of iron and clay, and brake them to pieces. Then was the iron, the clay, the brass, the silver, and the gold, broken to pieces together, and became like the chaff of the summer threshing-floors; and the wind carried them away, that no place was found for them; and the stone that smote the image became a great mountain, and filled the whole earth." [36]

Notice that there are four parts to this wonderful image: 1. The head of gold; 2. The breast of silver; 3. The sides of brass; 4. The legs of iron, the feet of iron and clay, and then finally the ten toes. Lastly comes the stone which destroys all these and fills the whole earth, and stands forever. Now read the prophet's explanation. In verses 37, 38, he says that this head of gold represents Nebuchadnezzar, or rather the kingdom, Babylon, of which he was the head. He goes on explaining: "And after thee shall arise another kingdom inferior to thee, and another third kingdom of brass, which shall bear rule over all the earth. And the fourth kingdom shall be strong as iron." [37] These four parts, then, represent four kingdoms. What do the ten toes mean? He continues: "And whereas thou sawest the feet and toes, part of potters' clay, and part of iron, the kingdom shall be divided." [38] The fourth, or iron, kingdom, then, was to be broken up into ten kingdoms. Now, reader, this is exactly what has happened. The next event is to be the setting up of God's eternal kingdom. [39] We inquire, How did Daniel know the history of the

---

[36] Dan. 2:31-35.
[37] Verses 39, 40
[38] Verse 41.
[39] Verse 44.

world so many thousand years in advance? Did he merely guess at it? Close guessing this must have been!

The same facts are again brought out in the seventh chapter of Daniel. Here the prophet saw four great beasts come up from the sea; the first was like a lion,[40] the second like a bear,[41] the third like a leopard,[42] the fourth a terrible beast, with ten horns.[43] After this he says the Judgment was set, and the books were opened.[44] Now, what do these beasts represent? In verses 17, 18, it is declared that these four great beasts are four kingdoms, which should arise, and then the kingdom of God should be established upon the earth, and should stand forever.

Twice, then, Daniel declared that there should be four great and leading kingdoms of the world before the end of time, and that the last, or fourth, should be divided into ten kingdoms. Reader, you know that these powers have thus arisen. With such unquestionable proof before you, will you not believe that these prophecies are the work of inspiration? Men are not gifted with the power of guessing so correctly as all this. We might select hundreds of such prophecies from the Bible, not one of which has ever failed in any particular, while nearly all of them have been minutely fulfilled, and the balance are fulfilling every year. We will close this chapter with one more evidence of the fulfillment of prophecy.

8. *The Messiah.* The prophecies of the Old Testament concerning Jesus Christ are so numerous as to take up a large share of those writings.

---

[40] Dan. 7:4.   [41] Verse 5.   [42] Verse 6.
[43] Verse 7.   [44] Verse 10.

Let us select a few, and notice their remarkable fulfillment. The first prophecy of the Messiah is found in Gen. 3: 15. It was promised that the seed of the woman should bruise the serpent's head. From this chapter to the very last in the Old Testament, there are innumerable references to both his first and his second advent.

It was promised that he should come of the seed of Abraham.[45] But Abraham had several sons; of which one of these should he come? It is plainly declared that he should come of Isaac. "For in Isaac shall thy seed be called."[46] But Isaac had two sons, Esau and Jacob; of which one of these was he to come? Here we are not left in doubt. He was to come of Jacob.[47] But Jacob had twelve sons; of which of these should the Messiah come? The word of God answers this question also. He was to descend from Judah. In Jacob's remarkable prophecy concerning Judah, he says, "The scepter shall not depart from Judah, nor a lawgiver from between his feet, until Shiloh come; and unto him shall the gathering of the people be."[48] All agree that this refers to the Messiah. He was to come of the tribe of Judah. But Judah had many descendants; of which of these families was Christ to be born? Again the Lord specifies. He was to come of the family of Jesse. "And there shall come forth a rod out of the stem of Jesse, and a Branch shall grow out of his roots."[49] But Jesse had eight sons; which of these was to be the father of this remarkable person? Once more the Lord particularizes. Christ was to be the son of David. "The Lord hath sworn in truth unto David; he

---

[45] Gen. 22: 18.   [46] Gen. 21: 12.   [47] Gen. 28: 14.
[48] Gen. 49: 10.   [49] Isa. 11: 1.

will not turn from it: Of the fruit of thy body will I set upon thy throne." [50]

Now, when Jesus did come it was exactly in the line here pointed out. He was the son of David, the son of Jesse, of the tribe of Judah, etc.

The very time when the Messiah was to come was also definitely located. In Gen. 49:10, before quoted, it was declared that the scepter should not depart from Judah until Shiloh came. Christ was born the very year when Augustus Cæsar imposed a tax upon the Jewish nation [51] as indicative of their subjection to the Roman government. Daniel is more definite still; he says: "Know therefore and understand, that from the going forth of the commandment to restore and to build Jerusalem, unto the Messiah the Prince, shall be seven weeks, and threescore and two weeks; the street shall be built again, and the wall, even in troublous times. And after threescore and two weeks shall Messiah be cut off, but not for himself." [52]

How remarkable is this prophecy! It plainly declares that the Messiah shall be cut off, but not on account of his own sins. How exactly this was fulfilled! He comes the very year when he should come. Commencing with the going forth of the commandment to restore and build Jerusalem, which was in the year 457 B. C., [53] it was to be sixty-nine prophetic weeks until the Messiah should come. Seven days to the week would be four hundred and eighty-three days, and as these were prophetic days, each day representing a year, it would be four hundred and eighty-three years. It was exactly that number of years from the going forth

---

[50] Ps 132:11.
[52] Dan. 9:25, 26.
[51] Luke 2:1-7.
[53] Ezra 7.

of that decree, to the baptism of Jesus, and the commencement of his ministry. Compare Ezra 7 with Mark 1. Reader, impostors do not risk their reputation in such definite statements as these.

Again: The Messiah was to be born of a virgin. Thus the prophet said, "Behold, a virgin shall conceive, and bear a son, and shall call his name Immanuel."[54] Jesus was born of the Virgin Mary.

The very town where he was to be born was definitely pointed out seven hundred and ten years before his birth. How remarkable is this fact! Now read the prophecy: "They shall smite the Judge of Israel with a rod upon the cheek. But thou, Bethlehem Ephratah, though thou be little among the thousands of Judah, yet out of thee shall He come forth unto me that is to be ruler in Israel; whose goings forth have been from of old, from everlasting."[55] Who is this personage who is to be the Judge of Israel? It is said that it is he "whose goings forth have been from of old, from everlasting;" or as the margin says, "from the days of eternity." This is none other than the Messiah. Moreover, it is the one who is to be ruler in Israel. It is the one who is to be smitten upon the cheek with a rod. This was the mighty Redeemer who was to come. Where was he to be born? Notice how definite is the statement: "But thou, Bethlehem Ephratah, though thou be little among the thousands of Judah, yet out of thee shall He come forth unto me that is to be ruler in Israel." From that day forward all Israel knew that the Messiah was to be born in Bethlehem. So, when Herod inquired of the chief priests where the King of Israel was to be born, they replied, "In Bethle-

---

[54] Isa. 7:14.   [55] Micah 5:1, 2.

hem," and then quoted this prophecy to prove it.[56] Jesus was born in that same little town.

Again: The Messiah was to go down into Egypt and be called out from thence; for thus the Lord said, "I loved him, and called my Son out of Egypt."[57] Out of Egypt he did come with his father.

A messenger was to be sent before the Messiah to prepare the way for him. "Behold, I will send my messenger, and he shall prepare the way before me; and the Lord, whom ye seek, shall suddenly come to his temple, even the messenger of the covenant, whom ye delight in. Behold, he shall come, saith the Lord of hosts."[58] John the Baptist did go before Jesus to prepare the people to believe on him.[59]

He was to ride into Jerusalem in a literal manner, sitting upon an ass, while the people were to shout and rejoice. "Rejoice greatly, O daughter of Zion; shout, O daughter of Jerusalem. Behold, thy King cometh unto thee; he is just, and having salvation; lowly, and riding upon an ass, and upon a colt the foal of an ass."[60] Every Sabbath-school scholar is familiar with the fact that it was just in this manner that Jesus did ride into Jerusalem while the multitude went before and after, shouting and praising God.[61]

The treachery of Judas was foretold.[62] The Messiah was to be betrayed for thirty pieces of silver, which were subsequently to be given for the potter's field. "And I said unto them, If ye think good, give me my price; and if not forbear. So

---

[56] Matt. 2:1-6.   [57] Hosea 11:1.   [58] Mal. 3:1.
[59] Luke 7:2.   [60] Zech. 9:9.   [61] Luke 19:30-40.
[62] Ps. 41:9; 55:12, 13.

they weighed for my price thirty pieces of silver. And the Lord said unto me, Cast it unto the potter; a goodly price that I was prized at of them. And I took the thirty pieces of silver, and cast them to the potter in the house of the Lord." [63] How plain this prophecy! All remember how it was fulfilled by the act of Judas in betraying Christ for thirty pieces of silver, and the appropriation of that silver to the purchase of the potter's field.

The Messiah was to die. "After threescore and two weeks shall Messiah be cut off, but not for himself." [64] Again: The prophet Isaiah, in speaking of the Messiah, says: "Who shall declare his generation? for he was cut off out of the land of the living. For the transgression of my people was he stricken. And he made his grave with the wicked, and with the rich in his death; because he had done no violence, neither was any deceit in his mouth." [65] Here it is plainly predicted that the promised Messiah shall be put to death; and Jesus was thus put to death.

At his death he was to be forsaken by his followers. "Awake, O sword, against my Shepherd, and against the man that is my fellow, saith the Lord of hosts. Smite the Shepherd, and the sheep shall be scattered; and I will turn mine hand upon the little ones." [66] Jesus was thus forsaken when he was crucified.

He was to be scourged and spit upon. "I gave my back to the smiters, and my cheeks to them that plucked off the hair; I hid not my face from shame and spitting." [67] Jesus was treated in just this manner, before his crucifixion. They scourged

---

[63] Zech. 11:12, 13. [64] Dan. 9:26. [65] Isa. 53:8, 9.
[66] Zech. 13:7. [67] Isa. 50:6.

him; they struck him on the check; and they spit in his face. All the important facts connected with his crucifixion are plainly foretold by the prophets, even to what his enemies would say on that occasion, how they would treat him, what they would give him to drink, how they would pierce his hands, his feet, his side, etc. Let us read a few of them:—

"All they that see me laugh me to scorn; they shoot out the lip, they shake the head, saying, He trusted on the Lord that he would deliver him. Let him deliver him, seeing he delighted in him." "They gaped upon me with their mouths, as a ravening and a roaring lion." "They pierced my hands and my feet. I may tell all my bones; they look and stare upon me. They part my garments among them, and cast lots upon my vesture."[68] How literally all these particularities of the prophecy were fulfilled!" Again: "And they shall look upon me whom they have pierced." And again: "And one shall say unto him, What are these wounds in thine hands? Then he shall answer, Those with which I was wounded in the house of my friends." "They gave me also gall for my meat; and in my thirst they gave me vinegar to drink."[69]

How can any person read these wonderful predictions, most of them written from seven hundred to a thousand years before Christ's time, and not be convicted that they must have been indited by the great God who knows the end from the beginning? How exactly and minutely every one was fulfilled in Jesus! Indeed, all the important events

---

[68] Ps. 22 : 7, 8, 13, 16–18.
[69] Zech. 12 : 10; 13 : 6; Ps. 69 : 21.

of his life are plainly pointed out in the Old Testament. It cannot be objected that any of these prophecies were dark, mysterious, or symbolical. No; they were clothed in the simplest language, and were literally fulfilled.

"This is a concise view of some of the predictions contained in the Old Testament, concerning the nature, birth, life, doctrine, sufferings, death, resurrection, ascension, and kingdom of the Lord and Saviour Jesus Christ. There can be no doubt respecting the priority of the predictions to the birth of Christ, because it is well known by every person who is at all conversant in these matters, that the Old Testament was translated out of Hebrew into the Greek language, and dispersed over the world, many years before Christ came; and that the latest of the predictions was upwards of three centuries before the birth of the Redeemer of mankind. Such a variety of circumstances, therefore, predicted concerning one man so many years before he was born, of so extraordinary a nature, and under such convulsions and revolutions of civil governments, all accomplished in Christ, and in no other person that ever appeared in the world, point him out with irresistible evidence, as the Saviour of mankind. I call upon and challenge the most hardened infidel in Christendom to refute the conclusion."[70]

"If the predictions did not originally refer to him, and only happened to be accomplished in him, it would be reasonable to suppose that out of the innumerable millions of men that have lived since they were published, some other individual, if not hundreds, would have appeared exhibiting the same

---

[70] Dr. Berg.

correspondence. Where is the record of such an event? Can the person be mentioned in whom there was even an approximation to the fulfillment exhibited in the history of Jesus? I need not say that no one ever pretended to be able to find such a person."[71]

Here we rest the argument. We believe it to be perfectly conclusive. If the reader has candidly weighed the mighty evidence here presented, he must be persuaded that the Bible originated with some higher intelligence than that of man; in fact, that it is what it claims to be, the word of God. If the prophecies which have been cited have all proved true, then we assuredly know that the balance will prove equally true; that those which plainly foretell the dreadful day of Judgment, the reward of the righteous, and the eternal death of the wicked, will be literally fulfilled. Reader, do you love that God whose word this is? Are you preparing to meet him? Have you given your heart to the Saviour? This is the grand question you should immediately settle.

CHAPTER XXX.

OBJECTIONS CONSIDERED.

INFIDELS are always urging us to answer their objections. This is their burden. As long as they can raise an objection to Christianity they feel very triumphant and self-satisfied; and they feel no interest to hear the vast amount of positive testimony

---

[71] M'Ilvaine's Evidences, pp. 271, 272.

which we have to offer in favor of the Bible and our religion. No; this has no weight with them. One trivial objection will outweigh it all. Hence their constant cry is, "What will you do with this objection? How will you answer that objection?" etc.

Now we have not room in this small volume to give even the shortest answer to the numerous objections which these cavilers raise. A recent writer has well said: "Many and painful are the researches usually necessary to be made for settling points of this kind. Pertness and ignorance may ask a question in *three* lines which it will cost learning and ingenuity *thirty pages* to answer. When this is done, the same question will be triumphantly asked again the next year, as if nothing had ever been written upon the subject. And as people in general, for one reason or other, like short objections better than long answers, in this mode of disputation, if it can be styled such, the odds must ever be against us; and we must be content with those of our friends who have honesty and erudition, candor and patience, to study both sides of the question."[1]

It is unequivocally true that every objection and cavil which the host of unbelievers have ever raised against the Christian religion has been candidly and thoroughly answered by Christians. These answers are published in books accessible to all. They will be found in the books recommended to the reader on page 16 of this volume. If doubters will not read those answers, they would not read the same if given here; hence I shall not attempt a task that would be useless.

The reader should remember that it is very easy

---

[1] Horne, Letters on Infidelity, p. 82.

to raise objections. Any simpleton can do that. Objections can be, and have been, raised against everything. When Fulton proposed to run his steamboat, thousands of objections were raised to it; and a host of doubters conclusively proved that he never could run a steamboat; but, nevertheless, the conception of genius was made a reality. And when the steam-cars were first invented, another crowd was on hand with unanswerable objections, thoroughly proving that such a thing as running carriages by steam could never be done; but the cars did run, notwithstanding. And when Morse proposed the telegraph, this race of doubting philosophers pronounced the thing impossible, and proved it so, as they thought. They raised objections which to themselves were perfectly satisfactory; but the telegraph was brought into successful operation, for all that.

Shall we reject the Bible and Christianity because of some seeming difficulty which every novice in religion cannot answer? Shall we throw away our Bibles because every simple-hearted Christian cannot solve every difficulty and reconcile every contradiction which we may imagine in the Bible? Infidels seem to think this a proper thing to do. But in following this plan they would have to reject every science in the world. Take the science of mathematics, the most undoubted and demonstrative of them all. Who does not know that it requires the very strongest minds and the most intense and thorough application to master its difficulties and to solve its problems? Addition, subtraction, multiplication, and division,—the fundamental principles of arithmetic, those which are necessary for every-day use,—are so simple that anybody can understand them by a very little application. But go beyond this, to fractions, decimal fractions, the rule of three, and then to problems in algebra and geometry, and how difficult the science becomes. Not one in a thousand, with the ordinary study which the most of men give the subject, could demonstrate one of these problems. Accost the first farmer, grocer, or common laborer you meet; open your algebra, and ask him to explain some of its difficult problems. Could he do it? No; he would be utterly confounded. He could tell neither its beginning nor its end. Would it be reasonable, because of this, to throw your algebra away, and pronounce the whole thing a humbug? "Oh, no," you say; "that would be foolish; these men have never studied algebra. Let us go to a scholar who has patiently and thoroughly studied this science for years; he can explain the problem." My friend, it is just so with the Bible. You expect farmers, mechanics, and day-laborers, who give the subject very little or no study, to be able understandingly and readily to clear up every difficulty in the Bible to your entire satisfaction, and that, too, in a word, or else you reject it as a humbug. Shame on you, unreasonable man! You would blush to be so unreasonable on any other subject.

As with mathematics, so with the Bible: the great, practical truths and duties of Christianity are so simple that any one may readily understand them. But there are other things not so readily understood, passages difficult of explanation. These require more study and learning. In this the Bible is just like all nature around us. Any one can warm himself in the light of the sun; but who can tell what the sun is, and how its rays come to us? It requires a profound astronomer for that. Any one can drop a stone to the earth; but who can tell why it drops,—can explain the mysteries of gravitation? Not one in ten thousand. Shall we, therefore, refuse to believe that it falls? So the fundamental facts and principles of the Bible are simple and plain to all, while some less important things are hard to understand.

Be it known, then, that a fair and reasonable answer can be and has been given to every objection which infidelity has ever raised against the Bible. But I have noticed that when you have answered the objections of one infidel, you have done nothing toward satisfying another. His objections are entirely of a different nature. You answer him, and a third one is on hand with something differing from both; and although his objection may have been answered a thousand times, yet he will urge it as triumphantly as though it had never been refuted.

But suppose we could not solve these difficulties, or remove these objections; would that settle the question in favor of infidelity? By no means; and why? Because, where infidelity can raise one objection, can make one argument against Christianity, Christians can propound a score of unanswerable questions to infidelity, can make a hundred sound arguments in favor of the Bible which unbelievers never have answered, and never can answer. So, dear friends, the objections are not all on one side. Do not think, therefore, that you escape all difficulty by adopting infidelity. You only increase your difficulty. Where you had one objection to answer before, you now have a score. Consider this fact well. If we have fairly proved the positions taken in the previous chapters of this book, and we are thoroughly satisfied that we have done so, then the Bible is the inspired word of God, Jesus

Christ is the Son of God, and Christianity is true. What will you do with all this mass of evidence? Will you throw it all away because of some apparent contradiction or slight objection, which, perchance, you have never seen answered? Be cautious how you act so foolishly.

It is the height of madness to seek to raise objections to positions fairly proved, especially such objections as those usually brought against the Bible. The plan of infidels has been to select a few isolated passages, which, perhaps from want of knowledge of oriental customs and habits, are hard to be understood, and upon the strength of these to deny the authority of the whole Bible, while the great chain of evidence by which its truthfulness is established continues unbroken, and the mass of proof offered in its behalf, untouched. The Saviour said that the gates of hell should not prevail against the church.[2] Neither shall they against the Bible. "As well might one attempt to destroy the giant oak by cutting away a few sticks of shrubbery about its roots, while he leaves the trunk unharmed. Such attacks, we repeat, are altogether ineffectual—they do not reach the question at issue, and the skeptic has made no progress in the overthrow of Christianity, until the historical facts by which it is established, and, with these, the very foundations of human knowledge, are all prostrated in the dust. Until he has accomplished this, every objection must fall short of the mark."[3]

Infidels in every age, from Celsus to the present time, have attacked the Bible; but have they fairly met and refuted the argument advanced in its favor? They have not. "Infidels have attacked

---

[2] Matt. 16:18.   [3] Christianity vs. Infidelity, p. 281.

Christianity; but anything may be attacked. They have slandered her doctrines, ridiculed her word, reviled her precepts, hated her holiness, and influenced many to go and do likewise; but neither hatred, nor reviling, nor ridicule, nor slander, is the test of truth. Have infidels ever resorted to the only fair and honest mode of meeting face to face the whole array of testimony which Christianity advances, by endeavoring coolly to prove, as a matter of historical evidence, that the authenticity of the New Testament and the credibility of its history are not sustained; that the miracles of Jesus have not been supported with adequate testimony; that the prophecies of the Scriptures have met their attestation in no accurate histories; that Christianity was propagated by human force alone, and its fruits are those of a corrupt and deceitful tree? I answer, No. There is no such effort in the books of infidelity. I read of speculations, opposed to our facts; insinuations, in answer to our testimonies; sneers, in reply to our solemn reasonings; assertions, where we demand arguments; levity and presumption, where an advocate of truth would have been serious and humble. But I know of no such thing as a book of infidelity in any sense corresponding in the nature, or grounds, or spirit of its reasoning, with such arguments for Christianity as those of Paley, or Lardner, or Gregory, or Wilson, and a thousand others, to which no man ever dared to attempt an answer. Infidelity, like an insect on the pillar of some stupendous temple, that can see no farther than the microscopic irregularities of the polished marble beneath its feet, may busy itself in hunting for little specks in the surface of the stately edifice of Christianity; but it has no such eye, and takes no such elevated stand, as would enable it to survey the whole plan, and judge of its pretensions by the mutual adaptation of its parts, the harmony and grandeur of its proportions." "Infidelity is all speculation. Reduce it to a residuum of inductive reasoning, and you bring it to nothingness. Strip it of its several envelopes of ingenious hypothesis and bold assertion and scoffing declamation, and you find nothing left but a man of straw,—an ugly shape to keep the hungry from the bread of life,—which you need only approach to discover that it is made of rags and stuffed with rottenness."[4]

The most formidable and deceptive form of infidelity comes in the shape of "philosophy;" not that true philosophy or science opposes the Bible, but that men hide their infidelity behind the sciences; and men that know but little of science, or the Bible either, talk as learnedly of the absurdities and incongruities of the Bible as though they had committed it to memory, and speak as fluently of science as though they had "ordained the laws that keep the planets in their courses." Some seem to think that they have only to reject the Bible and call it all "humbug," and they are philosophers at once,—that skepticism is an evidence of a great mind,—that there is no surer proof of intellectual superiority than to treat all religion as mere fable, fit only for the amusement of women and children. Hence come the groundless assertions concerning the Bible which are so confidently repeated. These things are regarded as an evidence of having arisen above the common herd of mankind, and outgrown their superstition. Would-be philosophers feel a kind of pride in plunging into the whirlpool of infidelity,

---

[4] M'Ilvaine's Evidences, pp. 481, 482, 485.

while many *great* minds tremble even to approach its brink. Many flatter themselves that they are fiends, who some day will be astonished to learn that they are only fools.

"Every little fledgling which has scarcely left its nest, or the care of its mother, hastens through the spelling book and primary reader, and then sets up for an oracle, discourses learnedly of spirit and matter, of the physical and moral worlds, the eternal and unbending laws of nature, the mysteries of time and space, the wonders and revelations of animal and spiritual magnetism, of the infinite and invisible, and deals with the profoundest questions of divine truth with more ease and familiarity, and not half the reverence of a Jesus or a Paul. He speaks as though he had sounded all the depths of knowledge, with an air of unquestionable authority. He talks of things known and unknown—mostly of the last. He uses coined formulas of speech, 'words of prodigious length and thundering sound.' He rises up into what he calls the spiritual view of all subjects. He expands, and becomes more and more transparent, till the inflation is so great as to end in the usual results of the law of expansion, or he passes off out of sight into infinite fogdum, and, like the comet that became entangled among the moons of Jupiter, never regains his orbit again, which, perhaps, is little cause for regret. The comet is scarcely needed to light up our evening skies, and its presence will not be missed while the fixed stars continue to shine on in their everlasting beauty.

"Now we are ready to say that we have no reverence whatever for this kind of philosophers, nor for their philosophy. It is a broad burlesque upon the name. It is all surface,—there is no depth to it. It does not come down into the earnest and solemn realities of life, and speak of our individual and social duties, relations, and responsibilities. It spends itself in asking questions, which, if answered, would lead to no valuable results. It apes the profound and mysterious. It occupies all its time in mere speculation, in weaving gossamer webs, and building rainbows on the ever-passing clouds. It talks like a parrot, but never works, never makes itself useful. . . . . In a word, this folly, absurdly called philosophy, is a mere baby, not to say idiotic, babbling sheer nonsense mostly, intelligible neither to itself nor to those who hear." [5]

"It is a phenomenon, like the advent of a great comet, to find a man profoundly versed in any science, attack the Bible. Your third or fourth rate men of learning attain distinction in this field. An anti-Bible writer or lecturer always has been promoted to that high eminence from the school-room, or the editorial sanctum of an unsuccessful newspaper, or his patients have not appreciated his physic, or he has failed in getting a patent-right for his wonderful perpetual motion, or possibly he has enlarged his practical knowledge of science in the laboratory of some Western College, and had his head turned by being asked to hear the mathematical recitations during the sickness of some professor. But to hear of men like Galileo, Kepler, Boyle, Newton, and Leibnitz, or of Lyell, Mantell, Herschel, Agassiz, Hitchcock, Balbo, Nichol, or Rosse, heading an attack upon Christianity, would be an unprecedented phenomenon. Such men are profoundly impressed with the thorough agreement between the facts of nature rightly observed, and the declarations of the Bible rightly interpreted.

---

[5] Christianity vs. Infidelity, pp. 6–8.

"Nevertheless, the other class, being both the most numerous and the most noisy, make up by perseverance for their deficiency of information, and counterbalance their ignorance by their assurance. Such writers, assuming that they have outstripped all the philosophers of former days, will tell you how foolishly David, and Kepler, and Bacon, and Newton, and Herschel, dreamed of the heavens declaring the glory of the Lord, and the firmament showing his handiwork; 'while at the present time, and for minds properly familiarized with true astronomical philosophy, the heavens display no other powers than those of natural laws, and no other glory than that of Hipparchus, of Kepler, of Newton, and of all who have helped discover them.' Theology belongs only to the infancy of the human intellect; metaphysical philosophy is the amusement of youth; but the full-grown man has learned to relinquish both religion and reason, and comes to the positive state of science in which the human mind, acknowledging the impossibility of obtaining absolute knowledge, abandons the search after the origin and destination of the universe, and the knowledge of the secret causes of phenomena. The crown of modern science is ultimately to be placed upon the brow of Atheism; but long before that eagerly desired achievement, the old Bible theology is to be buried beyond the possibility of a resurrection, under mountains of natural laws, and monuments of scientific discovery.

"These assertions, confidently made and perseveringly reiterated in the ears of ungodly men ignorant of the facts, of impetuous youths eager to throw off the restraints of religion, of Christians weak in the faith, and even poured into the unsuspecting mind of childhood, produce the most painful and often fatal results; and it becomes the imperative duty of the bishops of the church of Christ not to allow them to pass unchallenged, but to convince the gainsayers, and stop the mouths of these unruly and vain talkers; or, if that be not possible, to make their folly manifest to all men. The weapons for such a service are well-tried and abundant, and the difficulty lies only in making a proper selection."[6]

We now come directly to the question, Are the sciences really against the Bible? We answer, No. It is true that the Bible does not abound with lectures upon physiology, anatomy, hygiene, materia medica, chemistry, astronomy, or geology. It is not given for the purpose of teaching these subjects. God has given us the stars to teach us astronomy, the earth to teach us geology, and the Bible to teach us religion. Yet nothing in the Bible contradicts the sciences. As each new science has been discovered, it has been supposed by infidels that in it they would find a new ally; but, alas for infidelity, the older sciences have all proved to be of heavenly birth, and have given their testimony in behalf of God and the Bible; so will the new ones when more perfectly understood. Of all the sciences, geology, if it may be termed a science, has proved itself the most fallible; and yet its professors are the most noisy in their boasts of what they intend to prove.

As certain second-rate geologists are just now loudly boasting that geology overthrows the Bible record of creation, we will briefly consider that objection. One would think, to hear some of them

---

* Fables of Infidelity, pp. 190, 191.

talk, that in a few years the Bible would be buried beneath miles of stratified rocks which had been millions of ages in forming. The testimony of infidel geologists is, that the Bible teaches that the earth is now not quite six thousand years old, while geology teaches that it has been many millions of years in arriving at its present geological structure.

In reply to the above, we shall take the position that geology, unassisted by the Bible, cannot certainly prove the earth to be even six thousand years old. Geology is not a demonstrative science; hence it is incapable of teaching anything positively with regard to the age of the earth. Geologists themselves acknowledge it to be the most uncertain of all the sciences.

Sir David Brewster says: "The dry land upon our globe occupies only *one-fourth* of its whole superficies. All the rest is sea. How much of this fourth part have geologists been able to examine? and how small seems to be the area of stratification which they have explored? We venture to say not one *fiftieth part of the whole.*"[7]

"Abstract or speculative geology," says Mr. Chambers, "were it a perfect science, would present a history of the globe from its origin and formation, through all the changes it has undergone up to the present time, describing its external appearance, its plants and animals, at each successive period. *As yet, geology is the mere aim to arrive at knowledge*, and when we consider how difficult it is to trace the history of a nation, even over a few centuries, we cannot be surprised at *the small progress geologists have made* in tracing the history of

---

[7] More Worlds than One, p. 56.

the earth through the lapse of ages. To ascertain the history of a nation possessed of written records, is comparatively easy; but when these are wanting, we must examine the ruins of their cities and monuments, and judge of them as a people from the size and structure of their buildings, and from the remains of art found in them. This is often a perplexing, always an arduous, task. *Much more so is it to decipher the earth's history.*" [8]

Mr. Lyell says: "The canoes, for example, and stone hatchets found in our peat bogs, afford an insight into the rude arts and manners of the earliest inhabitants of our island; the buried coin fixes the date of some Roman emperor; the ancient encampment indicates the districts once occupied by invading armies, and the former method of constructing military defenses; the Egyptian mummies throw light on the art of embalming, the rites of sepulture, and the average stature of ancient Egypt. This class of memorials yields to no other in authenticity, but it constitutes a small part only of the resources on which the historian relies; whereas, in geology, it forms the *only* kind of evidence which is at our command. For this reason *we must not expect to obtain a full and connected account of events beyond the reach of history.*" [9]

Dr. Berg, in his debate with Joseph Barker, says: "Geology, as a science, is yet in its infancy. Its oracles are as contradictory as the sophisms of atheism. They contradict one another, and they contradict themselves. Whom shall we follow? Shall we go with Buckland, when, in company with Cuvier, Le Duc, Dolomien, and others, he tells us

---

[8] Rudiments of Geology, p. 10.
[9] Principles of Geology, p. 8.

the traces of the Mosaic deluge are indubitable, or shall we believe him when in his Bridgewater Treatise he somewhat modifies his views? Shall I take my stand with Hugh Miller, when, in his 'Old Red Sandstone,' he teaches that 'the system began with an age of dwarfs, and ended with an age of giants'? or shall I follow him in his 'Footprints,' another of his books, in which he reverses his former theory, and, at the very base of the system, 'discovers one of the most colossal of its giants,' and, instead of an ascending order of progressive development, asserts a descending order of progressive degradation? Which of Lyell's contradictory positions shall I take? There is one point at least in which all are agreed; it is this: *There is not a geological theory extant which would not be overthrown, and the whole science revolutionized, by the discovery of a single new fact.* Miller, in his 'Footprints,' p. 313, speaking of geology, says: 'It furnishes us with no clue by which to unravel the unapproachable mysteries of creation; these mysteries belong to the wondrous Creator, and to him only. We attempt to theorize upon them, and to reduce them to law, and all nature rises up against us in our presumptuous rebellion. A stray splinter of cone-bearing wood, a fish's skull or tooth, the vertebra of a reptile, the humerus of a bird, the jaw of a quadruped,— all, any of these things, weak and insignificant as they may seem, become, in such a quarrel, too strong for us and for our theory; the puny fragments in the grasp of truth form as irresistible a weapon as the dry bone did in that of Samson of old, and our slaughtered sophisms lie piled up, "heaps upon heaps," before it.'

"This is the testimony of a man who *is* a geologist. Whether my opponent is, or is not, I cannot say. If he is, instead of asserting things as geological facts, it would be his duty to *prove* them, for he may rest assured his assertions will carry very little force of conviction in a Christian community. The probability is, he is not a practical geologist at all. If he were he would not preach Hitchcock, praise Hitchcock, and, to all practical purposes, if not swear, at least affirm, by Hitchcock, as lustily as he does! And is this the kind of evidence upon which the Bible is to be discarded? Are we to take the mutterings of geological wizards, who peep out of the dust, as louder and better truths than the dictates of this Book, when the best of them, the man who stands in the front ranks of geologists, admits that a stray splinter of wood, or the wing-bone of a bird, would be weapon enough to beat the brains out of the best system geologists have ever devised? Oh! what faith my opponent has in Hitchcock; and yet I very little doubt, if the truth were known, other parts of Hitchcock's book might be used to show that in rejecting the Mosaic history of the deluge, he is at variance not only with the Bible, but with his own principles. Geologists must be more modest. Let them tarry in Jericho till their beards are grown; and when the science which they are cultivating is out of its cradle, and able to stand erect upon its own feet, the first impulse of its generous manhood will be to proclaim from the very heart of this great earth which Jehovah has made, that the Bible is the book of God, as surely as heaven and earth declare his glory and show his handiwork." [10]

Mr. Patterson sums up his remarks on geology in the following language:—

---

[10] Debate with Barker, pp. 251-253.

"Let it not be supposed that the progress of inductive science, and the prevalence of the Baconian philosophy, have banished absurdities and contradictions from the sphere of geology. It would require a man of considerable learning to find three geologists agreed either in their facts or in their theories. In a general way, indeed, we have the Catastrophists, with Hugh Miller, overwhelming the earth with dire convulsions in the geological eras, and upheaving the more conservative Lyell, and the Progressionists, who affirm that all things continue as they were from the beginning of the world. And there is perhaps a general agreement now, that the underlying *primitive* rocks, so-called, are not primitive at all, as geologists thought twenty years ago, but, like the foundations of a Chicago house, have been put in long after the building was finished and occupied. But then comes the question how they were inserted—whether, as Elie de Beaumont thinks, the mountains were upheaved by starts, lever-fashion, or, as Lyell affirms, very gradually and imperceptibly, like the elevation of a brick house by screws?

"Nor is there the least likelihood of any future agreement among them, inasmuch as they cannot agree either in the thickness of the earth's solid crust which is to be lifted, or the force by which it is to be done. Hopkins proves, by astronomical observation, that it is eight hundred miles thick. Lyell affirms that at twenty-four miles deep there can be no solid crust, for the temperature of the earth increases one degree for every forty-five feet, and at that depth the heat is great enough to melt iron and almost every known substance. But then there is a difference between philosophers about this last test of solidity—those who believe in

Wedgewood's Pyrometer, which was the infallible standard twenty years ago, asserting that the heat of melted iron is 21,000° Fah., while Professor Daniels demonstrates by another infallible instrument that it is only 2,786° Fah., which is rather a difference. In one case, the earth's crust would be over two hundred miles thick; in the other, twenty-four miles.

"But then comes the great question, What is below the granite? and a very important one for any theory of the earth. It evidently underlies the whole foundation of speculative geology, whether we assume, with De Beaumont and Humboldt, that 'the whole globe, with the exception of a thin envelope, much thinner in proportion than the shell of an egg, is a fused mass, kept fluid by heat,—a heat of 450,000° Fah., at the center, as Cordier calculates,—but constantly cooling, and contracting its dimensions,' and occasionally cracking, and falling in, and 'squeezing upward large portions of the mass,' 'thus producing those folds or wrinkles which we call mountain chains;' or with Davy and Lyell, that the heat of such a boiling ocean below would melt the solid crust, like ice from the surface of boiling water—and with it the whole theory of the primeval existence of the earth in a state of igneous fusion, its gradual cooling down into continents and mountains of granite, the gradual abrasion of the granite into the mud and sand which formed the stratified rocks, and all the other brilliant hypotheses which have sparked out of this great internal fire. Instead of an original central heat, he supposes that 'we may *perhaps* refer the heat of the interior to chemical changes constantly going on in the earth's crust.' Now if the very foundations of the science are in such a state of fusion, and floating on a *perhaps*, would it not be wise to allow them to solidify a little, before a man risks the salvation of his soul upon them?"[11]

The author of "Geognosy" in speaking of the uncertainties of geology, and the contradictions of its advocates, says:—

"There is not another question in the whole range of their system, in regard to which they do not entertain a wide diversity of opinion. They are not agreed, for example, whether the world, at its creation, was in a gaseous or in a solid form. They are not agreed in respect to the processes by which gneiss, schist, and the other primary rocks, were produced. They are not agreed in respect to the point at which the secondary series commences, the order of the strata, the sources from which some of their elements were drawn, nor the agencies to which they owe their peculiar structure. They differ in respect to the point at which vegetable and animal life commenced, and the forms which it first assumed. They entertain the most diverse and absurd opinions respecting the origin of lime, coal, gypsum, chalk, magnesia, iron, and salt. They hold conflicting views in regard to the state of the globe at the epoch of the different formations, the forces by which the strata were dislocated, the causes by which the mountains were upthrown, the period at which land animals were first called into existence, and the origin of the races that now inhabit the globe. They differ likewise, to the extent of countless ages, in regard to the period that has elapsed during the formation of the strata. In short, beyond the simple facts that the strata have been formed since the creation of the earth, that

---

[11] Fables of Infidelity, pp. 298, 299.

chemical and mechanical forces of some kind were the principal agents in their deposition, and that the fossilized forms that are imbedded in them once belonged to the vegetable and animal worlds,— there is scarce a topic of any moment in the whole circle of the science, in respect to which they do not maintain very diverse opinions; there is scarce a solitary point so fully ascertained as to be placed beyond a doubt. Their unanimity in assigning a vast round of ages to the world, while they thus disagree in respect to the *nature of the processes to which they suppose those incalculable ages were requisite*, instead, therefore, of giving strength to their induction, indicates that the grounds on which it rests are mistaken. What can be more absurd than to suppose that an inference, erected on such a mass of gratuitous assumptions and disputable theories, can be entitled to the rank of a philosophic induction? What can be more preposterous than to dignify a branch of knowledge in which there is so little that is settled, and so much that is in debate, with the lofty title of an '*accurate science*'? It cannot, as a whole, rise any higher, in a demonstrative relation, than the parts of which it consists; the conclusion cannot acquire any greater validity than the postulates possess from which it is drawn."[12]

"But how greatly diluted must the modified and hesitating conviction, possible to an actual observer, become, when, as is generally the case, a man is not an actual observer himself, but *learns his science at school*. Such a person leaves the ground of demonstrative science, and stands upon faith. The first question, then, to be proposed

---

[12] Geognosy, pp. 304, 305.

to one whose demonstrative certainty of the truths of physical science has disgusted him with a religion received on testimony and faith, is, How have you reached this demonstrative certainty in matters of science? Are you quite sure that your certainty rests not upon the testimony of fallible and erring philosophers, but solely upon your own personal observations and experiments?

"To take only the initial standard of astronomical measurements,—the earth's distance from the sun. Have you personally measured the earth's radius, observed the transit of Venus in 1769, from Lapland and Tahiti at the same time, calculated the sun's parallax, and the eccentricity of the earth's orbit? Would you profess yourself competent to take even the preliminary observation for fixing the instruments for such a reckoning? Were you ever within a thousand miles of the proper positions for making such observations? Or have you been necessitated to accept this primary measure, upon the accuracy of which all subsequent astronomical measures depend, merely upon hearsay and testimony, and subject to all those contingencies of error and prejudice, and mistakes of copyists, which, in your opinion, render the Bible so unreliable in matters of religion? * * *

"Or, after all your boasting about scientific and demonstrative certainty, have you been obliged to receive the certainties of science 'upon faith, and at second-hand, and upon the word of another;' when, to save your life, you could not tell half the time who that other is, by naming the discoverers of half the scientific truths you believe? What! are you dependent upon hearsay and probability for any little science you possess, having in fact never obtained any personal demonstration or experience of its first principles and measurements, nor being capable of doing so ? Then let us hear no more cant from you about the uncertainty of a religion dependent upon testimony and the certainties of experimental science. Whatever certainty may be attainable by scientific men,—and we have seen that it is not much,—it is very certain you have got none of it. The very best you can have to wrap yourself in is a second-hand assurance, grievously torn by rival schools, and needing to be patched every month by later discoveries. Your science, such as it is, *rests solely upon faith* in the testimony of philosophers, often contradictory and improbable, and always fallible and uncertain. * * *

"We are met at the very outset by the great fact that God has so constituted the world and everything in it, that *in all the great concerns of life we are necessitated to depend on faith*, without any possibility of reaching absolute certainty regarding the result of any ordinary duty. We sow without any certainty of a crop, or that we may live to reap it. We harvest, but our barns may be burned down. We sell our property for bank-bills, but who dare say they will ever be paid in specie ? We start on a journey to a distant city, but even though you insure your life, who will insure that fire, or flood, or railroad collision, may not send you to the land whence there is no return ?

"Science is the child of yesterday; but from the beginning of the world men have lived by faith. Before science was born, Cain tilled his ground without any mathematical demonstration that he should reap a crop ; Abel fed his flock without any scientific certainty that he should live to enjoy its produce; and Tubal Cain forged axes and swords without any assurance that he should not be plundered of his wages. All the experience of mankind proves that experimental certainty regarding the most important business of this life is impossible. By what process of philosophical induction is religion alone put beyond the sphere of faith and hope? If religious duties are not binding on us unless religion be scientifically demonstrated, then neither are moral obligations; for these two cannot be separated. Is it really so, that none but scientific men are bound to tell the truth and pay their debts, and that a person may not fear God and go to Heaven unless he has graduated at college? The common sense of mankind declares that we live by faith, not by science.

"*We demand the knowledge of truths of which science is profoundly ignorant.* Science is but an outlying nook of my farm, which I may neglect and yet have bread to eat. Faith is my house, in which all my dearest interests are treasured. Of all the great problems and precious interests which belong to me as a mortal or an immortal, Science knows nothing. I ask her whence I came; and she points to her pinions, scorched over the abyss of primeval fire, her eyes blinded by its awful glare, and remains silent. I inquire what I am; but the strange and questioning *I* is a mystery which she can neither analyze nor measure. I tell her of the voice of conscience within me; she never heard it, and does not pretend to understand its oracles. I tell her of my anxieties about the future; she is learned only in the past. I inquire how I may be happy hereafter; but happiness is not a scientific term, and she cannot tell me how to be happy here! Poor, blind Science!"[13]

Now, patient reader, permit us to bid you farewell. Our task is done. Not that we have presented all the evidences of Christianity, or all the outlines of the great chains which have been examined. But we trust that at least enough has been said to convince you that the book we call the Bible

"Is divine and unalterably sure."

If we have succeeded in awakening a spirit of investigation, so that you will examine other and more able writings upon this subject, we shall be satisfied.

Before taking our final leave, we would remind you that it is not enough merely to assent to the truth of the Bible. Thousands who sincerely believe the Bible to have been given by inspiration of God, will land in destruction. "O, taste and see that the Lord is good." Follow out the convictions which have now been formed in your mind. Read this book again. Get another work on this vital subject, and read it for the purpose of true investigation. Begin to serve God. Break off your sins. Cultivate faith in Jesus. Throw away your doubts. You have evidence enough if you will only build upon it. God gives the evidence: you must have the faith, and carry out your faith by your works.

---

[13] Fables of Infidelity, pp. 302-305.

CATALOGUE OF PUBLICATIONS

Issued by the Review and Herald Publishing Association, Battle Creek, Mich.

PERIODICALS.

The Advent Review and Sabbath Herald. A 16-page Religious FAMILY Newspaper, devoted to a discussion of the Prophecies, Signs of the Times, Second Coming of Christ, Harmony of the Law and the Gospel, What we must Do to be Saved, and other Bible questions. $2.00 a year.

Good Health. A monthly journal of hygiene devoted to Physical, Mental, and Moral Culture.
$1.00 a year.

The Youth's Instructor. A 4-page illustrated weekly for the Sabbath-School and the family.
75 cts. a year.

The Sabbath Sentinel. A live 4-page monthly quarto, devoted exclusively to the vindication of the Sabbath of the Bible. 25 cts. a year.

The Bible-Reading Gazette. A 24-page octavo monthly, devoted wholly to Bible Readings. Circulation limited. Terms may be had of Publishers.

Sandhedens Tidende. A 16-page Danish semi-monthly, devoted to expositions of Prophecy, the Signs of the Times, and Practical Religion.
$1.00 a year.

Sanningens Harold. A 16-page Swedish semi-monthly, magazine form, of the same character as the SANDHEDENS TIDENDE. $1.00 a year.

Stimme der Wahrheit. An 8-page German monthly devoted to the same topics as the SANDHEDENS TIDENDE and the SIGNS OF THE TIMES.
75 cts. a year.

☞ *The above are published at Battle Creek, Mich. Terms always in advance.*

The Signs of the Times. A 15-page weekly Religious Paper, devoted to the dissemination of light upon the same great themes treated in the REVIEW. Published in Oakland, Cal.
$2.00 a year.

Tidernes Tegn. A Danish-Norwegian monthly of the same size and character as the TIDENDE. Published in Christiania, Norway.
70 cts. a year.

Sundhedsbladet. A 16-page Danish-Norwegian health and temperance monthly. Published in Christiana, Norway. 70 cts. a year.

Helso-og Sjukvard. A Swedish monthly health journal of the same size and character as SUNDHEDSBLADET. Published in Christiana, Norway. 70 cts. a year.

Les Signes des Temps. A monthly Religious journal in French. Published in Bale, Suisse.
$1.15 a year.

Herold der Wahrheit. An 8-page German monthly. Published at Bale, Suisse.
60 cts. a year.

L'ultimo Messaggio. An 8-page Italian quarterly. Published at Bale, Suisse. 25 cts. a year.

Adevarulu Present. An 8-page Roumanian quarterly. Published at Bale, Suisse.
25 cts. a year.

BOUND BOOKS.

Complete History of the Sabbath, and the First Day of the Week. By Eld. J. N. Andrews. A mine of information on this all-important question. Treats the subject from a Biblical and Historical standpoint. 528 pp. $1.25

Thoughts on Daniel. Critical and Practical. By Eld. U. Smith. An exposition of the book of Daniel, verse by verse. 416 pp. $1.25

Thoughts on the Revelation. By Eld. U. Smith. This work presents every verse in the book of Revelation with such remarks as serve to illustrate or explain the meaning of the text.
420 pp. $1.25

Life Sketches of Elder James and Mrs. E. G. White. The early lives and Christian experience of both are given in this volume. Their subsequent history is so connected with the cause, that this book gives an outline of the rise and progress of our people and this cause. Has two fine steel portraits. This is the last work written by Elder White before his death. 416 pp. $1.25

The Sanctuary and the 2300 Days of Dan. 8:14. By Eld. U. Smith. This work explains the past Advent movement, and makes plain the present position of those who wait for the Lord.
352 pp. $1.00
Condensed edition, paper covers, 224 pp. 80 cts.

The Biblical Institute. This work contains a synopsis of the lectures given at the Battle Creek College by Eld. U. Smith, and at Biblical Institutes.
352 pp. $1.00

The Nature and Destiny of Man. By Eld. U. Smith. This work treats on the great questions of the condition of man in death, and his destiny beyond the resurrection. 356 pp. $1.00

The Spirit of Prophecy; or, the Great Controversy between Christ and his angels, and Satan and his angels, in four volumes. By Mrs. E. G. White. These volumes cover the time from the fall of Satan to the destruction of sin and sinners at the close of the one thousand years of Rev. 20. Each, 400 pp.
Vol. I. Old Testament Facts to Christ. $1.00
Vol. II. Life and Ministry of Christ. 1.00
Vol. III. The Death, Resurrection, and Ascension of Christ, with the Lives of his Apostles, 1.00
Vol. IV. (In preparation.) 1.00

The Coming Conflict; or, the United States to become a Persecuting Power. By Eld. W. H. Littlejohn. The Sabbath question fully discussed. A careful exegesis of Revelation 13, showing that the United States is soon to enter upon a career of religious persecution, for which the Sabbath question is to be made the pretext. 428 pp. $1.00

Spiritual Songs. A book of hymns and tunes. 537 hymns, 147 tunes. 416 pp. $1.00
Morocco, gilt, 1.50

Life of Wm. Miller, with portrait. This book gives interesting sketches of the Christian life and public labors of this pioneer in the Advent movement in this country. 416 pp. $1.00

Life of Elder Joseph Bates, relating his experience of twenty-five years on ship-board, with incidents of his rise from cabin-boy up to master and owner. The closing chapters relate to his labors in the ministry, and in the cause of temperance and other reforms.
Fine tint paper, 352 pp. $1.00
Plain white paper, 85 cts.

The Bible from Heaven. By D. M. Canright. An argument to show that the Bible is not the work of men, but is in deed and truth the word of God. 300 pp. 80 cts.

The Soul and the Resurrection, showing the Harmony of Science and the Bible on the Nature of the Soul and the Doctrine of the Resurrection. By J. H. Kellogg, M. D. 75 cts.

Sketches from the Life of Paul. By Mrs. E. G. White. 336 pp., muslin, 80 cts.

Early Writings of Mrs. White, 75 cts.

A History of the Doctrine of the Soul. Muslin binding. 75 cts.

Smith's Diagram of Parliamentary Rules. Indispensable to Parliamentarians. 50 cts.

The Song Anchor. A popular collection of songs for the Sabbath-School and praise service.
164 pp. 35 cts.
Bound in muslin, 50 cts.

Temperance Song Book. An unequaled book. All temperance people are lavish in its praise.
30 cts.
Bound with Song Anchor, muslin, 80 cts.

Better than Pearls. A superb collection of very choice music and words. Unequaled. 40 cts.
In boards, 30 cts.

Pearly Portals. A new book. 35 cts.

Songs for Class and School. A truly meritorious book. 35 cts.

Gems of Song. A vest-pocket song book containing hymns only. A choice collection. 96 pp., 119 hymns, bound in flexible cloth. 15 cts.

The United States in the Light of Prophecy; or, an exposition of Rev. 13: 11-17. By Eld. U. Smith. Dealing with our own land, and applying to our time. Of surpassing interest to every American reader. New edition. 225 pp. 75 cts.
Paper covers, 25 cts.

The Advent Keepsake. A collection of Bible texts for each day in the year, on the subjects of the Second Advent, the Resurrection, etc.
136 pp. 25 cts.

Thoughts on Baptism; Its Action, Subjects, and Relations. By Eld. J. H. Waggoner.
190 pp. 25 cts.

A Word for the Sabbath: or, False Theories Exposed. A poem by Eld. U. Smith. 60 pp. 30 cts.
Glazed paper covers, 15 cts.

Bound Volumes of Review and Herald, Each, $1.25

The Youth's Instructor for 1879-'80. Firmly bound. $1.00

SABBATH-SCHOOL HELPS.

Bible Lessons for Little Ones, No. 1. Flexible cover. 15 cts.

Bible Lessons for Little Ones, No. 2. Flexible cloth, with map. 20 cts.

Bible Lessons for Children, No. 3. 25 cts.

Bible Lessons, No. 4. With map. 25 cts.

Bible Lessons, No. 5, 25 cts.

Bible Lessons, No. 6, 25 cts.

PAMPHLETS.

The Atonement. By Eld. J. H. Waggoner. An examination of a remedial system in the light of Nature and Revelation. 168 pp. 25 cts.

Our Faith and Hope. Sermons on the coming and kingdom of Christ. By Eld. James White.
182 pp. 25 cts.

Facts for the Times. A volume of valuable Historical extracts. 25 cts.

Testimonies, Nos. 20-30, each, 25 cts.

S. D. A. Year Book for the year 1884. 25 cts.

Refutation of the Age to Come. By Eld. J. H. Waggoner. 168 pp. 20 cts.

The Ministration of Angels, and the Origin, History, and Destiny of Satan. By D. M. Canright. 144 pp. 20 cts.

The Nature and Tendency of Modern Spiritualism. By Eld. J. H. Waggoner.
184 pp. 20 cts.

The Visions: Objections Answered. 20 cts.

The Spirit of God, its Gifts and Manifestations to the end of the Christian age. By Eld. J. H. Waggoner. 144 p. 15 cts.

The Three Messages of Rev. 14:6-12. Particularly the third angel's message and the two-horned beast. By Eld. J. N. Andrews.
144 pp. 15 cts.

The Two Laws, as set forth in the Scriptures of the Old and New Testaments. By D. M. Canright. 128 pp. 15 cts.

The Morality of the Sabbath. By D. M. Canright. 96 pp. 15 cts.

Miraculous Powers. The Scripture testimony on the Perpetuity of Spiritual Gifts.
128 pp. 15 cts.

The Complete Testimony of the Fathers of the First Three Centuries Concerning the Sabbath and the First Day of the Week. By Eld. J. N. Andrews. 112 pp. 15 cts.

Matthew Twenty-Four. A clear and forcible exposition of our Lord's discourse upon the Mount of Olives. By Eld. James White. 64 pp. 10 cts.

Matter and Spirit. A philosophical argument on an interesting theme. By D. M. Canright.
10 cts.

Bible Sanctification. By Mrs. E. G. White.
10 cts.

The Seven Trumpets. An exposition of the subject, as set forth in Revelation, chaps. 8 and 9. 96 pp. 10 cts.

The Truth Found. The nature and obligation of the Sabbath. By Eld. J. H. Waggoner.
64 pp. 10 cts.

Vindication of the True Sabbath. By Eld. J. W. Morton, formerly Missionary of the Reformed Presbyterian Church to Hayti. 68 pp. 10 cts.

Hope of the Gospel, By Eld. J. N. Loughborough. 80 pp. 10 cts.

Christ and the Sabbath; or, Christ in the Old Testament, and the Sabbath in the New. By Eld. James White. 56 pp. 10 cts.

Redeemer and Redeemed. By Eld. James White. This work sets forth the plan of Redemption in its three stages. 40 pp. 10 cts.

Review of Gilfillan: or, Thoughts Suggested by the Perusal of Gilfillan and other Authors on the Sabbath. 64 pp. 10 cts.

Appeal to the Baptists for the Restitution of the Bible Sabbath. 46 pp. 10 cts.

Review of Baird. A review of two sermons against the Sabbath and Seventh-day Adventists. By Eld. J. H. Waggoner. 64 pp. 10 cts.

The Rejected Ordinance. A carefully prepared paper on our Saviour's Act of Humility in John 18, 10 cts.

The Position and Work of the True People of God under the Third Angel's Message. By Eld. W. H. Littlejohn, 10 cts.

Life of Christ and his Apostles, 8 books, paper covers. 90 cts.

The Saints' Inheritance. 10 cts.

The Ancient Sabbath. Forty-four objections considered. 88 pp. 10 cts.

Key to the Prophetic Chart. A valuable publication. 6 cts.

TRACTS.

5 cents each. Our Faith and Hope. Justification by Faith. Milton on the State of the Dead.

4 cents each. Redemption. The Second Advent. The Sufferings of Christ. The Present Truth. Origin and Progress of S. D. Adventists. Ten Commandments not abolished. Address to the Baptists. The Two Thrones. Spiritualism a Satanic Delusion. Samuel and the Witch of Endor. The Third Message of Rev. 14. Scripture References. Tithes and Offerings. Seventh Part of Time.

3 cents each. Second Message of Rev. 14. End of the Wicked. Lost-Time Question. Seventh-day Adventists and Seventh-day Baptists. Signs of the Times. Who Changed the Sabbath? The Spirit of Prophecy. The Millennium. Sabbaton.

2 cents each. Christ in the Old Testament. The Sabbath in the New Testament. The Old Moral Code not Revised. The Sanctuary of the Bible. The Judgment. Much in Little. The Two Laws. Seven Reasons. The Definite Seventh Day. Departing and Being with Christ. The Rich Man and Lazarus. Elihu on the Sabbath. First Message of Rev. 14. The Law and the Gospel. God's Memorial. The Sabbath Made for Man.

1 cent each. The Coming of the Lord. Perfection of the Ten Commandments. Without Excuse. Thoughts for the Candid. Which Day and Why? Can we Know; or, Can the Prophecies be Understood? Is the End Near? Is Man Immortal? The Sleep of the Dead. The Sinner's Fate. The Law of God. What the Gospel Abrogated. One Hundred Bible Facts about the Sabbath. Sunday not the Sabbath. "The Christian Sabbath." Why not Found out Before?

CHOICE JUVENILE BOOKS.

Sabbath Readings for the Home Circle. In four volumes, containing moral and religious reading for the household; carefully selected, and compiled for the use of Sabbath-school and family libraries. No better books for children in the market.
Each, 60 cts.
Put up in a neat box, $2.50

Sunshine at Home. A bright, sparkling book for the family circle, brimful of good sense, and perfectly free from "trash." 112 quarto pages, highly embellished. $1.50

Golden Grain Series. A choice collection of instructive stories suited to the wants of children from eight to sixteen years and older, illustrated and beautifully bound in three volumes.
The Hard Way, 160 pp.; The School-boy's Dinner, 160 pp.; Grumbling Tommy, 160 pp. Each, 30 cts.

The Child's Poems. Containing Little Will and other stories, teaching beautiful lessons of temperance and virtue. Bound in cloth, and richly embossed in gold and black. 128 pp. 25 cts.

Golden Grains in Ten Pamphlets, 32 pages each. 320 pp. 50 cts.

The Sunshine Series. Stories for little ones, in Ten Small Books, adapted to children from the ages of four to ten years.
In glazed paper covers, 320 pp. 50 cts.

HEALTH PUBLICATIONS.

Plain Facts about Sexual Life. A wise book, treating on delicate topics, for all ages, married and single. This is a *Christian* book, highly commended by the press and clergymen. 408 pp. $1.50
Condensed edition, flexible covers, 75 cts.

Manual of Health and Temperance. A book brimful of information on a hundred useful topics. Thirty-fifth thousand. Cloth. 244 pp. 75 cts.

Digestion and Dyspepsia. By J. H. Kellogg, M. D. This work embodies the results of the author's experience in dealing with all forms of the disease, in all of its stages, and is a thoroughly practical treatise on this prevalent malady.
In cloth, 176 pp. 75 cts.
Paper covers, 25 cts.

Uses of Water in Health and Disease, giving careful and thorough instruction respecting the uses of water as a preventive of disease, and as a valuable remedy.
In cloth, 166 pp. 60 cts.
Paper covers, 136 pp. 25 cts.

Lectures on the Science of Human Life. By Sylvester Graham. Three lectures of great value which should be in the hands of every individual. 174 pp. 30 cts.

Diphtheria. A concise account of the nature, causes, modes of prevention, and most successful mode of treatment of this now prevalent and fatal disease
Board covers, with 4 colored plates, 64 pp. 25 cts.

Alcoholic Poison; or, the Physical, Moral, and Social Effects of Alcohol as a Beverage and as a Medicine. The best compendium of the temperance question published. Its statements are brief, concise, and to the point.
Paper covers, 128 pp. 25 cts.

Evils of Fashionable Dress, and How to Dress Healthfully. This little work considers the subject of fashionable dress from a medical standpoint, and thoroughly exposes its evils. It does not stop here, but points out an easy and acceptable remedy.
Enamel covers, 40 pp. 10 cts.

Bound Volumes of Health Reformer, and Good Health. These valuable volumes contain more practical information of a vital character than any other of their size. Each volume contains 380 pages of reading matter, well bound. $1.25

Proper Diet for Man. A scientific discussion of the question of vegetable versus animal food. Ultra notions are avoided, and the subjects treated are handled with candor.
Paper covers, 15 cts.

Health and Diseases of American Women. 60 pp. 15 cts.

The Hygienic System. Full of good things. 15 cts.

TRACTS.

3 cents each. Wine and the Bible. Startling Facts about Tobacco.

2 cents each. Pork. The Drunkard's Arguments Answered. Alcoholic Medication. Twenty-five Arguments on Tobacco-Using Briefly Answered.

1 cent each. Causes and Cure of Intemperance. Moral and Social Effects of Intemperance. Tobacco-Using—Cause of Disease. Tobacco-Poisoning—Nicotiana Tabacum. Effects of Tea and Coffee. Ten Arguments on Tea and Coffee.

½ cent each. Alcoholic Poison. Tobacco-Using a Relic of Barbarism. True Temperance. Alcohol, What is It? Our Nation's Curse.

OTHER LANGUAGES.

The Association has 47 different works in Danish-Norwegian, 32 in Swedish, 35 in German, 15 in French, and 1 in Holland, besides the regular periodicals in those tongues already noticed.

☞ Full Catalogues of all our publications in English, and the various Foreign Languages, furnished *free*, on application.
For anything in this Catalogue address,

REVIEW AND HERALD,
Battle Creek, Mich.

SUNSHINE AT HOME:

Sparkling Pages for the Child, the Youth, and the Parent.
A Family Portfolio of Natural History
and Bible Scenes.

ONE HUNDRED AND SEVENTY ILLUSTRATIONS.

THE life mission of some people seems to be to "scatter sunshine" wherever they go. A happy disposition, which makes the best of everything, looks on the bright side, and ever bears in mind that "the darkest cloud has a silver lining," is the means of brightening the lives of all who are brought under its influence. The work entitled "SUNSHINE AT HOME" has been prepared for the purpose indicated by its title. Its mission is to brighten the lives of those who peruse its pages, by its cheering words, its entertaining sketches, and its beautiful pictures.

THE WORK OF ITS PREPARATION

Has been carefully performed, every page having been submitted to the most exacting scrutiny. The book comprises choice poetical selections, descriptive sketches accompanying the engravings, interesting geographical descriptions, entertaining articles on natural history, zoölogy, etc., short illustrated stories, designed for both old and young, together with biographical and historical sketches, pungent paragraphs, and lessons of wisdom.

THE ENGRAVINGS ARE GEMS

Worthy of the literary setting with which they are exhibited. As works of art, many of them will take high rank, being the product of the combined skill of designers and engravers at the head of their professions.

DESCRIPTIVE.

The work comprises 112 large quarto pages, and 170 engravings, and is printed on fine calendered paper, in the best style of the typographic art. It is handsomely and substantially bound in fine cloth, embossed in jet and gold, and is a handsome ornament to any center-table, and an adornment to any library.

ITS FIELD OF USEFULNESS.

The character of the work is well calculated to give it a wide circulation. Bright and sparkling, without being frivolous or trifling; moral in its tone, without being somber or dogmatical; religious, without sectarianism,—it finds ready sale in all classes of society. Agents meet with great success. Send for the book.

Price, post-paid, - $1.50.
Address, REVIEW & HERALD, Battle Creek, Mich.

TEACH Services, Inc.
PUBLISHING

We invite you to view the complete
selection of titles we publish at:
www.TEACHServices.com

We encourage you to write us
with your thoughts about this,
or any other book we publish at:
info@TEACHServices.com

TEACH Services' titles may be purchased in
bulk quantities for educational, fund-raising,
business, or promotional use.
bulksales@TEACHServices.com

Finally, if you are interested in seeing
your own book in print, please contact us at:
publishing@TEACHServices.com

We are happy to review your manuscript at no charge.

www.ingramcontent.com/pod-product-compliance
Lightning Source LLC
Chambersburg PA
CBHW071529160426
43196CB00010B/1717